Gender Relations

in Canada

Intersectionality and Beyond

Janet Siltanen & Andrea Doucet

OXFORD
UNIVERSITY PRESS

OXFORD
UNIVERSITY PRESS

70 Wynford Drive, Don Mills, Ontario M3C 1J9
www.oup.com/ca

Oxford University Press is a department of the University of Oxford.
It furthers the University's objective of excellence in research, scholarship,
and education by publishing worldwide in

Oxford   New York

Auckland   Cape Town   Dar es Salaam   Hong Kong   Karachi
Kuala Lumpur   Madrid   Melbourne   Mexico City   Nairobi
New Delhi   Shanghai   Taipei   Toronto

With offices in

Argentina   Austria   Brazil   Chile   Czech Republic   France   Greece
Guatemala   Hungary   Italy   Japan   Poland   Portugal   Singapore
South Korea   Switzerland   Thailand   Turkey   Ukraine   Vietnam

Oxford is a trade mark of Oxford University Press
in the UK and in certain other countries

Published in Canada
by Oxford University Press

Library and Archives Canada Cataloguing in Publication Data

Siltanen, Janet
Gender relations in Canada : intersectionality and beyond / Janet Siltanen, Andrea Doucet.

Includes bibliographical references and index.
ISBN 978-0-19-542320-4

1. Sex role.   2. Sex differences.   3. Gender identity.
I. Doucet, Andrea.   II. Title.

HQ1075.S556   2008   305.3   C2008-900800-6

Cover Image: Elena Genova/iStockPhoto

1 2 3 4 – 11 10 09 08

This book is printed on permanent (acid-free) paper ∞.

Printed in Canada

Contents

JS—To Margaret (Peggy) and Margrit

for helping me to get here, and to David and Calum

who make being here worthwhile.

AD—To three women who've made

all the difference: Norma Doucet, Carol Gilligan,

and in memory of Suzanne Mackenzie.

Acknowledgements

We offer our heartfelt appreciation to Lorne Tepperman and the late James Curtis for inviting us to be a part of this OUP series. We owe many thanks to the OUP editorial staff—to those who started us off on this project, Lisa Meschino and Roberta Osborne, and to Dina Theleritis, whose patience and determination helped us to bring it to an end. Thank you also to Dorothy Turnbull for her encouragement and copyediting.

We extend sincere thanks to Mary Ellen Donnan for her contribution of chapter 5. Mary Ellen completed her PhD in sociology at Carleton University in 2004, and it is a pleasure to work with her now on a fully collegial basis. A very special thank you to Riva Soucie for her supporting research, for the lion's share of the glossary, for reading and offering comments on each chapter, and for taking on many tasks at very short notice.

We are grateful for research and other assistance from Calum Dean, David Dean, Mike Graydon, Amanda Maurice, James Opp, Sarah Rayfield, and Jamie Walker. The book is significantly enriched by the excellent research contributions and personal reflections provided by sociology graduate students at Carleton University. For these, we thank: Aimee Campeau, Renuka Chaturvedi, Karen Foster, Kristen Gilchrist, Mike Graydon, Christopher Longtin, Perez Nyamwamge, Willow Scobie (PhD, 2007), Nick Scott, Riva Soucie, and Kevin Walby.

Finally, we wish to thank each other! While more hands did not always make for less work, they offered much more than what would have been possible otherwise. Parts of chapter 6 draw from some of our other work, specifically: J. Siltanen. 2006. 'Gender, Diversity and the Shaping of Public Policy: Recent Aspects of the Canadian Experience', *Scottish Affairs* 56: 88–101; A. Doucet. 2006. *Do Men Mother?* Toronto: University of Toronto Press; A. Doucet and N.S. Mauthner. 2006. 'Feminist Methodologies and Epistemologies', in Clifton D. Bryant and Dennis L. Peck, eds, *Handbook of 21st Century Sociology*. Thousand Oaks, CA: Sage Publications.

Mary Ellen would like to thank Janet, Andrea, Riva, and Gerry Coulter for their help in preparing her chapter.

Chapter 1

Sociology and the Analysis of Gender Relations

Chapter Objectives

1. To illustrate how the sociology of gender relations is grounded in everyday life problems and issues.
2. To demonstrate connections between agency and structure in experiences of masculinities and femininities and to encourage you to think about how these connections work in your own life.
3. To lay out two key conceptual shifts in the development of sociological thinking on gender relations. The first shift involves mainstream sociology accepting that gender matters, and the second shift involves identifying the interrogation of gender as a central sociological task.

INTRODUCTION

Fill in a school registration form, apply for a bank account, renew your driver's licence, send in your tax return, and the one question about yourself that you will always be asked is: are you male or female? Most of us are pretty clear about what answer we should give to this question. But are we clear about why the question is being asked at all? Why is it that in our society, one of the first things we notice about a person—say, a newborn baby, the latest Canadian Idol, a hockey player, or the governor general—is whether that person is male or female?

On the surface, the question may seem commonplace and mundane. But it can also be disturbing and dangerous. This sense of danger is powerfully portrayed in the movie *Boys Don't Cry* (1999) which, along with a 1998 documentary film (*Brandon Teena: A Story*), is based on the true life story of Brandon Teena, a 21-year-old male living in a small town. Brandon hangs out with the local guys, drinks heavily, gets into trouble with the law, and dates several women who come to love him as one of the most sensitive and considerate young men they have ever met. The story turns, however, from one of simple small-town life to a series of violent scenes when it is

accidentally revealed that Brandon's physiology is out of sync with his public gender identity. Brandon Teena is in fact Teena Brandon, and this discovery by others
tears his life apart as he suffers betrayal, humiliation, rape, and ultimately murder.
Issues of how gender matters to others are painfully portrayed in the film when
Brandon, turned over to the police, faces a large, surly male officer who repeatedly
interrogates Brandon with a pointed question: 'Well, what are you—a girl or a boy?'
The fact that Brandon has no clear answer to this question sends the police officer
into a rage, thus subtly illuminating how this simple question has enormous social,
political, and psychological dimensions. This scene, in which actress Hilary Swank
(who earned an Academy Award for the role) delivers an emotionally heart-
wrenching performance, reveals the tortuous consequences that can be faced by
those who do not have a straightforward gender identity, and why gender matters
profoundly in social life.

The police officer in *Boys Don't Cry* is actually an excellent metaphor for how
society more widely regards being a man or a woman as a basic, obvious, and taken-
for-granted biological fact—end of story. When these assumptions are troubled or
turned upside down, many people may find the resulting sense of turmoil difficult.
This is certainly not the case for sociologists. Attuned to the limitations of setting up
binary positions (man/woman, white/black, gay/straight) and open to the richness
of diversity and complexity, sociologists have a different view. We regard maleness
and femaleness, masculinities and femininities, as highly complex and rather inde-
terminate social accomplishments—and an apparently never-ending story.

In this book, we look in detail at sociologists' views about gendered identities and
the complex relationships between them. We shall explore the many ways that the cities
you live in, the families who raise you, the television shows you watch, the schools you
attend, the computer games you play, and the friends you have shape your sense of
who you are and what you are capable of as a girl, a boy, a woman, or a man. We shall
also look at how both individuals and groups challenge and attempt to change ideas
about what is appropriate male and female behaviour. We live our lives in particular
historical and social contexts, and these contexts of laws, rules, conventions, and expectations set out life paths that many follow. While there are well-trodden paths, our lives
are not predetermined. The choices we make, our determination to address the injustices we see, the ways we use opportunities that come our way, and the passions we
have, can direct us down paths of life that forge new ground and establish new ways of
being male and female.

Much of the history of Canada in the twentieth century, as elsewhere, has been
about experimenting with and testing new paths of male and female experience. Sociology has been deeply involved in this interrogation of the old and experimentation
with the new. It has made important contributions to understanding the need for,
and the consequences of, change in our ideas about men and women and the relationships between them. In fact, sociologists were among the first to insist that *it is
possible* for change to occur in how people understand and live being a man or a
woman. They were also among the first to use the term 'gender' to refer to those
socially produced differences between women and men that are open to debate, intervention, and change.

This book is organized to take you through some of the most significant contemporary sociological work on gender relations in Canada. We shall also draw on theoretical and research contributions in some international literature. We expect that you already have a basic familiarity with sociological ideas and concepts as well as some exposure to the sociology of gender relations. Our aim is to build on your foundational understanding by introducing you to the latest ideas and developments in the field.

Throughout this book, we feature areas of research and debate that are of current interest to sociologists. Moreover, since sociologists often respond to what is happening in their society, you will find that the issues we discuss are also featured in newspapers and magazines and debated on talk shows. In sum, we want to introduce you to the sociology of gender relations as an ongoing project of research addressing questions and experiences that people are grappling with today. As in sociology, our own ideas about gender have changed considerably over the years, and they continue to be challenged and explored.

To help make sense of this new and important material on gender relations in Canada, we have organized the book into chapters that follow the flow of an individual's life. We start with childhood and move on to adolescence and the transition to adulthood. We then focus on different aspects of adult life, beginning with the interrelationships between earning and caring and then examining how gender relations affect the way adult men and women engage in public life as citizens, as employees, and as individuals and groups who want social change. We do not take you any further along the life course than this, although significant work is being done in Canadian sociology on the gendered processes of aging and later life. However, we hope that by focusing on stages of life that you are more familiar with— through your own and your parents' experiences—you will be able to think about this sociological material in terms of your own life. That, after all, is the area in which many sociologists hope to make a difference—in the way individuals experience daily life.

This chapter introduces two conceptual shifts in the work on gender in sociology in Canada and elsewhere. The first shift occurred throughout the 1970s and into the 1980s. It involved accepting that gender mattered and had profound implications for sociological theory and research. We review four insights that form the main contours of this conceptual shift in part 1 of the chapter. This review will help you to appreciate the radical impact that work on gender has had on the discipline of sociology. It will also help you to understand what is new in the second conceptual shift.

In part 2, we introduce you to the revision and development of these four insights during the second shift in sociological theory and research on gender relations. This shift began in the 1980s, took hold in the 1990s, and is currently ongoing. It brought changes to thinking about gender itself, as well as changes to sociology more generally. The shift involved a move to interrogate the conceptualization of gender more closely and to treat gender in a more relational, contextual, specified, and contingent manner. This reconfiguration of how we think about and do research on gender has, to some extent, led the way in moving sociology towards the development of post-positivist research practices. In reviewing the main elements of recent theoretical and methodological developments, we bring you to the edge of where thinking is today on the conceptualization of gender.

We also use the four main insights of the second shift to ground the presentation of life course events and issues in subsequent chapters. In each of these chapters, we highlight and further elaborate aspects of the main insights of the second shift. Throughout the text, we also highlight how our own thinking and research around gender relations has been intertwined with these conceptual shifts. In this regard, we locate ourselves in the sociology of gender to highlight the issues—political, professional, and personal—that have been important to us over the years.

As educators, we believe that you will learn more deeply and more meaningfully if you can relate the material in this book to your own life. We hope to help you in this process by including short reflective pieces written by us and a number of students currently in or recently graduated from the sociology graduate programs at Carleton University. These reflective inserts are in all of the chapters. They show you how we, a diverse collection of women and men, think about gender in our own lives and in our academic research—and how we often find strong linkages between the two. We invite you to contemplate the meaning and relevance of the material in the book generally, but in the inserts especially, for how you are living your own life. You will understand the significance of gender relations and how they are articulated in multiple ways, in both social structure and agency, if you can begin to see and engage with gendered patterns and connections in the social world around you. We are convinced that the question posed by Nancy K. Miller, an American professor of English literature, is an important one: 'How is the narrative that unfolds in the book describing a story that is "like me," or "not like me"?' (Miller 1997). By sharing our own experiences with you, we want to demonstrate to you how the sociology of gender relations came to matter in our lives and how it came to occupy such a central place in our sociological work. In showing you how the narrative in this book is 'like us', we hope that you will be able to make similar though unique connections that link this sociological narrative on gender relations with your own personal life.

PART 1: THE FIRST SOCIOLOGICAL SHIFT— ACCEPTING THAT GENDER MATTERS

> If we date the women's movement in Canada from the late 1960s, it becomes possible to speak about 'before' and 'after' on virtually every topic that has been raised by feminists. This does not mean that everything changed in the way that the participants and supporters of the movement intended. But there was a sea change ... (Hamilton 1996, 42)

Whenever we teach gender studies within sociology or in women's studies, we detect a sense among many of our undergraduate students that the battle for gender equality happened quickly and easily and that the issue is now passé. It takes some work to convince them that at one time in Canadian society, women as persons, as well as issues of importance to women, were largely invisible, absent, or devalued. Students do not realize that tremendous changes occurred during the twentieth century and, perhaps most significantly, since the 1960s. As the quote above indicates, the impact of the women's movement and feminist thinking on sociological knowledge and the everyday practices of gender relations resembled a massive 'sea change'. The 'before' and 'after' topics that have been raised by feminists make up a long list, including fashion, health research, body care, music, media, sport, sexuality, housework, child care, employment, violence, war, politics, education, sex work, domestic architecture, dating, food, smoking, pornography (. . . we could go on!).

Throughout the 1970s and into the 1980s, feminist sociologists and other scholars interested in gender continually pushed at the boundaries and foundations of sociological knowledge, looking for ideas that could be used to study the social organization and experiences of masculinity and femininity. Four insights had the most profound impact on shifting and shaping the sociological understanding of gender during that period. They are:

1. Gender is a vantage point of critique.
2. Gender is a social construction.
3. Gender is realized in social roles and institutions.
4. Gender is a relation of power and inequality.

Insight 1: Gender is a vantage point of critique

The history of sociology in Canada, as in many other countries, is a history of contestation about gender. While the analysis of women's circumstances and gender inequalities is now fairly well accepted as an important part of the discipline today, it was not so long ago that sociology was a male-centred discipline, undertaken overwhelmingly by men and focused on areas of social life where men were dominant and women absent or invisible. The impact of this world on female sociologists was twofold. First, they had to confront the fact that the daily lives of most women were not represented in the discipline. Marylee Stephenson justified her 1973 collection of articles on *Women in Canada* by stating that both were underdeveloped areas of academic work. She said (1973, xiv), 'We don't know yet what it is to a Canadian for many of the same reasons we don't know what it is to be a woman. Canada . . . like women, has traditionally been defined by others.' Canadian sociology was not alone in thinking the world was a masculine world. Ann Oakley, one of the (grand)mothers of British feminist sociology, observed that women were simply a 'side issue' within sociology: 'The male orientation may so colour the organization of sociology as a discipline that the invisibility of women is a structured male view, rather than a superficial flaw. The male focus . . . reduces women to a side issue from the start' (Oakley 1974b, 4). In the United States too, similar frustrations with the absence of women's experiences in sociological theory and research were being expressed. Reflecting on this time, Joan Acker comments about an area in which she taught and researched: 'I had been teaching courses on class and stratification and on organizations; these were the areas in which I began to see inconsistencies, contradictions, and absences of women. How, then, could these theories pretend to conceptualize society-wide economic and status structuring?' (Acker 1997, 34).

The second impact, closely related to the first, was that women found being in the discipline an alienating experience. Whether as students or professors, women found themselves immersed in very male academic environments. Feminist sociologists realized that the debates and struggles they were studying in the daily lives of other women were reflected in their own marginalized experiences within sociology departments and within the Canadian professional association. Women were a small minority within the sociology profession. In the early years of the Canadian Sociology and Anthropology Association (founded in 1965), women comprised about 10 per cent of the membership. In the association's first 15 years, only one woman (Gillian Sankoff) had been elected as president, the highest executive office, and only one female sociologist (Aileen Ross) had been entrusted with the important job of co-ordinating the annual conference (Eichler 1992, 75–6). Eventually, women's participation and representation would pick up, but in those early days, it was not unusual for a woman to be either alone or among only one or two other women in her sociology department.

Dorothy Smith was among those who wrote about the disjuncture women sociologists experienced between wanting to engage with women's everyday lives, including their own, and having no conceptual basis or institutional support within sociology with which to do so. Smith's book, *The Everyday World As Problematic* (1987), grew out of this sense of marginalization and disconnection. It is one of the best sources for learning about the ways by which women were made invisible in the discipline of sociology and ways that women-centred domains (housework, child care, informal work, community work) were absent from sociological knowledge. The subtitles in her first chapter alone are highly revealing: 'A Peculiar Eclipsing: Women's Exclusion from Man's Culture'; 'Text, Talk and Power: Women's Exclusion'; 'Men's Standpoint Is Represented As Universal'; and 'The Brutal History of Women's Silencing'.

Smith identified this disconnection as one of *bifurcated consciousness*, a concept that captures how women in academia were compelled to learn and to think in ways that erased what they knew from their everyday experiences, with no vocabulary or language to capture the texture and nuances of women's lives. Yet from this place with no language or words to speak, feminist academics like Smith, Oakley, Eichler, Acker, Stephenson—and many others—began to 'talk back' to sociology (DeVault 1996). In challenging the discipline, they also offered the possibility of something exciting and new. They were not just tinkering with the edges of sociological knowledge. They were asking questions and assessing answers that were fundamental to the core of the discipline. Smith captured this sense of possibility and importance when she wrote: 'Thinking more boldly . . . might bring us to ask first how a sociology might look if it began from the view of women's traditional place in it and what happens to a sociology that attempts to deal seriously with that. Following this line of thought, I have found, has consequences larger than they seem at first' (1974, 7).

A sociology that 'began from the view of women's traditional place in it', and with 'consequences larger' than anticipated, was evolving into a sociology in which gender was a *critical vantage point* from which to view the development of the discipline itself. Yet there would be many challenges ahead for feminist scholars as they began to attempt to make women visible within sociology and to think about how to transform sociology with perspectives drawn from women's lives.

One of the greatest challenges at the time was attempting to fit women into already developed theoretical concepts and arguments. British sociologist Hilary Graham captured this dilemma eloquently when she observed that women's experiences were being researched with surveys designed for men's lives and asked, 'Do her answers fit his questions?' (Graham 1983). Also in Britain, sociologist Rosalind Edwards commented some years later that the oft-repeated attempts to fit women's lives into male theories were much like trying to 'fit a round peg into a square hole' (Edwards 1990).

A good example of the round peg/square hole phenomenon was, as Acker's comments earlier suggest, the awkward fit between women and existing analyses of social class. Social class classifications were constructed largely on the basis of male occupational groupings and hierarchies. Further, if class was analyzed at the level of households, it was the man's occupation (as head of the household) that was taken to be the determinant of the household's class position. Thus, women's own occupational experiences were marginalized in social class classifications and ignored altogether in studies of class structure based on households. Because housework was not part of the paid economy, it was difficult to know how this form of work fit into hierarchies of social class. Several attempts were made to try to connect housework with class schema, but the need to do so was more an illustration of the problem of women's exclusion than a longer-term solution to it.[1] While claiming to be *general* theories, these sociological approaches were in fact *gendered* theories in that they systematically foregrounded men's experience. It is not surprising, then, that many aspects of society that interested students of gender were simply not being captured by conventional sociological analysis. At the time, these aspects included issues of sexuality, the medical domination of women's reproductive health, their experiences of violence, and the silencing of women's creative and political voices.

Arguments in the first sociological shift challenged what counted as important sociological phenomena and the adequacy of existing sociological concepts to explain gender patterns. As identified by Heather Jon Maroney and Meg Luxton (1987, 9, 11), there was a need to move 'beyond the stage of "adding women on" to make a genuine attempt to theorize gender'. Thus, a key challenge for sociology was *how* to include women's experiences within the discipline and *how* gender could be theorized and researched.

Insight 2: Gender is a social construction

Sociologists have had a lot to say about the role gender relations play in organizing the daily lives and fundamental social structures of society. How they have thought about gender, however, has gone through some transformations. Traditional sociological analyses in the 1950s and 1960s presented being male or female as an 'ascriptive' characteristic: that is, as a 'natural' attribute beyond the influence of individuals or societies. Today, it is quite extraordinary to think that a discipline devoted to the social construction of human experience would section off some aspects of that experience as beyond reach. But such was the state of sociological thinking at the time that several aspects of personal identity were treated in this way—not only gender but race and age as well. 'Ascriptive' characteristics were contrasted with other attributes such as class position or professional status, which were regarded as 'achieved' character-istics. One of the earliest developments in thinking about gender in sociology was to challenge this notion of 'ascribed' status and to insist that gender was 'achieved' or socially constructed.

Where you sit on a bus, who you start conversations with, who your friends are, what you wear, how late you stay out at night, what sports you play, whom you dance with, whom you have sex with, how old you are when you first have sex, whom you marry, whom you have children with—these are all activities structured by societal conventions concerning appropriate female and male behaviour. In some cases, the activities are also regulated by more formal procedures, rules, and laws about which relationships between men and women are socially sanctioned and which are not. Both the more informal and the formal regulation of appropriate gender behaviour varies according to the wider structural context, be it at the level of, for example, neighbourhood, religious group, social class, or nation.

This observation was a very early insight in the first shift that has shaped all sub-sequent sociological thinking about gender. It was argued that views in society about masculinity and femininity, and about appropriate behaviour for women and men, boys and girls, have a social foundation independent of biological necessity. 'Gender' was introduced as a term distinct from 'sex': sex referred to biologically based differ-ences, primarily related to differences in chromosomes and reproductive functions, while gender referred to socially produced differences, primarily of character, ambi-tion, and achievement.

Ann Oakley was the first to bring a sustained analysis of the differentiation between sex and gender to the attention of the sociological community. In her classic 1972 book *Sex, Gender and Society*, Oakley drew on anthropological, psychological, biological, psychoanalytic, and sociological evidence to make the case that distinctions of sex are not as clear-cut and straightforward as people typically think and that the cultural and psychological features of gender are so variable historically and cross-culturally that it is impossible to map these features onto biological sex difference.

In Canada, the social construction and inequalities of gender were initially stud-ied as 'sex roles' and 'sex stratification' (Stephenson 1973). However, it was not long before the concept of gender was established as the more common conceptual lan-guage for sociologists.[2] One reason that people were so keen on this particular way of thinking about men's and women's experiences of masculinity and femininity was that it put the possibility of change in the forefront.

First and Lasting Impressions

Janet Connects with the First Shift in the Sociology of Gender

Sociology's willingness and ability to problematize gender is the basis of my attachment to and respect for the discipline. As an undergraduate in Toronto and then Waterloo in the 1970s, I was drawn to the study of sociology. In the beginning,

I didn't know much about the subject except that it had something to do with 'people', and in all honesty, I found the endless definitions about social roles, institutions, the family, and bureaucracy in first-year sociology more than a little boring. But there were parts I found very exciting. My sociology professors were speaking about large, exciting things—social change, social conflict—that were important and happening in the world around me. But the biggest thing I encountered in sociology as an undergraduate, and the thing that motivated my study of sociology from that point on, came in a second-year course on 'sex roles' taught at the University of Waterloo by Professor Margrit Eichler.

Encountering the idea that as a girl, there was a social script for me, an identity and an appearance that I was expected to embrace and fulfill—no matter how well it suited my own talents, inclinations, and ambitions—struck home hard. It made sense of all those fights I'd had with my parents and schoolteachers about what I wanted/what they expected me to do, how I wanted/was allowed to look, and how I did/should behave. It helped me to have the courage to examine things that had, or had not, happened to me and to wonder whether the politics of gender was at the heart of these experiences. Why was I sent home in grade 8 because I wore a necktie to school? Why were the smokers at the edge of the school property mainly girls? Why did only boys get invited to participate in special extracurricular science experiments? Why were girls at my high school required to wear skirts, even in the middle of winter? Why did the Royal Bank hire female university students as tellers for summer employment and male students as management trainees? Why did no one ever come out to watch the University of Waterloo girls basketball team, and yet the boys' games were always packed? Why did we go in mixed groups to watch the female stripper at the Kent Hotel in downtown Waterloo? Why were young women who went to the university medical service for birth control fitted with the Dalkon Shield? That there existed within sociological thinking the means to answer all of these questions, and the inspiration to ask even more, was a revelation and a liberation.

While the study of gender in sociology has moved on enormously since those early days in Professor Eichler's sex roles class, there remains in sociology a critical impulse to assess how, for what purpose, and with what consequences gender continues to structure our personal lives and our society. Feminist sociologists in the 1970s in Canada battled the prevailing winds, cleared the ground, and set up a safe house for those who came after, eager to hear more about a sociology that spoke to women's experience and challenged social arrangements that systematically discounted women's hopes and concerns. I have benefited, in my personal and professional life, from their determination to be heard and from the sociological space they created for critical reflection and action on gender inequality. In return, I have tried in my own sociological teaching and research, and in my day-to-day life with colleagues, family, and friends, to honour their efforts by doing what I can to help further enlarge and enrich the social space for a critical engagement with gender.

Insight 3: Gender is realized in social roles and institutions

With gender well-established as a social construction, there was more conceptual work to do to identify just what form of constructed phenomenon it is. Gender was identified as part of everyday lived experience as well as a feature of how the societies in which people live are organized. A gender perspective thus regards being masculine or feminine as a social achievement that requires intense effort and scrutiny on the part of individuals and societies. More specifically, attributes and inequalities associated with being male and female came to be seen as socially created consequences of the way society is organized around gendered identities. For example, the fact that doctors have traditionally been male and nurses female is not a consequence of natural abilities or chromosome patterns. It is a result of how ideas of gender enter into the social organization of social institutions such as the family, paid work, the state, the courts, and the media. The structure of gender was studied as forms of organization, systems, and institutions that make up the larger envelope of people's lives. The lived experience of gender began to be studied by sociologists as questions of identity (who and what am I?) and questions of agency (how can I direct my life?).

Throughout the 1970s and early 1980s, questions of gender identity were explored largely through 'sex role theory', which was one of the most popular accounts of the construction of gender identities in sociology. The concept of 'role' was centred around a distinction between people and the social positions they occupy. That is, society provides different gender roles or scripts, which men and women learn and follow. A related term was socialization, a term that was very popular in sociology at that time because it seemed to explain how people learn their gender identities through a process of subtle or explicit sanctions or rewards (Parsons and Bales 1955). This approach pointed to how gendered norms and social expectations had a significant impact on the way women and men made choices and acted in society. Social institutions—the family, schools, the media—acting as agents of socialization were said to reward boys and girls who behave in ways deemed appropriate to their gender and punish those who did not.

Residues of socialization theory and sex role theory still remain in sociology, and certainly public perceptions persist that socialization is a key tenet of sociology. Nevertheless, sociologists did begin to realize the limitations of 'sex role theory' and accounts of gender identity that relied too heavily on socialization. The American feminist sociologist Barrie Thorne, perhaps best known for her book *Gender Play* on gender and childhood, has commented aptly on these limitations. While her comments are about children, they relate equally well to thinking about problems with the concept of gender socialization in general:

> For one thing, the concept of 'socialization' moves mostly in one direction. Adults are said to socialize children, teachers socialize students, the more powerful socialize, and the less powerful get socialized. Power, indeed, is central to all these relationships, but children, students, the less powerful are by no means passive or without agency. As a parent and as an observer in schools, I have been impressed by the ways in which children act, resist, rework, and create; they influence adults as well as being influenced by them. (1993, 3)

Although the critique of socialization is a significant development in the sociology of gender and would continue for some time, it is important to recognize that it grounded an important insight of the first shift. Individuals are gendered because society is organized in such a way as to make gendered identities meaningful. At the level of social institutions, a lot of effort is expended on trying to ensure that individuals adopt and conform to gender-appropriate behaviour. Socialization was criticized for emphasizing a 'top-down' image of the relations between individuals and their society. However, at the time, it provided a much needed idea of how gendered identities are reproduced from one generation to the next. It began a line of thinking that identified gender as a systemic feature of society.

Andrea Connects (Belatedly) with the First Shift in the Sociology of Gender

My connection with the first shift in sociological thinking on gender relations occurred in a rather delayed way. Indeed, it shocks me now when I think about how I went through my undergraduate degree in the late 1970s with so little focus on gender. As described in this chapter, varied factions within the feminist movement and different strands of feminist theory were in existence all around me, and yet I was, at that time, only interested in social class and Marxism. The only way I can account for this is to say that we are often moved intellectually and politically by the questions that plague us at a personal level.

The mix of the personal and the political wove together my working-class background in northern New Brunswick and the intellectual climate that I found at York University in the late 1970s. In the months before boarding the train that took me from my small Maritime town to the big city of Toronto, I graduated from high school as class president, winner of the gold medal for academic achievement and leadership, and, like all five of my siblings, the recipient of a full-tuition scholarship from the paper mill where my father worked. It never occurred to me at the time that gender was an issue that translated into inequality or disadvantage. In a family of six children, three girls and three boys, we were treated equally by my parents and were evenly rewarded for our efforts. I did have some niggling concerns about why my brothers had well-paid jobs at the paper mill each summer while I laboured for minimum wage at the Dominion grocery store as a cashier and why there wasn't a girls' soccer league or hockey team in my town. And I certainly noticed my mother's fatigue as she pieced together a labourer's wage while cooking all the meals 'from scratch', housecleaning, washing clothes in an old-fashioned wringer-washer, hanging out loads and loads of laundry, making most of our clothes, and volunteering at church and school events. Yet I was equally concerned about the pressure on my father, earning his wages through 12-hour shifts at the paper mill and with the constant threat of its closure hanging over our heads. It was the latter issue that first fuelled my political interests. At the age of 17, I was completely taken up with Marxist theory and class analysis. While I did study with a handful of Marxist female professors in political science at York (Judith Hellman, Himani Bannerji,

Ellen Wood) and I am sure that they wove issues of gender, race, and class into their analysis, it was mainly class issues that spoke to me then.

It was years later, after completing my BA in political theory and my MA in international development studies, during a six-year stint of working in Central and South America, that the profound centrality of gender as a vantage point of critique and understanding of the social world hit me, metaphorically, like a ton of bricks. I suddenly tuned in to stark divisions of paid and unpaid labour between women and men and to the constant intersections between gender and power. These realizations came to me through stories, which I heard and witnessed throughout my years of working and travelling in Latin America, including: stories of physical abuse that I heard from women in poor rural villages in Bolivia and Peru; the contradictory treatment of women in revolutionary Nicaragua where they were both revered as soldiers but also treated as sexual objects; the crippling illiteracy levels in women throughout poor rural communities; and the palpable absence of women in positions of power both in local community settings and all the way up to national politics throughout Latin America.

This strong awakening meant that I began to read back through my own biography using gender as a lens, which ultimately created *revised memories* and a completely different biographical narrative. I suddenly saw my own life (and that of my two sisters) as well as that of my mother and my grandmother with new understandings that extended into my work and later my scholarly life. These new ways of seeing were further sharpened when I combined my doctoral studies at Cambridge University with the raising of three young children. Sociology had changed enough that I did not face that extreme sense of 'bifurcated conscious-ness' that Dorothy Smith referred to. Yet I had glimpses of this dissonance between the world that I occupied at home with my children and the world of academia. With Janet, I share a strong sense that the struggles of early feminists have mat-tered enormously in clearing a path for new generations of feminist scholars and activists. This has allowed us to move with some ease into research areas that challenge male-defined understandings of paid and unpaid work, that interrogate divisions between the public and the private, and that point to the importance of valuing care work.

Insight 4: Gender is a relation of power and inequality

Early studies in sociology, especially from the structuralist functionalist school, emphasized the complementarity of male instrumental and female expressive gen-der roles. Interventions from feminist sociologists challenged this view to highlight the inequality embedded in definitions of masculinity and femininity and to insist that the unequal features of gender relations be acknowledged. The argument that gender identities are fundamentally unequal propelled much of the sociological work on gender from the 1970s onward.

Some forms of traditional sociology did acknowledge the profound inequality in how women's and men's lives were positioned in cultural, economic, and political spheres. Thorstein Veblen, a late-nineteenth-century American social theorist and satirist, was a very early outspoken critic of the way women were dressed and displayed as tokens of conspicuous consumption and conspicuous leisure. In *The Theory of the Leisure Class*, Veblen (1953, 232) described the life of a leisure-class woman: 'She is petted, and is permitted, or even required, to consume largely and conspicuously—vicariously for her husband or other natural guardian. She is exempted, or debarred, from vulgarly useful employment—in order to perform leisure vicariously for the good repute of her natural (pecuniary) guardian.' The German social theorist and Marx's collaborator Friedrich Engels was another early critic of the position of women in society. In *The Origin of the Family, Private Property and the State* (1942), Engels described how a 'historic defeat of the female sex' ushered in a societal structure of male domination. Feminist sociologists drew inspiration from some of this earlier critical work but also forged new conceptual ground in setting out two claims that related to gender inequality.

The first claim was that 'sex differences' had often been exaggerated, and this often occurred to the detriment of women's opportunities and self-esteem. It was observed that discussions of 'sex differences' in temperament, in attitudes, and in capabilities overstated the extent of difference between men and women as social groups. These overstatements hindered women's abilities and achievements and contributed to men's claims of power and authority in all things and in all places. One vigorous debate at this time had to do with the extent to which one could attribute observed sex differences to naturally based patterns of behaviours. For example, in the late 1960s the appropriately named Lionel Tiger wrote about the significance of male bonding in both animal and human communities for the survival of the species. In describing his own argument, he asserts:

> I tried to suggest the importance of male bonding in human communities and its possible biological basis and significance. In the latter connection, the proposition was put that ceremonies of initiation reflect a pattern of unisexual selection for work, defence and hunting purposes comparable to sexual selection for reproductive ones. (1969, 246–7)

Much energy was directed at refuting the scientific and logical bases of such research, which developed later as sociobiology. Kaplan and Rogers (2003, 39) note that some early critiques of the biological determinism of sociobiology were particularly motivated to challenge the idea that any variation from identified sex differences was abnormal and that attempts to bring about change were futile. They identified the popularity of such arguments as a form of backlash against women's growing independence during this period. Other sources of 'sex difference' research, such as psychology, also came under intense scrutiny. The extensive review and debunking of such research by psychologists Maccoby and Jacklin (1974) helped to fuel arguments by feminist sociologists against the exaggeration of difference in the analysis of women's and men's character and personalities. As British feminist Juliet Mitchell (1980) famously remarked, compared to giraffes, women and men are very much alike. The conclusion was that the overstatement of sex difference was becoming itself a form of discrimination and oppression that largely worked to the advantage of men.

The second claim was that inequality in women's and men's life chances is a consequence of how society is organized and of the particular ways in which gender is created and sustained as a significant feature of social and personal life. In Canada, three streams of work developed this idea. One focused on the more organizational aspects of inequality, with an emphasis on inequalities in education, employment, income, and the amount and types of work that women and men do. Monica Boyd's early work (1982; 1985; Boyd et al. 1985) on occupations is a good example of this interest. The second was concerned with larger systemic foundations of gender inequality, captured by analyses of capitalism, patriarchy, and what came to be called the sex/gender system. The work of Roberta Hamilton sits within this research trend very well, from her early work on relations of patriarchy and capitalism (1978) to her more recent 'gendering' of the vertical mosaic (2005). The third investigation of gender inequality focused on issues of identity construction and the constitution of gendered selves and bodies. Mary O'Brien undertook this type of investigation, exploring how men's efforts to compensate for their existential alienation from reproduction underlies gendered power relations. She wrote (1981, 8): '[I]t is not within sexual relations but within *the total process of human reproduction* that the ideology of male supremacy finds its roots and rationales.'

Conclusion: The first shift in the sociology of gender

The first shift in the approach to gender in sociology involved acknowledging that the discipline had been male-focused, finding ways to include women's experience, and accepting that gender mattered a great deal to the sociological enterprise. Often associated with feminist politics of the 1960s, 1970s, and 1980s, this first shift in sociological thinking exhibited a sense of movement, exhilaration, possibility, and potential. It constituted a sea change in sociological thinking. Such sentiments are captured by Joan Acker's recollections of the time: 'Feminism helped me . . . to understand why sociology had been so alienating and confusing to me. . . . Finally I was asking myself questions that made sense to me, that were interesting. They were my questions, not questions dredged from some "body of literature" and couched in the concepts of some bodiless "theorist" ' (1997, 35). The significance of this shift in sociology is acknowledged by later generations of women scholars who see their relationship to the discipline as defined by a mutual interest in gender. Barbara Marshall comments on this connection in the introduction to her book *Configuring Gender* (2000, 10): 'Thanks to the intrepid feminist sociologists who preceded me and my peers, carving out gender as a legitimate area of sociological concern, I have had the opportunity to focus my academic career around the sociology of gender. . . . "Gender" has, in large part, been the mediating concept between the political interests of feminism and the intellectual interests of sociology.'

As described in the next section of this chapter, there were many concerns and many persons who were *not* caught up in this sea change, however. Issues of exclusion and inclusion, challenges to assumptions of common experiences among women, and discontent with the theoretical limitations of gender conceptualizations—all of which had been swirling underground for some time—began to surge and break in the 1980s. We now turn to the main insights of the second shift in sociological thinking about gender relations.

PART 2: THE SECOND SOCIOLOGICAL SHIFT— INTERROGATING GENDER

By the early 1980s, gender was quite solidly in place as a key feature of sociological theory and research, and the argument that gender mattered was accepted in most sociology courses and programs. However, the conceptualization of gender and gender inequality had not remained static. Strong and compelling arguments about the need to interrogate gender—both as a sociological concept and as a focus of policy development and political action—began to emerge from several quarters. For example, such critiques have come from racialized women, colonized women both within Canada and in Third World settings, pro-feminist men, women with disabilities, the GLBT (Gay, Lesbian, Bisexual, and Transgendered) community, and young women and activists fighting the feminization of poverty. Criticisms also came from postmodern and post-structuralist positions, which were radically transforming ways of thinking and knowing across the academy. Thus, new ways of thinking and speaking about gender were surfacing alongside of, as well as within, larger intellectual challenges and changes to how individuals, social relations, and societies were understood.

In general, this second shift in sociology can be characterized as involving a movement from more homogeneous, static, category-focused, and deterministic ideas of gender to more heterogeneous, dynamic, relational, and contingent conceptualizations. Four insights in this second shift are driving much of the current research in sociology. Each of these insights revises, extends, and deepens the four insights of the first shift, as described in part 1 of this chapter.

The four insights key to the second shift in the sociological understanding of gender are:

1. Gender is a vantage point of critique—but we need to recognize multiple vantage points.
2. Gender is a social construction—but it is actively constructed in fluid and diverse ways.
3. Gender is realized in social roles and institutions—but we need to see these as dynamic, multi-layered, and relational contexts.
4. Gender is a relation of power and inequality—but we need to analyze these as intersectional phenomena and recognize that equality must accommodate difference.

Insight 1: Gender is a vantage point of critique—but we need to recognize multiple vantage points

As work on gender in sociology moved through the 1980s and into the 1990s, it became clear that the earlier idea of gender as a vantage point of critique must mean including a broader array of vantage points. Just as Dorothy Smith felt a sense of 'bifurcated consciousness' between her everyday life and the life reflected within malestream sociology of the 1960s, particular groups of women felt much the same way as they watched feminist theory, and gender studies, in sociology unfold in ways that did not speak to them or about them. Voices of women who occupy varied positions within Canadian society were quite justifiably wanting to be heard. They argued strenuously for the significance of their unique individual and collective experiences of gender relations as specified by, for example, class, ethnicity, race, sexuality, generation, religion, immigration status, citizenship, language, and disability. We cannot address all of these concerns here—most will be covered in the following chapters. For the moment, to give you a flavour of how the arguments are running, we focus briefly on race, generation, and the multiple voices of masculinity.

In Canada, racialized women drew on earlier work conducted by pioneering scholars in the United States and pointed to how the seemingly harmonious Canadian multicultural mosaic was marred by exclusion, discrimination, and, at times, brutality. The work of Himani Bannerji and Sherene Razack stands out in this regard. Bannerji (1991; 1995) brought together critical reflections on the compound impact of gender, class, and race oppressions in Canadian society and posed powerful critical challenges to how feminist and sociological analysis had to date ignored or trivialized these experiences. Razack (1998) offered critical theoretical perspectives that were useful for understanding how racialized women are viewed and the varied ways that they respond to racism in diverse sites—in classrooms and courtrooms, in parks and slums, in spaces where prostitutes and pimps assemble, and in parliaments. Both of these authors employ the evocative metaphor of the *gaze* to capture relations of both oppression and resistance. Bannerji's *Returning the Gaze* (1993) and Razack's *Looking White People in the Eye* (1998) both depict the active agency, response, and resistance of racialized women who stare back at and challenge injustices in Canadian society. Work with and by Aboriginal women represents an important project to have the gender struggles of some of the most marginalized individuals in our society recognized and addressed. These efforts have helped to put the many forms of racialization and racism in Canada, and the way they intertwine with gendered hierarchies, on the sociological agenda. They have also pushed sociology towards a more complex and nuanced understanding of gender.

Another interesting development in the push for more varied vantage points in the sociological treatment of gender has come from across the generational divide. Feminist sociologists who struggled in the first shift for the acknowledgement of gender were also caught up in a politics that reflected problems and issues of their time. Younger women have taken up different issues that are particularly salient to the social and cultural agendas of more recent times and to those who grew up in the 1980s and 1990s. These issues include body image, transgressive sexualities, eating disorders, and male sexual responsibility, as well as recent cultural phenomena like Riot Grrrls, the *Bust* and *Bitch* zines, and Eve Ensler's *Vagina Monologues*. Such concerns have also been highlighted in numerous books by young women focusing on what has been identified as Third Wave feminism.[3] The story of how Richards and Baumgardner, two 30-something feminists who met while working at *Ms* Magazine, came to write their influential book, *Manifesta: Young Women, Feminism and the Future*, reflects the experiences of many younger feminists growing up in Canada and the United States who felt alienated from the feminism of the 50-somethings. They note the divide between older feminists and those their own age 'with tight clothes and streaky hair, who made zines and music and Web sites' (Baumgardner and Richards 2000, 24). The insert below by Alana Wingfoot from the 3rdwwwave website sets out some of this divide in terms of what is identified as issues for feminist politics. This generational divide was also felt within sociology, as younger women coming into the discipline began to reflect on and challenge the distance between existing gender formulations and their own generation's interpretation and understanding of gender issues.

In recognizing the significance of diversity among women, it is important also to draw attention to the positioning of multiple men's voices in the sociology of gender. If the study of gender came to take on the vantage point of a critique within sociology, where are men's voices in this critique? The short answer is that since the study of sociology had been the study of men's lives and interests for such a long time, then men's place within the study of gender relations would have to be a process of delicate and steady negotiation. Both Janet and Andrea have memories from the 1980s of male colleagues wanting to join feminist reading groups or male academics putting their names forward to teach courses in women's studies or gender studies. Feminist sociologists did and still do vary in their responses and conclusions on these issues. Nevertheless, there is substantial recognition that men's views on and struggles with masculinity need to be a component of gender studies. One impulse in this direction came from racialized women, who argued that they shared with racialized men oppressions stemming from both race and gender hierarchies. In the US, Patricia Hill Collins, for example, pointed to how '[f]or African Americans, the relationship between gender and race is intensified, producing a Black gender ideology that shapes ideas about Black masculinity and Black femininity' (2004, 6). Similar views of the common interests between particular groups of women and men because of the shared oppression of gender and race ideologies and hierarchies have emerged in Canada—particularly with respect to highly marginalized and pathologized groups. A second impetus for thinking about the place of men in gender studies came from men themselves, who began to theorize and research multiple forms of masculinity. A male pro-feminist theoretical and activist perspective began to take shape in sociology through the 1980s and 1990s. These male scholars (Frank, Messner, Kimmel, Kaufman, Morgan, and Connell, among many others)[4] have pioneered studies of men and masculinities and in doing so have not only added to the rich scholarship of gender studies in sociology but also offered views on where sociological work needed to advance and improve.

Voices expressing their discontent with the too white, too heterosexual, too middle-class, too old, too female conceptualizations of gender represent a significant dynamic in the second shift in gender's place in sociological theory and research. There is an increasing awareness within sociology of the need to specify gender categories with reference to more particular situated experiences. We now try to talk specifically, and recognize the particular circumstances, of Aboriginal women, new immigrant women, black women, women with disabilities, lesbian women—and we are increasingly aware that even these categories can be too heterogeneous to be meaningful. Also, as we try to move the understanding of gender in society forward, it is

Different Generations, Different Issues

by Alana Wingfoot
29 June 1998

We grew up in a different world. We run into different problems than you did. Is it any wonder that we work with different issues?

SECOND WAVE FEMINISM	THIRD WAVE FEMINISM
Getting paid work, even if you're married or a mother.	Getting better-paid work so we can support ourselves and our families.
Securing the right to an abortion.	Maintaining that right and learning how to use it properly.
Breaking the glass ceiling.	Leaving the building and climbing up to the roof.
Getting women into positions of political power.	Getting women into positions of economic power.
Getting day care.	Changing our family and work structures so day care is less necessary.
Finding ways for women to have loving sexual relationships with other women.	Finding ways for women to have loving sexual relationships with whatever gender they prefer, and yes, that includes the individuals with prominent external genitalia and obvious body hair.
Breaking the silence about rape and sexual abuse.	Breaking the silence about consensual sex.
Giving women divorce and singlehood as options to het marriage.	Making het marriage a better choice for the women who want it, while still keeping those other options.
Making it acceptable for women to delay or space their children with birth control, or even to not have children at all.	Making it possible to be a mother AND have a life.
Making it acceptable for mothers to work.	Earning enough money so we can afford to become mothers.

clear that gender studies must include the experiences of men and forms of masculinity. That experiences of more specific forms of masculinity and femininity have been ignored or marginalized considerably reduced the ability of sociology, including feminist sociology, to give convincing and comprehensive accounts of the configurations and dynamics of gender in society.

Insight 2: Gender is a social construction—but it is actively constructed in fluid and diverse ways

Recognition that the categories 'woman' and 'man' could no longer be used in sociological analysis as if they had a singular and universal meaning led to a burst of activity exploring how gender identities and relations are produced in their varied forms. Throughout the past two decades, theoretical and empirical investigations into the social construction of multiple gender identities have been lively and exciting. The 'gender-bending' that was taking place culturally over this period was in effect also happening in sociological analysis, with explorations into the fragmenting, blending, reversing, and stretching of gender categories. For many, however, it became clear that 'bending' was not enough, because it left unexamined and unchallenged too much of the original gender formulations. In particular, scholars started to interrogate more closely the processes by which gender is produced and becomes meaningful as a social phenomenon and personal identity. A key feature of the second shift in thinking about gender in sociology is a rethinking of what is meant by the 'social construction' of varied forms of gender. In contrast to being conceptualized as a rather static and top-down process, there was movement towards ideas that emphasized the fluidity and diversity of gender construction.

Janet Recalls Early Encounters with the Second Shift—Different Ways of Being a Privileged White Woman

I lived in England in the early 1980s. Two English women were constantly in the news at that time: Margaret Thatcher and Diana Spencer. Thatcher's career as Conservative party leader and prime minister was a challenge to the existing system of class and patriarchy. She was the daughter of a shopkeeper and the first female British prime minister—transgressions of both traditional class and gender hierarchies. She was admired by some—mocked by others. A popular TV satire of the time—'Spitting Image'—played on the gender-bending involved in her historic political position. She was always shown in a man's pinstriped suit, with a spectacularly coiffed hair-do, smoking a fat cigar, wearing gaudy oversized rhinestone rings, and ordering her all-male cabinet around as if they were a collection of pet poodles. As a woman, she had personal success, but she did little during her time as prime minister to help the cause of other women in Britain. 'Maggie, Maggie, Maggie—Out! Out! Out!' was a political slogan shouted at many rallies and marches throughout the UK with equal conviction by women and men.

At the time of her marriage to the Prince of Wales, Diana Spencer was not at all unconventional in class or gender terms. She was a young girl of good breeding destined to be a good breeder. We were all assured that the future queen of England was a bona fide virgin who loved children. She did not listen for a second to the feminist 'Don't do it, Di!' campaign that occurred before the royal wedding. She showed up on the day wearing the most speculated-about wedding dress in history—bedecked in bows and ribbons and puffy bits—looking like a girl child playing grown-up. She was, of course, only 19. As time passed, she appeared to be revelling in her pampered, clothes-horse, glamour role, but this did not last long. We soon learned that her marriage was collapsing, unable to stand the strain of her husband's persistent infidelity. She broke with convention and started to talk in public about how limiting and restricting it was to be a female member of the Royal Family. While we might have dismissed Diana's troubles as just desserts for the undeserving rich and famous, she was doing other things that garnered her much admiration and respect. She showed a lot of courage in taking on and actively championing unpopular and dangerous causes. In particular, she defied stereotypes and ignorance about AIDS patients and was a vocal and passionate advocate on their behalf. She also acted as a spokesperson for the campaign against landmines and was photographed many times visiting areas of conflict suffering the consequences of this cruel technology of war. She also became a sincere campaigner for the fight against eating disorders—a predominantly female affliction and one she herself suffered. No one would have predicted that the young, naive, privileged teenager who married the Prince of Wales and was expected to be content with mothering the next British monarch would become a woman with ideas and convictions and have the character to speak about these issues publicly. Of course, as all of you must know, Diana died in a car crash in Paris in August 1997. When they heard of her death and during the procession to her funeral, the outpouring of emotion from the people of Britain, as well demonstrated in the popular movie *The Queen*, was nothing short of overwhelming.

Watching these two women comply with and defy the class-conditioned conventions of femininity into which they were born and present two very different scenarios of what it means to be a woman, I saw the embodiment of a sociological insight that was becoming very prominent. 'Woman' could not be regarded as a unified, static category of experience. At any one time, and over any one individual's lifetime, what it means to be a woman could mean different things and be experienced differently in different contexts. Gender identities are both diverse and fluid.

Can you think of an example of a woman, or a man, whose life illustrates the complexity of gender identities or how the ways in which people live their femininity or masculinity can change over a lifetime?

There are two main focal points to the rethinking of gender as a social construction. First, the idea that gender as a social phenomenon can be distinguished from sex as a biological phenomenon underwent an intense interrogation. Second, much work focused on the active social construction of fluid and diverse gender identities. We shall discuss each of these briefly in turn.

By the 1980s and early 1990s, feminist sociologists began to widely question the validity of distinguishing gender and sex, as well as the utility of overlaying this distinction onto a division between the social and the natural. The Canadian feminist sociologist Margrit Eichler expressed early versions of this disquiet. Her 1980 critique of feminist social science sets out analytical problems caused by separating biological sex and social gender. More elaborate versions of this argument soon developed. Connell argued in *Gender and Power* (1987, 79) that 'social practices that construct gender relations do not express natural patterns, nor do they ignore natural patterns. . . . reproductive biology is socially dealt with in the historical process we call gender.' Sandra Bem (1993, 2–3) argued similarly that biological facts 'have no fixed meaning independent of the way that a culture interprets and uses them, nor any social implications independent of their historical and contemporary context.'

An important component of this interrogation was the examination of how women's biology is understood and presented. Emily Martin's (1987) very influential research on the ways in which women's (and men's) bodies are described in medical textbooks revealed what she called the 'cultural grammar' involved in the creation of the so-called 'natural' female reproductive system and of biological sex differences. Martin pointed out, for example, that such texts describe reproductive functions using productionist metaphors that cast the creation of multitudes of male sperm as an ongoing achievement of heroic proportions in contrast to the comparatively passive and paltry one-off production of the female ova (Martin 1987, 48–9).

The interrogation of the division between the natural and the social also focused on the place of this dualism, and its gender overlay, in traditions of Western intellectual thought. The early intervention by Canadian feminist sociologist R.A. Sydie (1987) set an important benchmark in this endeavour. Her analysis of the representations of 'natural women' and 'cultured men' in the sociological tradition traced, in the work of Durkheim, Weber, Marx and Engels, and Freud, separations and assumptions about the primacy of the social over the natural, of the rational over the emotional, of the masculine over the feminine. As Sydie concluded (1987, 210–11), what was required was a complete rethinking of the conceptualization and explanation of the construction of the social world and women's and men's place in it. This interrogation of the division between the natural and the social in the conceptualization of gender has been explored more recently in Marshall (2000), who also takes issue with how post-modern challenges to sociology have positioned themselves in this debate.

A feature of these interrogations is the idea that 'nature' is what we understand it to be. This insight is important, for it suggests that we must view nature as a social construction—or at least as a phenomenon that we understand in ways that are structured, limited, and facilitated by our traditions and conventions of thought. It also pushes the body to the forefront in gender analysis as a practice of gender construction. As Nicholson elaborates (1994, 101), the body 'becomes a historically specific variable whose meaning and importance are recognized as potentially different in different historical contexts.' Thus, the body is itself a social construction, and its particular forms, meanings, and significance are questions for research. The construction of gendered bodies, and bodies that transgress gendered conventions, has been a tremendous area of sociological activity in recent years.

The decoupling of the sex/gender distinction from a division between the social and the natural also loosened the association of gender and sexuality and ushered in a torrent of research activity on sexuality as a socially constructed phenomenon that may or may not have a gendered form. While much of the 'sexual revolution' of the 1960s and 1970s reproduced conventional understandings of gender and sexuality (witness the infamous phrase by a male student leader that women's most significant position in the student movement was prone), the 1980s saw a stronger development of woman-defined female sexuality and other explorations of sexuality that were not gender-defined. The trend now is to see a more dynamic relationship between the 'biological' features of sexed bodies and what these features come to mean in social situations and in personal identities. With the social construction of gender released from more limited notions of heterosexuality and reproduction, a greater range of gendered behaviours emerged that expressed a more varied relationship to sexual orientation and the gendered/sexed body.

With this more diverse array of social aspects of gender came questions of how to see gender as an active social accomplishment. The idea of 'roles', as discussed in part 1, was too confining for this more dynamic and open-ended conceptualization of gender. Moreover, the idea of socialization seemed too programmatic and fixed as a description of a process whereby gender identities were formed. An important part of this opening up of the gendering of selves and bodies was the idea that gender is an accomplished social activity. Gender is far more likely now to be used as a verb than as a noun. Two useful ways to think about gender as an active accomplishment are the concepts of 'doing gender' and of 'gender as performative'.

In sociological formulations that stress the 'doing' of gender, everyday activities are regarded as highly skilled accomplishments. Gender is something that individuals must work at to achieve—in relation to themselves and to others. Gender has been studied in these sociological formulations for some time, and classics include Kessler and McKenna's study (1978) of sexuality and Goffman's work on gender advertisements (1979). West and Zimmerman's oft-cited work on 'doing gender' argues, drawing on Goffman, that gender is an 'accomplishment, an achieved property of situated conduct' (1987, 141). Rooted in ethnomethodological analyses of gender relations, 'doing gender' contains vestiges of a performance element. That is, when women and men 'do gender', they partake in activities and expression that befit their gender. As stated by Thompson and Walker, 'Women and men participate together to construct the meaning of gender and distinguish themselves from each other *as* women or *as* men' (1989, 865).

'Doing gender' shares some features of the performative approach to gender. The main proponent of the latter approach is Judith Butler, who presents one of the most radical departures from the idea that sex, gender, and sexuality exist in relation to each other. Her approach has given rise to an elaboration and exploration of queer theory, which challenges more fundamentally the place of gender in understanding relations of identity and sexuality. Butler (1990) argues that both gendered and sexed identities are performative. Being a woman, a lesbian, transgendered is something we 'do' rather than something we 'are'. Butler's approach distinguishes between performance and performative. She suggests that performance implies a pre-existing actor, whereas performative does not. As Salih explains (2002, 11), the idea that the subject is not a pre-existing, essential entity and that our identities are constructed means that it is possible for identities to be reconstructed in ways that challenge and subvert existing power structures. Thus, Butler sees the potential for change and transformation in the performative character of gender—the possibility of challenging the regulatory power of the fiction of gender (Butler 1990).

Emphasis on the doing and performative aspects of sex and gender, as fluid and diverse social phenomena, has added considerable richness and insight to our sense of how we actively gender our everyday selves and activities. This is not all there is to current conceptualization of gender as a social construction, however. It is central to the second-shift sociological approach to gender that this active gendering happens in contexts and circumstances that both offer and constrain choices. In other words, there is a structural aspect to the creation and re-creation of gender that continues to be of interest, albeit in a more extended and refined way than appeared in sociology previously.

Insight 3: Gender is realized in social roles and institutions—but we need to see these as dynamic, multi-layered, and relational contexts

The recognition of multiple genders and of the fluid nature of gender production connects with the idea that context matters. We actively construct our gendered and sexed identities but do so in specific contexts bounded by time, space, and other ways of structuring social relations. These contexts are themselves gendered, perhaps in multiple ways, so that they offer particular gender possibilities and do not offer others. For example, hairdressing salons and barbershops are highly constrained gender-specific domains. The men who frequent hairdressers, either as customers or employees, have to contend with the rather narrow set of identity options offered to men in such places. In contrast, women are rarely seen working in or getting a haircut at a barbershop—there are almost no identity options on offer for them in this setting except as servicing agents who drop off, pick up, or wait for a customer of the more appropriate gender. There are other social contexts that offer a wider range of gender possibilities. An example is schools. In the case of feminine identities, individual girls may have a range of gender negotiations to try out and draw on—sporty girl, caring girl, brainy girl, and so on—although some of these identities may be more possible in some contexts than in others (for example, brainy girl may be more possible in single-sex versus mixed-sex schools). Boys too have access to a range of male behaviours—cool guy, nerdy guy, sporty guy, music guy. As Marshall says (2000, 159), gender 'is only available as an identity—collective or individual—because of the social and cultural formations that make it so.' While acknowledging the need to emphasize gender as an enacted everyday social practice, many sociologists wish to attend as well to the character and dynamics of the social contexts in which actors 'do' gender. A fundamental concern for the second shift in the analysis of gender in sociology is how to identify the 'social and cultural formations' that contextualize action and, once they are identified, how to study their reproduction and transformation.

Andrea Connects with the Second Shift in the Sociology of Gender

In my teaching and writing about gender issues, my research explores and interrogates how both women and men are gendered subjects in social institutions such as the family and the workplace and in relation to state policies. It was my interest in the social institution of the family and mothering that led eventually to a decade-long research program on fatherhood. As discussed throughout this book, gender is realized in institutional and in relational contexts. I was confronted with this insight several years ago when a course that I taught underwent a name change and with it a change in the gender composition of my class.

In the fall of 2004, the course that I had taught for years under the title 'men and masculinities' changed to the more generic title 'advanced studies in gender'. This was part of a decision in my department to move towards broader titles so as to allow for a number of topics to be taught under the same course name. While the course content remained largely focused on men and masculinities, the change in title caused something that was not altogether unexpected. Under the name 'men and masculinities', the course usually had an enrolment of about one-third to one-half men, but under the title of 'gender', it was exclusively attended by women. This apparently small institutional change in the title of my course inadvertently changed the perception of what my class was about; it transformed it from a space open to both men and women to one that was apparently women-only.

While male students were clearly interested in taking courses that addressed questions of masculinity, they appeared to equate gender with something that was not about such issues. In sociology's second shift, gender increasingly came to include the study of men and masculinity, but I was beginning to sense that these ideas had not yet filtered into everyday perceptions. When I talked to the women who did take my class, they were both unsurprised that there were no men in the class and interested in seeing that so much of our time would be about men and masculinity. 'It will be interesting to find out about the other half of the world,' they said. They seemed to view gender as an essence or a property that people have or 'are' rather than as a set of dynamic processes wherein gender is enacted in relational contexts within which both women and men continually engage in creating and recreating gender, masculinities and femininities.

As I now reflect back to that class in the fall of 2004, I realize that two issues in the second shift of sociological thinking on gender were staring me in the face. One is that the vantage points of men and masculinities need to be incorporated routinely into gender studies. It seemed so ironic that having begun my interest in gender studies because of women's exclusion from sociology, I was looking at a specialization in sociology that had become the preserve of women. The second is that gender needs to be understood not as an essential property of individuals but as dynamic, multi-faceted, and relational social processes.

In the first sociological shift in the study of gender, it was a radical move to suggest that societies had a gender structure as a defining characteristic (societies could, for example, be patriarchal) and that apparently gender-neutral structures (such as the law or the state) were fundamentally shaped by assumptions about available and suitable gender identities and social positions. For the most part, gendered society and structures were seen as constraints on individual action and were problematized as external sources of gender oppression. As sociology and the progress of the gender critique developed, however, analysts wanted a more dynamic concept of structure—one that had a more direct and reciprocal relationship with the everyday actions of individuals—and the whole idea of society as an appropriate focus of analysis for sociology came under question.

Questioning the validity of more abstract levels of sociological analysis is an issue currently shared by many throughout the discipline—it is not an issue puzzled over only by gender analysts. Sociology has been struggling over the past two decades or so with challenges to its basic categories of analysis, including one of the most fundamental—society itself. By the beginning of the twenty-first century, because of processes such as globalization, the 'disappearance of society' was generating considerable debate. In addressing this debate, William Outhwaite offers an interesting perspective. His position is that a societal level of analysis is necessary but we must also recognize that society is layered. We need to look at how these layers interact and interconnect with one another to form complex multi-layered contexts of social action. Drawing on the case of globalization, he uses the example of young people's clothing styles to illustrate this point (2006, 96): 'dress styles for young people may be shaped at a global . . . level, yet also noticeably different in Flanders and Wallonia.' Accounting for these differences requires looking at the mediating levels of experience and how they engage both with the global and with more specific local circumstances.

The idea of multiple layers of society fits very nicely with Connell's conceptualization of layered social levels in the analysis of gender. In *Gender and Power*, Connell set out the first version of a formulation of how to think about gender as a relational phenomenon at different, though interacting, social levels. In this work, the concept of a 'structural inventory' is introduced, and Connell argues that such inventories are an important feature of a gender analysis. 'Where structural models push towards comparisons across situations at a given logical level, structural inventories push towards a more complete exploration of a given situation, addressing all its levels and dimensions' (Connell 1987, 98). Connell introduces two concepts to help identify more abstract levels of analysis required as part of a structural inventory: the 'gender order' refers to the 'structural inventory of an entire society', and 'gender regime' refers to 'the structural inventory of particular institutions'(1987, 99). Central to gender analysis are the layered contexts of the division of labour, power, cathexis (emotion), and symbolism. In later work (2000), Connell adds further layering to the contextualization of gendered practice. More attention is paid to the body, and 'body-reflexive practices' as a significant layer of gender-configured practice within specific gender regimes and gender orders. The concept of society is also extended to the global level: 'Locally situated lives are now (indeed have long been) powerfully influenced by geopolitical struggles, global markets, multinational corporations, labour migration and transnational media' (Connell 2000, 40). Therefore, gender analysis needs to engage the global level, attending to the gender order of a global society. Connell is very careful to point out—and we need to take special note of this point—that there is nothing essential or fixed in the conceptualization of gender regimes and gender orders: 'It is implicit in these concepts that gender regimes and gender orders are historical products subject to change in history' (Connell 2000, 29). The modifications and refinements to these ideas over the course of Connell's life work are a testament to this point.

Smith also articulates the position that in everyday experiences we can discern the workings of structural phenomena. She sets out a very powerful case for a method of analysis called 'institutional ethnography' and in doing so has inspired a new generation of sociologists to uncover structured contexts through an analysis of every day/every night gendered practice. She calls these structured contexts the 'relations of ruling', by which she means the 'internally coordinated complex of administrative, managerial, professional, and discursive organization that regulates, organizes, governs, and otherwise controls our societies' (1989, 38).

These newer approaches to the investigation of how gendered practice structures and is structured by more abstract levels of social organization have generated new strands of research into, for example, the sexuality of social organization (Hearn et al. 1989), the subversion of gender identities (Bruckert 2002), and new technologies of power (Davis et al. 1991).

Researchers are becoming increasingly aware that the meaning of gender, and even its salience, can be highly varied depending on context and the particular circumstances being investigated. There is, in other words, a trend towards regarding the relevance and substance of gender as questions for, and not assumptions of, research. This point is significant for all investigations of gender, but it has perhaps been most controversial and contested in the analysis of gender inequality.

Insight 4: Gender is a relation of power and inequality—but we need to analyze these as intersectional phenomena and recognize that equality must accommodate difference

When we explored insight 1 of the second shift (gender is a vantage point of critique, but we need to recognize multiple vantage points), we highlighted how different voices came to trouble and ultimately transform feminist theory and the analysis of gender relations. The recognition that gender does not involve homogeneous categories of experience—that in addition to the hierarchy of gender itself, there are dimensions of oppression and inequality that run through gender categories—has had a profound impact on the analysis of inequality. We consider three aspects of this impact here: the move toward an analysis of gender inequality that emphasizes how it intersects (or interconnects and interlocks) with other dimensions of inequality; reconsideration of the connection between difference and inequality; and finally, a questioning of what equality means and might look like.

While there is strong debate about how different dimensions of inequality interrelate with one another (see, for example, Acker 2006 and Glenn 2002), there is a concerted attempt to explore what the analysis of intersectionality could bring to understanding the relations between multiple structures and identities. The focus on intersectionality also draws attention to the need to move beyond the 'trinity' of gender, class, and race as *the* definitive mapping of inequality. Over the past two decades, analysts have argued that issues of citizenship, nationhood, ability/disability, age, religion, ethnicity, and generation need to be added to the mix. Recent reviews of Canadian contributions highlight several of these multiple dimensions (McMullin 2004; Zawilski and Rasky 2005). For scholars trying to work with formulations of intersectionality, a key aspect has been the rejection of any notion of conceptual hierarchy or predetermined salience. This means that the analysis does not presume from the start which dimensions have greater influence, or even which dimensions are important enough to be included in the analysis. As the Canadian feminist sociologist Daiva Stasiulis has argued (1999), given the importance of variations in structures and identities over time and place, there are simply no grounds on which such a determination can be made a priori.

An attraction of intersectional analysis is that it allows for recognition of inequalities within as well as between categories of gender, race, class, sexuality, and so on. For example, significant work is being done in Canada that begins to pull apart categories of race and ethnicity to see variations within communities in how gender is constructed and negotiated. In doing so, research points to the considerable diversity within racialized communities in the reproduction and transformation of masculinity and femininity. The research by Handa (2003) and Rajiva (2006) on generational and class differences in the negotiation of gender in Canadian South Asian communities are excellent examples of this trend.

However, the attraction of intersectional analysis comes with a significant challenge—exactly how are we to do intersectionality research when we have to take so many dimensions into account, consider inequalities within them as well as between them, and deal with such a high degree of complexity in the configuration of both social contexts and identities? Sociologists and others trying to work with the concept of intersectionality have commented that while it has had reasonably extensive development as a theory, it is not clear how this concept can be mobilized in research projects and analysis. Interesting attempts to address this problem are starting to emerge. Two contributions are particularly worthy of note—one from a Canadian feminist activist organization (CRIAW 2006) and one from an American sociologist (McCall 2005). This is an area of sociological work on gender inequality that will be fascinating to watch over the next years.

The work on intersectionality has underlined an idea that has been developing for some time and is now well-grounded in the sociology of gender. This is the idea that, for some women, gender difference may not be the most significant difference in configurations of social inequality. Growing recognition of and attention to the heterogeneous nature of the category 'woman' reveal deep and significant divisions and inequalities among women. Canadian work on employment relations within the domestic sphere are a powerful example of these inequalities. For example, Sedef Arat-Koc (1989) examined the lives of immigrant women working as live-in domestic workers in Canada, a situation in which housework 'becomes the responsibility of *some* [women] with subordinate class, racial and citizenship status, who are employed and supervised by those who are liberated from the direct physical burdens' (1989, 53). More recently, the work of Stasiulis and Bakan as well as Denise Spitzer exposes a deepening of these divisions of inequality among women because of systemic race discrimination in immigration programs and policies (Bakan and Stasiulis 1997; Stasiulis and Bakan 2003; Spitzer et al. 2003).

Equally, there is a need to consider that difference does not always mean inequality. Legal scholars such as Deborah Rhode have contributed to this thinking, pointing out that rather than simply focusing on 'difference per se', it is more useful to consider 'the disadvantages that follow from it' (Rhode 1990, 204). She argues, 'The difference dilemma cannot be resolved; it can only be recast. The critical issue should not be difference, *but the difference difference makes*' (Rhode 1989, emphasis added).

This is an intriguing point that moves beyond a common assumption that plagued the first shift in thinking around gender about the perceived necessity for women to adopt the behaviour, attitudes, and ambitions of men. Several variations on this theme have been explored in theoretical and empirical research. Do women need to be the same as men in order to have equality? Are there contexts and times in which gender differences are present but are just differences and not necessarily disadvantages (or do not lead to disadvantages)?

This idea leads us to the even larger discussion about the meaning of equality. We know that we would like to see the end of gender inequality, but what would gender equality look like? In the second sociological shift, attention is focused on a critique of those approaches to equality that are male-centred ways of thinking and being, or what some commentators have called *malestream* values and activities. That is, there is a significant realization that the *quality of equality* is often framed in male terms and thus needs to be constantly scrutinized. Many authors concur with Elizabeth Meehan and Selma Sevenhuijsen (1991, 28), who argued that 'the employment of equality as a concept and as a goal supposes a standard or a norm which, in practice, tends to be defined as what is characteristic of the most powerful groups in society.' Putting the point more succinctly, Alison Jaggar wondered whether women *should* want a larger piece of the pie (social, economic, political) if the pie is a carcinogenic one (Jaggar 1990). Canadian scholars have explored these ideas in relation to the meaning of equality generally and specifically as defined by the Canadian Charter of Rights and Freedoms (Jhappan 2002). The issue here is neatly summarized by the 1980s political slogan: 'Women who want to be equal to men lack ambition!'

While addressing the challenges of thinking through the interplay between differences and equality, and of thinking about what sort of equality we are aiming for, it remains important to draw attention to continuing issues faced by many Canadian women in their day-to-day lives. Indeed, it is a mistaken assumption that gender equality, even of a rudimentary form, has been attained. There is strong consensus that progress towards gender equality in Canada is unfinished business. Canadians are rightly very proud that the United Nations ranks their country highly in its assessment of the top places to live in the world. On the other hand, Canada does rather poorly in the United Nations ranking of the top nations in terms of gender equality.

Furthermore, equalization has often been achieved through a deterioration of men's circumstances so that women and men are 'equal' in that they share women's more disadvantaged circumstances. This, for example, has been the case in many areas of employment, including wages, benefits, employment security, and health and safety. The negative effects of 'equalizing down' can be severe. For example, in Ontario, the obligation for employers to provide transportation home for women who work late hours was challenged in court on the grounds of sex discrimination. The court agreed that the practice was discriminatory against men, and the upshot was to release employers from any obligation to provide such transportation. When a young woman in Ottawa was murdered as she walked home from her night shift at Wendy's in 2005, the issue of safety for employees working late hours re-emerged.

Backlash has occurred in some areas where progress toward gender equality had been achieved. Many issues, such as sexual assault, pornography, and other forms of commercialization and exploitation of women's bodies, remain stubbornly difficult, with little progress. Moreover, as societies change and develop, new forms of gender inequality emerge and need to be tackled.

Mary Ellen Connects with the Second Shift in the Sociology of Gender

By the time I was in my mid-20s, I had lived and witnessed a pretty devastating series of episodes in which gender played a starring role. Yet I had no effective way of theorizing those events. My BA in history, completed in 1987, offered few insights to the experiences. I had known some feminist activists and gained a lot of inspiration working alongside of them, but I was hungry for theories that could help me link the disparate pieces of experience together.

The statistics tell us that one in three women experiences violence at the hands of a man in her lifetime, but they offer no suggestions about how to reconcile that reality with the popular depictions in movies and books portraying men's relationship to women as protective and/or romantic. The contradiction can be pretty confusing and in my case contributed to a sense of self-blame, which is common for sexual assault victims. I had to find a way to accept that what had happened to me was not my fault, despite the fact that the society in which the violation of my core self occurred was unlikely to punish a perpetrator of sexual violence and almost undoubtedly add to my suffering if I decided to pursue justice through the courts. But these experiences of my own were not issues of survival. Furthermore as a middle-class member of the cultural and linguistic majority population where I lived as a young woman, I had access to social supports and advantages which the most frequently assaulted women in the country, Aboriginal women, do not. As I looked at the country I saw in my 20s, even worse was the indifference of our government to the lives of women and children fleeing abuse.

While working for a small television station, I interviewed some of the volunteers working in a women's transition house in Swan River, Manitoba. It was a house that was about to close its doors because of a short-term lack of funds. The existence of that fully furnished house, spacious enough for several families and perfectly located near a hospital and a police station, had saved the lives of women and given children a chance for a happy future. It was several months since the rent had been paid, and the landlord could not or would not keep waiting.

Budgeting for the transition house required that its residents pay the expenses but did not include the accumulation of a surplus to carry them through times when the house did not have a rent-paying occupant. The volunteers who had brought women to the house, equipped it, and gave social support had already extended themselves financially and emotionally as far as they could. Exhausted and heart-broken, many of them were women who had escaped violence themselves. Their continuing strength, resilience, and commitment amazed me. It is difficult for any abused women to rebuild her life and her self after abuse, but when we pay attention to numerous factors of oppression as intersectional analysis calls on us to do, we start to see how the disadvantages can accumulate for First Nations women and women who have recently immigrated. Social and economic marginalization means these women tend to have lower levels of education, poorer quality employment and worse employment opportunities than mainstream women have (Harper 2006, 35; Blum et al. 2006). There is a need for supplementary and culturally appropriate services for the women who experience intersecting oppressions.

The sad end of the Swan River Transition House story is that the house closed for the lack of a few thousand dollars. Despite press coverage and lobbying by women's groups, the local member of the legislature did not even try to intervene. It was 1989, and I struggled to understand how in Canada, supposedly one of the best places in the world to live, the Manitoba government refused to provide the few thousand dollars needed to keep a critically important women's transition house open.

Witnessing this series of events planted questions in my mind about the continuing gender power inequities in Canadian society. I knew that I needed some theory to make sense of the issue of violence against women and the govern-ment's seeming indifference to it. Working with women's groups directly trying to address the problems was a positive experience, but it sometimes felt like just bandaging wounds that were infected instead of treating the infection and stopping the violence that created the injuries. Several years later, when I had the opportunity to return to school and study gender through a sociological lens, I wel-comed the chance.

As I had hoped, in sociology I discovered gendered theories of social change that not only explained how our society could be so flawed but offered hope and strategy for building better societies. It helped me to see both the disadvantages I had experienced and the relative advantages I had over other women. Becoming a scholar was for me the result of very determined and vigilant efforts supported by a loving partner, strong family of origin, good friends, and the social advantages of being of British/Polish family background. The new society we work towards must make room for women of all backgrounds to be able to pursue their own ambitions and preferences.

Conclusion: The second shift in the sociology of gender

The second shift in sociological thinking about gender and gender relations has grappled with, and still does, a broad range of differences among and between women and men. Like the first shift, it has moved sociological thinking substantially ahead by revising, reconfiguring, and reconceptualizing the identities, relationships, and activities of women and men. Beginning in the early 1980s, new voices from multiple social locations increasingly expressed the need to interrogate gender as both a sociological concept and as a tool for policy development and political action. Thus, the second sociological shift in the conceptualization of gender comprises tremendously exciting developments that continue to open up to and embrace the perspectives of women and men in diverse social, political, cultural, and geographic locations. In addition, general movements in the discipline of sociology itself—movements spurred on by post-modernist and post-structuralist engagements with sociological traditions of thought—were felt within the study of gender. As we have indicated, the second shift in theorizing and researching gender relations within sociology has involved moving from conceptualizations of gender that were homogeneous, static, category-focused, and deterministic to those that understand gender as heterogeneous, dynamic, relational, and contingent. We have identified four specific insights that capture the main developments of the second shift. They highlight the impact of multiple vantage points, of the fluid and diverse character of gender identities, of a dynamic conceptualization of structure, and of revisiting the meaning and social significance of difference and equality.

CONCLUSION: SOCIOLOGY AND THE ANALYSIS OF GENDER RELATIONS

This chapter has laid out the contours of past and contemporary thinking in Canada and in other countries on gender and gender relations. Central to the chapter is the presentation of two conceptual shifts that have occurred in the sociology of gender. In the first shift, the discipline of sociology faced deep challenges in the form of calls to incorporate women's experience and the ubiquitous realities of gendered social relations (including those within the discipline itself). In the second shift, sociology again faced challenges to its central ideas and approaches—this time from a more diverse range of vantage points but with a similar message. What had been developed as the sociology of gender was too narrow, too static, and too limited in its reach. Insights about the social nature and impact of gender were revised and transformed to create conceptualizations that could address issues of division, diversity, and change. We fully expect further shifts and developments in how gender and gender relations are conceptualized in sociology. The ways this will happen depend very much on students like yourselves who, in thinking about how gender impinges on your life, can begin to document and construct your own narratives about what it means to be a woman or man in the twenty-first century.

In the chapters that follow, we focus on the four insights of the second shift in sociological thinking about gender and point to how and where they are being deepened and developed through the study of the lives of children, adolescents, and adults. The book follows the flow of our everyday lives, and we hope that you will see much, or at least some, of yourselves in this material. Chapter 2 focuses on the change and continuity in how gender features in the lives of children in Canada. In chapter 3, we enter a period of the life course when gender issues become intensified as adolescents struggle with gender identity and face intense pressures to conform to the norm. We also discuss in this chapter the way gender plays out in general trends in the transition to adulthood. Chapters 4 and 5 focus on themes of central importance to how we understand and live adulthood. Chapter 4 looks at the complex and changing relationships of earning and caring and how these relationships are shifting in women's and men's lives. In chapter 5, written by our colleague Mary Ellen Donnan, we look at other features of adult life in which gender is a strong element—being a citizen, having a career, and engaging in politics. Throughout the book, we continually confront the need to think of gender as a more specific and complex phenomenon. We address this need head-on in chapter 6. Here we pull together the key insights of the second shift and examine the challenges of doing sociological and policy research with conceptualizations and questions inspired by theories of intersectionality.

Research Questions

1. The *Canadian Review of Sociology and Anthropology* has been in operation since 1964 and will be available in your university library and, more recently, electronically. Find articles that discuss 'gender' written in each of the decades since the journal began. Do a content analysis of these articles to trace how the treatment of 'gender' has changed over this time period.
2. The conversations and debates about the sociological conceptualization of gender are international. Can you design a research study that would trace the engagement and the impact of Canadian contributions to these conversations and debates?

Discussion Questions

1. Which of the insights from the second shift in sociological thinking about gender do you find the most meaningful to you? Why?
2. This chapter opens with events in the film *Boys Don't Cry or The Teena Brandon Story*. Do you know of similar stories occurring today in Canada? Do you think North American society is becoming more tolerant of or open to persons and behaviours that challenge us to think outside the 'two gender boxes'?
3. What explanatory benefits does the move toward intersectionality bring for the analysis of gender? Is there anything negative in this move?
4. Can you think of an instance in which gender differences exist but do not necessarily lead to gender inequality?

Further Reading

Disch, Estelle, ed. 2006. *Reconstructing Gender: A Multi-cultural Anthology*, 4th edn. New York: McGraw-Hill. Analyzes gender in terms of intersectionality; focuses on both men and women.

Goldman, Paula. 2006. *Imagining Ourselves: Global Voices from a New Generation of Women*. Oakland, CA: New World Library. Third Wave essays answering the question 'What defines your generation of women?'

Hamilton, Roberta. 2005. *Gendering the Vertical Mosaic: Feminist Perspectives on Canadian Society*, 2nd edn. Toronto: Pearson. Important contribution to outlining the development of gender studies and issues in Canadian sociology and women's studies—the title is a reference to the famous metaphor for inequality in Canada as coined in the classic book by John Porter, *The Vertical Mosaic*.

Jackson, Stevi, and Sue Scott, eds. 2002. *Gender: A Sociological Reader*. London: Routledge. Useful collection of sociological work on gender, including contributions from Britain, France, Australia, Canada, and the United States.

Marshall, Barbara L. 2000. *Configuring Gender: Explorations in Theory and Politics*. Peterborough, ON: Broadview Press. Excellent consideration of the second shift in the sociological analysis of gender, including an assessment of the impact on gender studies of post-structuralist and post-modern critiques.

Chapter 2

The Multiple Genders of Childhood

Chapter Objectives

1. To identify dimensions of the gendering of children's lives in post-modern society.
2. To understand in greater depth arguments against essentializing and dichotomizing the concepts of sex and gender.
3. To acknowledge the complexity and fluidity of gender identities.
4. To appreciate the significance of multiple femininities and masculinities.

From There to Here: How Gendered Is Contemporary Childhood?

Dr Benjamin Spock's 1946 publication, *The Common Sense Book of Baby and Childcare*, challenged traditional notions of parenting by discouraging rigid feeding and sleeping schedules and promoting the idea that children need love more than they need discipline. While revolutionary in these ways, Spock's approach to raising children was very conservative in other ways—particularly in its consideration of gender roles. He presented gender identification as an early and straightforward event in a child's life, with the ambitions and skills of girls and boys soon showing their gendered form. A pre-school girl, Dr Spock wrote:

> ... realizes that it is her destiny to be a woman, and this makes it particularly exciting and challenging for her to try to be like her mother and other women. . . . In caring for her dolls, she takes that very same attitude and tone of voice her mother uses toward children. She absorbs her mother's point of view toward men and boys. By the age of three a boy is beginning to realize more clearly that he is a boy and will grow up to be a man like his father. . . . In his play he concentrates on propelling toy trucks, trains and planes, pretending his tricycle is a car, being a policeman or fireman, making deliveries, building houses and bridges. He is preparing himself to play a man's part in the world. (Spock. 1960. 'A Child's World'. *Ladies Home Journal*, June, 50)

While it was important for both mothers and fathers to model appropriate gender attitudes and behaviours for their children, Spock addressed his child-rearing advice mostly to mothers.

Fast-forward a number of decades, and the current parenting guru, Barbara Coloroso, presents a very different scenario concerning the prominence of gender in children's lives:

> It is important that chores not be gender-biased. Boys and girls can and need to learn to mow the lawn, take out the trash, do the dishes, clean their rooms, do the laundry, cook, sew, use yard and shop tools, baby-sit, scrub the bathroom, pull weeds, plant a garden. For too long, housecleaning and cooking have been seen as feminine chores, outdoor and repair work . . . as masculine. With these stereotypes we risk raising girls who think that a woman's place is in the kitchen and boys who think that certain types of work are beneath them—as well as men who couldn't sew on a button competently if their life depended on it. There are no biological imperatives where chores are concerned, except possibly those requiring great physical strength. Kids don't need lectures on gender roles though. They just need to see their parents doing all kinds of chores, and to have the opportunity themselves to do them. (Barbara Coloroso. 1995. *Kids Are Worth It!* Toronto: Somerville House Publishing, 171–2)

In this rendition of how to raise happy and well-adjusted children, the gender of the child (as well as the gender of the parent) is of little consequence. In fact, an even stronger message about the dysfunctional character of traditional gender roles is conveyed. Coloroso highlights differentiated and strictly enforced gender roles for girl and boy children as characteristic of 'brick wall' families. Such families are identified as producing 'children who as adults will believe themselves to be powerless and unable to live truly satisfying lives' (Coloroso 1995, 38).

Advice regarding the place of gender in children's lives and child-rearing practices has clearly shifted in popular parenting manuals, but is this an attempt to *create* a less gendered approach to child-rearing, or does it reflect an *already changed* attitude towards what is appropriate to encourage boy and girl children to feel, express, and do?

The significance of gender continues to be a highly contested aspect of our contemporary lives. Those on one side of the argument believe rigid gender roles are detrimental to children's well-being, while those on the other side fear the consequences of a genderless, or gender-transformed, world. Certainly, there has been some general change and convergence in our sense of how to raise happy and healthy boys and girls. We are more likely now, for example, to encourage boys to explore and express their feelings and to take on activities previously associated with girls' interests—such as babysitting, cooking, and reading. Similarly, we help girls to be assertive and to strive for non-traditional careers, and we champion their access to and achievements in arenas typically associated with boys, such as science fairs and competitive sports. The response to a question posed on the newer on-line version of Dr Spock reflects this sense of the need to encourage individual exploration beyond the confines of gender borders. A parent asks, 'At what age, if at all, should I stop my four-year-old son from putting on my lipstick and playing with my purses, etc.?' The expert response highlights the value of imitative play in personality development and concludes, 'As grown-ups, if [children] have done their pre-school work well, they will have a whole range of feelings and behaviors to call upon, not only those that are narrowly associated with "maleness" or "femaleness" ' (www.drspock.com/'Ask Our Experts About Your Pre-schooler', 6 June 2000).

At the same time, however, the importance of gender difference, and even traditional notions of masculinity and femininity, have their current advocates. For example, recent debates about the 'trouble with boys' highlight differences of opinion about the reality and desirability of the demise of traditional gender identities—with some arguing that the real trouble with boys is the feminist attack on traditional male characteristics and pursuits, leaving boys with an ambivalent and ill-defined sense of their masculinity. Patterns of gendered child-rearing continue, as do strongly contrasted cultures of boyhood and girlhood. Much of what children play with, do, and wear continues to be gender-coded. There may be some 'gender-bending' when children are very small (dressing boys and girls in more similar clothes, giving them the same early education puzzles, or reading them the same bedtime stories, for example), but it is not too long before the pink, sparkly regimen for girls and the sports logo regimen for boys makes a strong appearance. The fairies and princesses who go out to trick or treat on Halloween night are girls, while the ghouls, grim reapers, and other agents of death are boys (Nelson 2000). War-related toys continue to be the most popular selling toys for boys, and according to Wikipedia, Barbie dolls—that long-standing icon of hyper-femininity—sell at a rate of three per second (although Barbie's collector value means that not all sales would be for the purpose of children's play!). Thus, in spite of the changes Coloroso points to, there remains some doubt as to how transformed the role of gender in children's lives is at present.

Sociologists interested in the study of gender are fascinated by the dynamics of both change and continuity. They study processes and events that encourage change in the understandings and practices of gender, as well as the configurations of experience and interests that work to keep traditional understandings and practices in place. The purpose of this chapter is to explore forces of change and continuity in the ways that children's lives are structured by gender. We begin by considering in more detail what gender means for children and childhood today. To do this, we explore aspects of gender identity as constructed in our current post-modern society. Here we will discuss specific issues in the lives of children that raise significant points about the continued contestation over the necessity and desirability of gender as a feature of personal identity and a structure of society. Many of the issues discussed raise questions about the theoretical approach sociologists should take when investigating the role of sex and gender in children's lives. To consider these questions in greater detail, the chapter moves to a more extended discussion of how the sociological conceptualization of gender has developed in recent years. We pay special attention to the confrontation with essentialist and dichotomous thinking, especially in relation to sex/gender and male/female. These ideas are further developed in an examination of the significance of multiple definitions of femininity and masculinity. This theoretical discussion helps us to better understand the social context in which children are confronting the constraints and opportunities of a gendered society and, in doing so, forging their personal identities.

GIRLHOOD AND BOYHOOD IN A POST-MODERN WORLD

Every child is born into a specific historical and social context. We (Janet and Andrea) grew up in the 1950s and 1960s when Canada was in the process of expanding the public provision of education, health care, and financial support to families. In our childhoods, television was a new invention. We called it 'the tube', because that's what was inside. Computers did not exist. Store-bought clothes and eating out at a restaurant were occasional luxuries. Most telephones had dials! To travel by airplane was something very special. As we moved towards adolescence, American, and especially British, music and clothing styles were very exciting, and things from India were incredibly exotic. We listened to the Kinks, learned to do the bugaloo, and tried to get our parents to buy us Madras shirts and Levi jeans.

Most of you were born in the last decade of the twentieth century at a time when Canada was redefining its role as a state, embracing ideas of government that challenged notions of public provision and promoting the individual as the basic social unit. Technology is something you've grown up with. How old were you when you started to carry a cellphone in your backpack or chat with friends on MSN? Dinner can often mean eating out, possibly while riding in the back seat of a car! By the time you left elementary school, you were probably already a well-seasoned traveller. Growing up into adolescence is still very much about music, dancing, and clothes, but your choices were those of a generation linked worldwide by the information highway and chains of globalized production and distribution.

To talk about what it means to be born a boy or a girl, we have to contextualize this experience, at least in terms of time and place. Currently, the world is transforming into a global space, and Canada is deeply implicated in the realization of a post-modern society characterized by neo-liberal politics and priorities. Sociologists interested in children and youth are exploring what the move to post-modernism means for how children experience their childhood and the place of gendered identities in this experience.

The very idea of childhood is a modern one. We have all seen pictures of upper-class families in Victorian times in which the children look like miniature adults. In Canada at that time, it was common for children from poorer families to work alongside the adult members of the family. Much of Canada's population was still rural, and boys would help with farm chores while girls would help with cooking, cleaning, and looking after younger siblings. With compulsory education introduced for all children (Janovicek and Parr 2003), we have the beginning of childhood as Andrea and Janet experienced it: a time for learning and exploring, a time to think about what you want to be when you grow up, and a time to hang out with friends, doing not very much.

However, the transition to post-modern society includes transitions and transformations in what we understand and expect childhood to be. Since childhood is the time when gender identities are formed, it is important to consider how transitions to post-modern society affect the gendering of identities. Post-modern society affects how girls and boys encounter gender as a result of five factors: 1) a fast, competitive pace of life, with a focus on achievement; 2) blurring of the division between adulthood and childhood; 3) the invasion of consumer culture; 4) intensification of the crisis of masculinity; and 5) increased attention to issues of risk and safety.

A fast, competitive pace of life, with a focus on achievement

Post-modern society is a fast-paced, competitive society. As the book jacket for *In Praise of Slow* (Honoré 2004) says, 'In a world where speed rules and everyone is under pressure to go faster, anything that gets in our way or slows us down becomes an enemy.' Children are not exempt from this whirlwind of activity and break-neck pace. Observers of children's lives have noted that, compared to even the recent past, children today lead highly scheduled and busy lives. Pressures to compete and achieve slide down the age range so that even in pre-school activities, there is an emphasis on getting it right, doing it faster, and being the best. Time for play and the quality of play has seriously decreased (Stephens 1995, 33) to the point where people have started to talk of 'missing childhoods'.

The individualization of post-modern society requires individuals to regard themselves as 'projects' that they must invest in and promote in order to get ahead. Children are increasingly regarded as 'projects' by various social institutions as well as themselves, with their accomplishments being used as markers of adult success. A key example here is schooling. With post-modern society closely associated with information, schooling has become an even more contested area of children's experience.

Children's achievements are being used as the measuring stick for the effectiveness of schooling—a key indicator in a system increasingly focused on quantifiable, standardized deliverables as the educational equivalent of fast food (Honoré 2004; Davies and Guppy 2006). Standardized testing in primary and high school grades is not about what children have learned, but rather it is a means to assess, and reward or punish, the adults responsible for delivering education to children and adolescents. The main stakeholders in standardized testing are the government, teachers, and parents. Many discussions have taken place about how a 'management by results' focus for schools has intensified in recent years. The results of an educational process are notoriously difficult to quantify—and yet it is only quantitative data that governments collect and publicize.

Sociologists looking at this situation see a shift in the focus of education from attention to 'the whole child'—including social, emotional, physical, and artistic needs—to the 'performing child' whose test results communicate to parents and the government that taxes are being well spent. Many argue that this is a retreat from moves made in the 1960s and 1970s towards pushing back competitive pressures within the educational system so that children would have a space where they could really learn. A now-famous treatise on schooling at the time explored 'how children fail' and argued that they do so because we give them no room to truly engage in a learning process—where getting the answer wrong is a positive learning experience (Holt 1964).

Scott Davies and Neil Guppy (2006) identify an increase in competitive schooling strategies among parents of school-aged children. Signs of this include a greater number of private schools in Canada, higher enrolment in private schools, and a private tutoring business that is burgeoning across the country. For those who cannot afford full-time private schooling, individual tutoring is being sold as a strategy to give students a competitive edge. One study in 2002 estimated that up to one quarter of Ontario parents hired private tutors for their children, and another found an increase in private tutoring business by more than 100 per cent over an eight-year period (Davies and Guppy 2006, 90). There are even on-line tutoring opportunities for elementary students 'designed to help kids achieve higher grades'.

While both boys and girls are becoming more stressed as a result of the increased pressure to perform at school, research shows that they tend to deal with this, and are dealt with, differently. Boys have become the pariahs of schools and classrooms. They act out their stress, disrupting classroom routines, behaving badly to teachers, defacing school property. They are suspended from school more often than girls, are perceived to be more aggressive and disruptive, and are more likely to be medicated as a way of controlling their behaviour in the classroom. Perhaps not surprisingly, boys give up on school to a much greater extent and earlier than girls (Davies and Guppy 2006, 116; Nelson 2006, 144ff). This pattern is compounded by experiences of classism and racism. African-Canadian and Aboriginal boys are the least likely to remain in Canada's educational system.

For their part, girls are excelling scholastically at all levels of schooling. In many ways, this is a wonderful achievement for them—compared to the past. However, while girls are now more likely than boys to complete schooling up to university graduation, there is still a strong pattern of gender segregation in course and program selection. Also, the potential for success in school for girls is mediated by other factors, which impinge on how they are seen by themselves, their peers, and their teachers. Goli Rezai-Rashti (2005), for instance, describes how Muslim girls are subject to the misconceptions and simplifications of persisting colonialist ideas in schools. And the literature on bullying indicates that it is the successful girl who is often a target.

Blurring of the division between adulthood and childhood

With increasing pressure to 'grow up fast', children are exposed sooner to adult versions of gender identity. One concern with this is that it leaves little time for exploration and discovery of one's inner feelings, sensibilities, and inclinations. At younger and younger ages, children assume the postures and trappings of culturally presented, and commercially driven, adult female and male identities. One example is young girls with 'sexy girl' logos on their T-shirts and luscious glitter on their lips; the participation of young boys in paintball and laser gun games is another. If children are pressured to take on too much too soon, people argue, it favours the reproduction of status quo gender identities and inhibits explorations that may challenge and change what gender is all about.

Several researchers have noted the sexualization of girls at younger and younger ages. The prime culprits here are pursuits that emphasize, or at least require, the display and beautification of girls' bodies—including aspects of the sports played by girls (figure skating, cheerleading) and the beauty pageant industry. The presentation, and one could argue encouragement, of precocious sexuality is not just an extracurricular activity. The promotion of Lil' Bratz books in Canadian schools—with titles such as *Lil' Bratz Dancing Divas* and *Lil' Bratz Catwalk Cuties*—has been challenged precisely because they present an 'objectified sexuality . . . for the very young girls who represent the market for these dolls' (*Ottawa Citizen*. 2007. 'Parents Want Lil' Bratz Kept out of Schools'. 28 February, A12). With blurred boundaries in the display of sexuality, an accompanying concern is the effects this has on sexual activity. Girls and boys are becoming sexually mature at younger ages, when their understanding of social relationships are still quite basic and their self-images very other-dependent. With little experience at standing up for themselves and knowing what is best for themselves, the fear here is that girls become vulnerable, and boys become encouraged, to act out the more regressive forms of adult sexuality routinely portrayed in online, Playstation, and X-box games, as well as on DVDs and TV.

Preteens Parading in Pageants

by Gillian Judkins

Long, flowing hair, cascading down onto a petite body covered in a shiny sequined dress. She turns to the left, pivots to the right, and walks a little further, striking her pose. Her eyelashes flutter, thick with mascara. She is the epitome of the male sexual fantasy—however, she is only five years old.

This describes a typical scene at a beauty pageant for young girls. But just how healthy is this kind of competition for a young girl's development? And what does it do to their body image?

Co-ordinator of Western's Women's Issues Network, Kelly Guitard feels these competitions are not at all healthy for young girls. 'I think stressing competition can be damaging itself but especially dangerous when you're placing emphasis on physical appearance,' she says.

In a similar frame of mind is Sandra Aylward, sociologist and co-ordinator of the Women's Studies program at King's College. 'If they don't have the money, if they have a disability, or if they are seen as ugly, they can't get in [to the competition]. Beauty is considered good, and not fitting that definition of beauty is seen as bad.'

Not surprisingly, individuals involved in the modelling industry do not share the same sentiments. Former Miss Canada (1974) Blair Lancaster, owner of Modelling and Fashion Agency, explains, 'It depends on the pressure and expectations we [as adults] put on them. Pageants can do a lot of positive things but can also do negative things if not handled properly.'

Regardless of how parents may handle the pageant scene, young girls are still paraded in front of judges who assess them on their physical attributes. What might this scrutiny do to their perception of body image?

Lisa Rozak, co-ordinator of Western's Body Image Team, expresses extreme concern. She agreed that this can definitely teach youngsters to place emphasis on their body over personality or intellect. Rozak points out more and more research shows that 'girls as young as five years of age are restricting their food intake.'

Lancaster disagrees. 'My feeling is that beauty has nothing to do with body shape. It has to do with personality, frame of mind—it really has to come from inside.'

The fact remains that an average-sized woman or a slightly overweight one rarely appears on the cover of *Cosmopolitan* or *Vogue*. Society continues to show young women it is all right to put value on their body by encouraging young girls to enter competitions where they are judged on physical attributes. 'They're given a message that their body is for sale. It's an object separate from their personality,' Aylward says.

Lancaster feels, on the other hand, that there is nothing wrong with teaching young children to carry themselves properly and allowing them to enter pageants.

So the question then becomes, just how much should parents encourage their children to enter beauty pageants? Many people will argue that spending hundreds and thousands of dollars on pageants is no different from spending money on hockey or any other sport. But the difference is that with sports, children are not using their body as the object by which they are solely judged—young girls aren't being sexualized into beautiful little women.

And so she continues to pose and smile, eager to please the eyes of the judges. As onlookers, contributors, parents, and concerned friends, one can only hope that she will escape without causing her body harm.

Do you think that beauty pageants are a positive or negative activity for girls? Would you think the same for boys? Why or why not?

Source: *The Gazette*, 11 February 1997, 90, 77. London, ON: University of Western Ontario.

Post-modern society promotes individualization in ways that leave kids confused about the boundaries between childhood and adulthood. We can follow this argument by looking at the family. Sociologists have always been concerned about the state of family life. The family has never been in decline—as some sociologists have feared—but it certainly has undergone profound changes. Some of these changes have been intensified with the transition to post-modernity. The time crunch on family life has intensified. Both parents are working for pay, usually outside the home, and for longer hours. Joe Kincheloe (1998) argues that *Home Alone* has become the norm for Western children, who now increasing take on the responsibility of raising themselves. Faced with the routine absence of adults in the family home, children take their cues about appropriate grown-up behaviour from their encounters with electronic media:

> The new era of childhood, the postmodern childhood, cannot escape the influence of the postmodern condition with its electronic media saturation. . . . Thus, media-produced models replace the real. . . . Boundaries between adulthood and childhood blur to the point that a clearly defined, 'traditional', innocent childhood becomes an object of nostalgia—a sure sign that it no longer exists in any unproblematic form. (1998, 170)

Since its invention, TV has always been an important socialization agent for children, but programming trends in recent years expose younger and younger children to what should arguably be adult-only viewing. Programs that were adult hits several years ago—like *Sex and the City*—are now shown during after-school and dinner times. Daytime TV talk shows and so-called reality shows present scenarios of family life that the young viewer has no means to contextualize or assess—'I had my sister's husband's baby'; 'My 12-year-old son is having sex with his teacher'; 'My 10-year-old daughter is a prostitute'; and so on. Issues such as the sexual abuse of children, domestic violence, sexual addiction, and adultery are standard fare for the *Dr Phil* show aired just as kids are getting home from school and turning on the TV for their after-school chill time. There are no children in Dr Phil's studio audience, but this is not the case among his home viewers.

Researchers report increasing confusion and uncertainty among children regarding appropriate adult behaviour. In some circumstances, confusion about gender might be celebrated—if it led to a questioning of dominant patterns. However, researchers note that more often than not, confusion and uncertainty tend to resolve into a reproduction of the norm. Positive images of both masculinity and femininity vie with the negative dominant ones; however, as Marnina Gonick comments (2004, 207), the individualism of contemporary neo-liberalism creates tensions for young girls between the alleged fluidity of identity and the continued preference for the masculine. She concludes:

> . . . the individualism that underlies the possibility of subjectivity in 'global times' offers girls new positions previously denied them, as well as constraint on what it is possible to become. Traditional femininity is being undone through its inclusion in discourses of individualism, rationality and adulthood, even as it is being rearticulated through an ever increasing array of contradictions, the juggling of which has always shaped experiences of femininity.

The invasion of consumer culture

Researchers are in general agreement about the invasion of contemporary childhood by consumer culture. Shopping malls have become a community space where baby buggies can be pushed no matter what the weather, where toddlers can have fun on indoor climbing frames and rides, and where child care can be bought for some moments of child-free browsing. Older children meet friends at the mall and spend their allowance or babysitting money on DVDs, clothes, or junk food. In many ways, shopping malls have been constructed as a social space for women and children. Although malls do have stores that cater to men's clothing and entertainment interests, mall stores typically address themselves to the female shopper. Also, women are more likely to visit malls with a social as well as a shopping agenda in mind and with children in tow. Thanks to efforts to make shopping malls parent- and child-friendly, for many children their sense of neighbourhood includes home, school, and the shopping mall.

On the one hand, there is a good community service element to this development—appreciated particularly by seniors, those with mobility challenges, and families with young children. Just about every Canadian who has lived through winter temperatures of 30 below knows what a relief it is to step into a large, well-heated interior space that provides some respite from struggles with ice-covered sidewalks and flesh-freezing temperatures! On the other hand, this development means that more and more of our sense of community, our experience of socializing, our time together, is structured by, and within, the priorities and parameters of consumerism. Ultimately, shopping malls are for shopping. To the extent that young children and adolescents eat, play, sleep, and meet friends within a context of consumerism, this context becomes heavily implicated in their socialization and personal development. While this situation affects boys, it is more likely to be a heavier factor in the socialization of girls. From a young age, girls are encouraged to be, and praised for being, 'good shoppers'. As Anne Cranny-Francis and her co-writers remark, femininity has become associated with consumption (Cranny-Francis et al. 2003, 200). 'Born to shop' is a statement of *female* destiny!

Consumer culture is also, of course, the lifeblood of television. Stephen Kline (1993) sets out a fascinating account of how the use of television to advertise products and services has transformed. Initially, television advertisements conveyed messages about products and services that were intended for a generalized, primarily adult audience. But this proved to be a marketing strategy that lacked focus and was limited in its appeal. Marketing specialists started to promote the idea of more focused messages targeted at more specialized audiences. As this idea took hold, so too did the development of specialized TV programs for children and, with it, the realization that children constituted a specialized audience for product marketing. Kline argues that commercial television programming for children is driven entirely by marketing purposes:

> Television does provide a distinctive cultural product for young children. But these children have been furnished with a cultural product of their own not out of the magnanimity of broadcasters nor a sense of moral purpose. Commercial television is a business lodged in a competitive market place. This means that any analysis of it might well begin with the programmer's primary business considerations—audiences and what they purchase—which circumscribe their interest in children and shape all commercial television content. (1993, 74)

Targeted marketing for children basically means creating and selling toys that appeal to what Kline (1993, 288) calls 'consumption tribes'. The boundaries of these tribes are formed by gender and age distinctions. Boy children form a particular market, as do girl children. Only in very exceptional circumstances are toys marketed as suitable for both boys and girls. One notable exception is the 'slinky'—an enduring but hardly hot play item! Kline observes that gendered targeted marketing has left the narrow confines of television advertisements and has become the raison d'être of television programming itself. Product placement within programs is a soft version of this dynamic—such as TV characters eating a particular brand of cereal or drinking a recognized soft drink. Programming designed with accompanying products, or explicitly to promote products to boys or to girls—*Teletubbies, She-Ra, My Little Pony, Dino-Riders, Toy Story, SpongeBob SquarePants*—is the harder and more cynical manifestation of this phenomenon.

Of course, it is not only highly stylized gender images that are produced and sold via commercial television. As Ellen Seiter notes, much of children's TV is centred around whiteness, frequently male whiteness. 'Children of color and girls of all races are dispersed to the sidelines as mascots, companions and victims' (1998, 315). Perhaps this is less the case for programming aimed at very young children, which tends to be characterized by fantasy characters often of no apparent gender or race. As Kline observes, there are fewer and fewer real children in TV programming aimed at the youngest age groups. But Seiter's comment has resonance for programming aimed at older children. Affluence is certainly a big seller as well, and the possession of particular toys is one way children sort out the position of themselves and others in the social hierarchies of wealth and worth (Kline 1993, 348).

No one who watches commercial television can be in much doubt that commercial priorities are its primary driving force. The question is: how do audiences respond to and process the commercial content and products of television? In particular, how do boys and girls relate to the highly gendered messages and objects promoted by commercial television? Answers to this question provide a little good news—and quite a lot of bad news.

First, the good news. Kline argues that while marketing strategists are explicit in their attempts to exploit gendered tendencies in toy preferences and play styles, children can be selective in how they use, absorb, and play with gendered messages. Furthermore, commercial TV is not the only sort of TV produced for children, and community educational broadcasting stations like TVOntario play an important role in providing commercial-free (though not necessarily product-free) programming. Finally, even within commercial TV, messages about gender can be more ambiguous and even courageous in their promotion of non-traditional choices.

Now, the bad news. The gendered culture of TV programs and products creates and reinforces gender-segregated play modes so that even if they wanted to play together, boys and girls have a difficult time finding a common ground and language in which to do so (Kline 1993). Are there many girls who can mimic with equivalent gusto that *vroom, vroom* car sound that boys seem to have perfected by the age of three? Are there many boys who would have the first clue what to do with Mattel's Hair Salon? Boys and girls do play together (Thorne 1993) but rarely via the medium of toys—particularly TV toys—because of their intense gender saturation. The more these sorts of toys are produced and sold to children via the medium of television, the more gender-segregated play is reinforced.

There is more bad news. With television such a major agent in presenting children with ways to perceive themselves and their social relationships, we must ask what impact on psychological and social development the commercialization of children's socialization is having.

We have been talking about the role of commercial television in the reproduction of gendered images and behaviours through its impact on children's socialization. Before leaving this discussion, we must examine the wider context of television production itself. Sociologists have argued that culture and the technologies of its production obviously have a major role in defining our society. However, they are also defined by our society. While it is common to blame TV, or toy manufacturers, for contributing to the maintenance of gender stereotypes, they do so in part as a reflection of wider social processes and priorities. As Stephen Dale has warned (2005), we wring our hands about the pernicious influence TV has on our children without asking questions about larger policy priorities and issues that shape our children's lives. He cautions us to monitor campaigns against TV images and programming, because these campaigns are increasingly coming from the right. We do need discussion and debate about what is 'good' television for children, but we also need to be mindful that there are many political interests in such a debate. This point is very important for gender transformation. Programs like *Degrassi High* raise issues such as abortion, sexual harassment, contraception, and homosexuality that need to be discussed and deliberated on by older children and adolescents. Yet some would have such topics barred from broadcasting. Any kind of programming that presents movements away from traditional gender roles can come under similar attacks. In this sense, television reflects, rather than creates, the significant issues that need to be debated and contested in our society. Its role in reproducing traditional gender identities can carry on only as long as larger social forces allow it. To challenge gender imaging on commercial television is to take on the wider and deeper problems of gender construction in society more generally.

As children—particularly older children—switch their play activity towards the Internet, similar issues of commercialization and exposure to inappropriate content arise. Here, however, the problem may be even more pernicious, because there is less supervision and control over what children are exposed to. For example, anyone on the Internet might be interrupted by a pop-up featuring pictures of young women in suggestive poses, revealing most of their bodies, and be invited to join some 'friend finding' organization to get to know them. Whether or not these images are meant for children, they can routinely be seen by children. They are certainly meant to convey the message that women's bodies are commodities and to normalize the idea that the bodies of young women are commercial lures.

Intensification of the crisis of masculinity

Whereas it was once the lives of girls that gave parents and professionals of all sorts cause for concern, more recently the spotlight has turned on boys. Dr Fred Mathews, the keynote speaker at the First National Conference on the Status of Male Children in Canada noted (2002, 2) that 'the problems faced by boys remain largely invisible to the public and professionals alike.' He further emphasized the 'seriousness of the plight of boys and how urgent the need is for us to respond as a society'. It is interesting to note that the problems raised at this conference about boys sound very much like the alarms and concerns raised in the past about girls: the restricted nature of adult options, a systematic bias in elementary and high schools, the exposure of those with less-than-perfect body images to demeaning and belittling treatment both in real life and in the media, the loneliness and vulnerability of any who stray from the accepted norms of gendered behaviour, the relentless expectation to conform to a narrow definition of ability, personality, and aspirations. In this post-feminist backlash age, however, we hear these calls to realize the plight of boys and rescue them from their trials and tribulations with some caution.

Is the problem really that girls are finally getting their share of the pie and therefore there is less to dish out among boys? Is it a case of the previously privileged raising alarm when it is clear that their privilege has been breached? Or are there genuine social issues confronting boys that we as a society do need to recognize and resolve? Judging from the literature and the research on these issues, we could plausibly answer yes to all three questions. Girls' needs, abilities, and promise are now a focus of many policies and programs aimed at realizing their hopes and potential. They have not only caught up to boys in a vast range of children's and early adolescent activities (e.g., school, sports), but in many areas are surpassing boys in levels of both involvement and achievement. As part of the general anti-feminist backlash, some may be disgruntled at the girl-only focus of this attention and feel that rather than addressing an existing inequality, this girl-focus creates a new inequality. However, sociological research does support the idea that there is a genuine need for concern about what is happening to boys. And in many cases, this concern is linked to a celebration of the advances made by girls and an interest in promoting gender equality further by addressing where and how the lives of boys are in crisis. In other words, we can have concerns about the negative consequences of the social constructions of masculinity for boys without taking away from our efforts to promote positive identities for girls.

David Morgan (2006) asks us to be cautious in our use of the word 'crisis' when we talk about what is happening to masculinity. He notes that the possibility of crisis needs to be specified by contexts of class and ethnicity. Particular forms of masculinity, and particular groups of men, may indeed be experiencing a challenge to their sense of themselves as masculine. Whether this means that there is a more general threat to hegemonic masculinity (a term we shall discuss in more detail in chapter 3) is open to question. And what this means for boys is an important aspect of the larger debate. What is interesting—and this is a point also commented on by Hearn and Kimmel (2006)—is that the study of boys' encounters with masculinity has been a relatively neglected area of research, even among those who pioneered the field of masculinity studies. There are, however, some notable exceptions to this state of affairs—academics who have focused their research on how boys struggle for and against masculinity and what it means these days to grow up into manhood. A strong focus of this work has been on the stunting of boys' emotional intelligence—that is, the systematic denial of feeling and the limited repertoire of acceptable displays of emotion.

One of the first studies to bring the problematic state of contemporary boyhood to the attention of the general public was by Angela Phillips, a British journalist and academic. Her book, *The Trouble with Boys—Parenting the Men of the Future*, opened with some of her personal reflections on what it was like to be a mother watching her son grow up:

> One of the things that struck me so forcefully as the mother of a son is that growing up male is hard, very hard. Men may still grow up to inherit the earth but they give up a great deal on the way. I began to see that, for many boys, the process of attaining manhood is a process of de-sensitization, in which the openness of the small child shrinks further and further into the shell of the man. (1993, 9)

In the late 1990s, an American clinical psychologist at Harvard Medical School, William Pollack, published a popular book on boyhood that would be on the *New York Times* bestseller list for weeks. Despite the somewhat more alarming title, *Real Boys— Rescuing Our Sons from the Myths of Boyhood*, Pollack was conveying a similar message about the harm caused by the emotional withdrawal expected as boys matured:

> In my work I have tried to understand what boys are really saying about their lives and to get behind the mask of masculinity, a mask that most boys and men wear to hide their true inner feelings, and to present to the world an image of male toughness, stoicism, and strength, when in fact they feel desperately alone and afraid. (1999, xxii)

During the 1990s, sociological studies were also focusing on what was happening to boys. One well-known report is R.W. Connell's book *The Men and the Boys* (2000), a discussion of boyhood which focuses on schooling as a key site for social change. As primary institutions in which dominant forms of masculinity are fostered and encouraged, schools are both an obstacle to and an opportunity for positive change. It would be progress in itself, Connell argues, if schools were to act on the idea that all boys are not the same, that they encounter forms of masculinity that vary by class and culture, and that they need to be encouraged to explore a broader sense of themselves, their bodies, and their relationships.

Boys suffer from limited gender scripts that reduce their ability to explore who they are and embrace all that they find within themselves. This limited script—what Pollack calls the 'gender straitjacket'—narrows boys' social capacities so that when they need help and good advice, they cannot show that they need it, ask for it, or be seen to be following it. They are told to 'suck it up and crush it down'. Whereas the gender script of femininity has undergone a radical transformation in the past 50 years, shedding many aspects of its former straitjacket, there has been no comparable revolution in the masculinity gender script. While change has occurred, it has been slower and more subterranean compared to the women's movement and the reshaping of female identities.

One drag on the transformation of the masculine gender script is a society steeped in homophobia. According to E.W. Kane (2006), for example, parents of girls tolerate non-traditional behaviours and activities, while boys' activities and interests continue to be much more constrained for fear of encouraging homosexuality. Heterosexual fathers have been most concerned about socializing boys in traditional ways. Heterosexism limits the exploration of male identity (see Martin's discussion [2005] of whether William will get his doll). For boys, launching themselves into the world of sexual relations is fraught with pressures to conform to narrow ideas of sexual identity and orientation. 'Gay' continues to be a favoured put-down even among elementary school-aged boys. Heterosexuality must be asserted and done so unequivocally—particularly in the world of sports. Even in areas where costume and artistic expression have been important features of the activity, there is pressure to conform. Mary Louise Adams (1998) has described the 'macho turn' that is 'straightening' up men's figure skating, with efforts to emphasize figure skating as more sport than art form. To the extent that emotions are associated with the feminine—or with the effeminate—boys are systematically steered away from them. There are class and cultural differences that modify the script of masculinity, but the narrowness of what is acceptable behaviour is remarkably resilient to change (Kane 2006).

Uncovering strategies and possibilities for change has become an important focus of sociological investigation. Anthony Giddens (1992) has argued that post-modern society makes definitions of masculinity and male sexuality based on strength, force, and aggression redundant. Stephen Whitehead (2002, 178) identifies changes in family forms as one of the positive influences in shifting traditional expectations of male behaviour and, presumably with it, expanding the ways of being male that are observed and emulated by boys.

Janet Reflects on the Masks of Masculinity

My son, like most children, loved to draw pictures of things he saw in the world and of people he was fascinated by and wanted to be like. For several of his young years, just about every picture he drew was of a goalie. The image was always the same—pads, stick, glove, blocker, hockey sweater, and face mask. We have many, many of these drawings in our keepsake box! He got very good at drawing in meticulous detail the webbing of the glove, the exact angle of the stick, the team emblem on the sweater, the cage of the goalie mask, the stance of the goalie's body. He never got any practice drawing faces, however, because of course the goalie always had his mask on. Sometimes you could see two little eyes peeking out from behind the goalie mask, but there was never a full face showing. I never thought anything of this until I started to notice a similarity between these goalie pictures and the drawings of other male figures that he'd also do occasionally. They all were faceless. They all wore masks.

It occurred to me that many of the masculine figures that young boys are encouraged to admire are often masked. Firefighters, policemen, spacemen, hockey players, football players. While there are notable exceptions, boys' toys are often faceless or in some way non-human (like the transformers), and many of the television and movie male heroes are masked. Sometimes hiding or distorting the face is how the 'bad person' or 'evil' is presented—Darth Vader, the Joker, robbers. But good guys also hide their faces—especially when they set out to do their good deeds. Who is that masked man? The Lone Ranger! Spiderman, Batman, Zorro, the Incredibles all mask their faces when they step up to save the day.

The face is the main means by which we communicate with each other. While there is meaning communicated in the positioning and movement of the body and by the clothes and accessories we wear, the face is the most potent and powerful communicator of emotion. I wondered what it meant for the development of empathy and interpersonal skills that many of young boys' toys and heroes had no faces. They act—for good or evil—without revealing who they are, without looking at people directly, without showing a smile or grimace, a knowing look, a yearning in their eyes, or a meaningful scowl. Studies show that boys (and men) are less attuned to emotional cues in interpersonal relationships. Perhaps some of this inability to see, and to regard as important in interpersonal relations, the joy or the hurt in someone's face can be traced to the faceless hero world that boys inhabit?

Increased attention to issues of risk and safety: The case of bullying

New forms of risk are a prominent feature of post-modern society. Sociologists have observed that the reconfiguration of childhood occurring in the context of post-modern society involves increased anxiety about safety and an emphasis on risk as a feature of everyday social relations and experiences (Stephens 1995). An initial and ongoing focus of these anxieties is pathologies in the relationships *between adults and children*, especially in terms of the possibility of physical and sexual abuse. One could argue that the more recent explosion of attention on patterns and consequences of bullying represents an expansion of these anxieties to the relationships *among children*.

Bullying is not a new phenomenon, and yet it is receiving unprecedented attention from academics, the media, popular lifestyle writers, schools, governments, and international agencies. Popular literature presents stark contrasts: *Your Child: Bully or Victim?* (Sheras 2002); new terms have been created to capture the dramatic consequences of unidentified and unaddressed bullying: *Bullycide, Death at Playtime* (Marr and Field 2001); and every self-help guru writes about how to address the plague now rampant in schoolyards. Barbara Coloroso begins her book *The Bully, the Bullied and the Bystander* (2002, xxi) with a list of horrific things done to children by children that 'could go on for many pages, detailing incidents from around the world'. Technology is identified as a new aid to bullying behaviour, with cyber-bullying pointed to as 'a whole new virtual place to hide, where there are no witnesses, no scene of a crime and nobody can be certain who is wielding the knives' (Karen von Hahn. 2005. 'There Is No Safe Place'. *The Globe and Mail*, 25 March, F5).

We are not suggesting that bullying or any of the other safety issues faced by children today are not serious phenomena. However, we would like to use the example of bullying as a case in which there has been a tendency to revert to using gender categories in a way that emphasizes the contrast between boys and girls and neglects differences among girls and among boys in expectations, behaviours, and attitudes depending on a complex range of social and cultural variations.

There is no doubt that bullying is a nasty phenomenon that injures the individuals targeted and poisons the social settings in which it occurs. In examining the recent explosion of interest in the phenomenon, however, a number of academic researchers have adopted a cautionary approach. Two related issues in the discussion of bullying have drawn critical comment: the tendency to focus research on individuals and pay less attention to broader social issues and contexts, and the tendency to draw on gender stereotypes in characterizing both types of bullies and types of responses to bullying.

The significance of gender in contemporary forms of bullying is a ubiquitous observation. The Government of British Columbia presents the typical portrait:

'Studies show that both girls and boys bully. Boys generally tend to rely more on verbal and physical intimidation. Girls generally use tactics like teasing, gossiping, insulting, or excluding their victims from social events' (1998; 2000, 4).

Coloroso elaborates on this gendered pattern of bullying behaviour:

> There are three kinds of bullying: verbal, physical, and relational. Boys and girls use verbal bullying equally. Boys tend to use physical bullying more often than girls do, and girls use relational bullying more often than boys. This difference has more to do with the socialization of males and females in our culture than with physical prowess or size. Boys tend to play in large, loosely defined groups, held together by common interests. They establish a pecking order. . . . Physical prowess is honored above intellectual ability. Thus we see boys shoving smaller, weaker, often smarter boys into lockers, calling them 'wimp,' 'nerd,' 'sissy.' . . . Physical bullying is not exclusive to boys. Bigger girls are known to trip, shove, and poke smaller boys or smaller girls. Girls just have a more powerful tool in their arsenal to use against other girls—relational bullying. Compared with boys girls tend to play in small, more intimate circles with clearly defined boundaries, making it easier to harm a girl merely by excluding her from a social circle. (2002, 14–15)

While there is clearly some validity in the contrast between girls' and boys' experience as bullies and as bullied, this form of gender talk can verge on using gender categories in an essentialist way. Such talk, as Alexa Hepburn argues (1997), can serve to maintain existing power relations that support bullying behaviour. She suggests (1997, 46) that the 'focus on individual personalities as the source of the problem also brings with it a danger of seeing bullying behaviour out of context.' The research on bullying experiences shows a much more nuanced picture of the role of gender—one that is modified by, among other issues, social setting, age, class, relational context, sexual orientation, and race. If bullying is about power, then clearly not all boys and not all girls are equally placed in relation to power resources and opportunities.

Paul O'Connell et al. (1999) and others observe that much of the research into bullying is focused on the individual child and has left the significance of social context relatively unexplored. For example, O'Connell et al.'s research focused on the activities and interaction patterns in a sample of elementary school playgrounds in Toronto. Children participating in their study wore small video cameras in a waist pouch during recess. Researchers were then able to see and hear actual bullying events and to observe the whole complex of social relations surrounding such events. They discovered that bullying is a very public phenomenon, at least in terms of occurring in front of other children. In particular, they noted that peers play a very significant role in encouraging or thwarting the bullying event. 'On average, four peers viewed the schoolyard bullying . . . peers spent 54 per cent of their time reinforcing bullies by passively watching, 21 per cent of their time actively modeling bullies, and 25 per cent of their time intervening on behalf of victims' (O'Connell et al. 1999, 1). The researchers were also very interested in gender and age patterns, and indeed they noted that gendered responses were specified by age. Older boys tended to join in with the bully more than younger boys and older girls. Younger and older girls were more likely to support the victim than older boys.

Many authors (Rigby 2002; Duncan 1999; Nelson 2006) observe that gendered patterns of bullying are complicated by other factors associated with power differentials. Bullying among older children is frequently homophobic, with young gay males particularly at risk. It is also racist—not only in terms of the content of bullying but also who is targeted. The intersection of gender and race is a powerful combination in the more aggressive and destructive behaviours that adolescents exhibit towards one another. The tragic case of Reena Virk is remembered for the particularly violent behaviour towards a brown-skinned girl exhibited by a group of white boys and girls (Godfrey 2005). We further discuss the significance of inter-secting relations of race and gender in Reena Virk's death in chapter 3.

The case of bullying raises for us the difficult notion of how power enters into children's lives and is used by them to negotiate their everyday experiences. It also requires us to ask why displays of power have become more prominent in children's lives—and more worrying for the adults in their midst. In the case of gender rela-tions, power has always been a source of concern because of the gender imbalances typically associated with it. Indeed, Barron and Lacombe (2005) situate recent con-cerns over girl bullies as the product of a moral panic about shifting power differen-tials in gender relationships and a backlash against feminism.

We have been reviewing how features of post-modern society are exacerbating existing issues in gender relations in Canada and creating new issues as children discover what sorts of people they will become. As we investigate these patterns of continuity and change in society generally, we must take care to conduct the analysis of gender with an appropriate sociological approach. Bullying is a case in which some forms of analysis draw on types of gender concepts that have been identified as prob-lematic. We turn now to elaborate more fully the ways in which the study of gender has developed to address a more fluid and varied experience.

SEX/GENDER AND MALE/FEMALE: MOVING BEYOND DICHOTOMIES AND ESSENTIALISM

In her excellent analysis of what she calls the 'romance' between sociology and gen-der, Barbara Marshall (2000) identifies the legacy of the adoption of gender as a soci-ological concept as 'mixed'. She comments:

> . . . feminist sociology uses gender not simply to describe differences between men and women, but to expose its links to power and inequality. The intent is to problematize gender as a social relationship, and to transform not only sociology as an academic discipline, but the social world as well. However, categorical and essentialized conceptions of gender have not always functioned in an emancipatory way, and may act to shore up, rather than disrupt, the opposition between masculinity and femininity. (2000, 42)

As discussed in chapter 1, the concept of gender came into widespread use in soci-ology during the 1970s. While its use was by no means universally accepted (some feminist sociologists preferred to use the term sex—and still do), it was the norm in the discipline to make the distinction between sex and gender. Sex was used to refer to the biological distinctions between males and females, particularly chromosome patterns (XY or XX), secondary sex characteristics (hairy chests, breasts), and reproductive organs (testicles and penis, ovaries and vagina). Gender was reserved as a term for socially created differences between the identities and social roles associated with masculinity and femininity (for example, the competitive and tough football player versus the cute and supportive cheerleader, or the hard-nosed businessman versus the caring social worker). The identification of gender as a social phenomenon was an important advance over previous sociological thinking, which emphasized the link between biological attributes, particularly those associated with childbearing, and social roles of women and men. As Marshall points out, feminist sociologists not only had to confront sexist thinking in society more generally but also had to rout it out within the discipline of sociology itself. This new idea of produced masculinity and femininity highlighted the socially constructed, and therefore changeable, character of gender. For example, it was pointed out that the fact of women's childbearing bore no necessary relationship to who might be best equipped to care for and parent the child. Indeed, it was argued that gender equality would require men's active involvement in parenting and that there was no biological reason why men could not acquire the appropriate skills, emotional attachments, and priorities for active parenting.

However, the conceptualization of gender as a social construct distinct from sex as a biological fact of nature has also come under critical review. Most sociological work has moved on to consider sex, as well as gender, as a social construction. As well, most recent sociological work approaches both sex and gender as more ambiguous, varied, and fluid phenomena compared to the previous, more fixed, categorical approach. Two important aspects of this critical review will be discussed here: arguments against the essentializing and dichotomizing of sex and arguments against the essentializing and dichotomizing of gender. These critical arguments played a central role in moving the conceptualization of gender forward. Research focused on children's negotiation of sex and gender provided some of the important evidence supporting these critical arguments.

Against essentializing and dichotomizing sex

As important as the earlier conceptual advances were in establishing the significance of gender as a social construction, sociologists have had to revisit and rethink the division between the biological category of sex and the social category of gender. By leaving sex (as well as nature) out of the realm of the social, it was essentialized. This meant that sex was regarded as having given and fixed characteristics. It was regarded as having essential properties that were not subject to human intervention or thought. However, strong social constructionists wanted to argue that any notion of sex preceding gender should be abandoned and indeed reversed. They argued that it is gendered understandings that shape our perceptions of biological sex. In the early 1980s, Liz Stanley and Christine Delphy were among the first to present this idea. Stanley asked the question: should 'sex' really be 'gender'? She argued that ' "Sex" constructed as a natural order is thus conceptualized in ways which cut out the possibility of conceptualizing it as "really gender", really socially constructed and so mutable' (2002, 39). Delphy argued a similar point but from a somewhat different position. She proposed reversing the more usual causal ordering between sex and gender and hypothesized that it is gender that precedes sex. To this she further proposed to 'add to the hypothesis that gender precedes sex the following question: when we connect gender and sex are we comparing something social with something natural, . . . or are we comparing something social with something which is *also* social (in this case, the way a given society represents "biology" to itself)?' (2002, 55).

To understand this point, you might want to think about how our ideas about gender are acted upon in order to transform the sexual identity and appearance of our bodies. Much of what we identify as gendered behaviour and power dynamics is expressed on and with the body. This would include manipulation and alternation of 'natural' sex characteristics such as menstrual cycles, the look of the clitoris, breast and penis size, the longevity of erections, the location and density of hair, the size and shape of the vagina, and muscle mass. With strongly gendered ideas of what is appropriate for women and men to look like, we routinely intervene into all of these 'natural' characteristics in order to enhance size, appearance, timing, frequency, and so on.

The idea that both gender and sex are socially constructed is nicely summarized by Joan Scott, who draws on Donna Haraway and Judith Butler to identify gender, sex, and indeed nature itself as forms of knowledge and, therefore, concepts with traceable social origins and historical trajectories of use. Scott goes on to elaborate:

> If sex and gender are both taken to be concepts—forms of knowledge—then they are closely related, if not indistinguishable. If both are knowledges, then gender cannot be said to reflect sex or to be imposed on it; rather sex becomes an effect of gender. Gender, the social rules that attempt to organize the relationships of men and women in societies, produces the knowledge we have of sex and sexual difference (in our culture by equating sex with nature). Both sex and gender are expressions of certain beliefs about sexual difference; they are organizations of perception rather than transparent descriptions or reflections of nature. (1999, 72–3)

Another area of innovation in our understanding of 'biological sex' is the increasingly complex picture of how many sexes there are and how difficult it can be to unambiguously identify the sex of a person. It is clear from recent investigations that the idea of sex as a dichotomous phenomenon is not correct. As Adie Nelson has observed:

> Biological sex is not a unitary phenomenon with two simple dichotomous categories of 'male' and 'female'. Rather, it comprises a number of variables that must be considered together: chromosomal, gonadal, hormonal, reproductive, genital, brain and assigned sex. . . . These variables operate and interrelate in intricate ways. (2006, 38)

Information from organizations supporting individuals with ambiguous sex identities reveals the extent of the ambiguity. For example, the Intersex Society of North America indicates that in one of every 1,666 births, the child has neither an XX nor an XY chromosome pattern. They also assert that one of every 100 people has a body that does not conform to a standard male or female form.[1]

Sex testing at Olympic sports competitions is an interesting example of how difficult it can be to determine whether a particular individual is male or female. As the boxed text below reveals, despite attempts to use increasingly sophisticated scientific testing to establish an athlete's sex, no tests have proved sufficiently conclusive. This is not the fault of the tests per se, although their relevance in identifying performance-related sex characteristics is questionable. It is rather a reflection of Nelson's point—that being biologically female or male is a multi-dimensional phenomenon and that all dimensions do not necessarily point in one conclusive direction. Try to 'sex' an Olympic athlete at <www.hhmi.org/biointeractive/gendertest/gendertest.swf>, and you will see that it is not so easy to do! This was indeed the conclusion reached by the International Olympic Committee in 1999 when it decided to abandon sex testing.

Sex Testing at the Olympic Games

Sex testing was introduced in competitive sports in the mid-1960s, amid rumours that some competitors in women's events were not truly female—especially two Soviet sisters who won gold medals at the 1960 and 1964 Olympics, and who abruptly retired when gender verification testing began.

The first tests, at the European Championships in 1966 and the Pan-American Games in 1967, required female competitors to undress before a panel of doctors. Other methods used during this period included manual examination or close-up scrutiny of the athlete's genital region.

When athletes complained that these tests were degrading, the IOC at the Mexico City Olympics in 1968 introduced genetic testing in the form of a sex chromatin (Barr body) analysis of cells from a buccal smear. The procedure was further modified at the Barcelona Games, using the polymerase chain reaction to amplify the DNA extracted from a specimen to allow detection of a Y chromosome gene, SRY, that codes for male determination.

While this procedure was far less humiliating for competitors, geneticists and other experts argued that the test is pointless at best and has the potential for causing great psychological harm to women who, sometimes unknowingly, have certain disorders of sexual differentiation.

A case in point is the condition called androgen insensitivity syndrome (AIS) or testicular feminisation, which experts estimate affects about 1 in 500–600 female athletes. Although such individuals are genetically male because they have both an X and a Y chromosome, their tissues cannot respond to androgens and they develop as women. The irony is that the tests would not identify women with medical conditions that, in theory, might give them a competitive advantage over 'normal' women, such as congenital adrenal hyperplasia and androgen-secreting tumours that could result in greater muscle mass.

Source: Excerpt from J. Stephenson, 'Female Olympians sex tests outmoded', *Journal of the American Medical Association*, 17 July 1996, 276, 3: 177–8.

In light of the insight that biological sex is a far more complex and potentially ambiguous phenomenon than has been assumed in the past, important questions arise as to how children whose biology is sexually ambiguous should be raised. The tragic story of David Reimer is often told as a cautionary tale against those who would argue that nurture plays a stronger role in gender development than nature. The subject of CBC and BBC television documentaries, books (Colapinto 2001), interviews (including one in *Rolling Stone* magazine), and a potential Hollywood movie, David's complicated and painful life was the subject of much curiosity and controversy. David was born in Winnipeg, one of two male twins. While born unambiguously male, David suffered a horrendous injury to his penis during a circumcision procedure, and a decision was taken to raise him as a girl. The details of the David Reimer story reveal the incredible measures taken to convert David's male body into a female body—and only because he suffered an injury to his penis. Not until he was well into puberty, and as a result of his refusal to undergo further feminizing treatments, was David (living as Brenda) told that he was born a boy. With this knowledge, David eventually reverted to living his life as a male, a process involving further medical intervention to reverse earlier surgical procedures and hormone therapy undertaken to feminize his body.

But does David's story represent the 'social' exception that proves the 'biological' rule—is this really a case of biology winning out over social conditioning? The answer to this question has to be no. When the details of the case are examined carefully, there seems to be many other factors about how David lived his life as a girl that could explain his preference to return to a male gender identity. Even though he underwent several operations to make the conversion to a female body, his biological sex was ambiguous. For example, while his testicles were removed, the remaining stub of his penis was left in place so as not to interfere with his urinary function. And so 'Brenda' was the only child in the girls' washroom who peed standing up. Given the continued ambiguity of David's biological sex, and the extreme amount of medical intervention (we may even argue, abuse) he experienced in the effort to create for him a female body, we can hardly point to his case as a clear and straightforward test of the power of nature over nurture.

David Reimer—The Boy Who Lived as a Girl

CBC News Online | 10 May 2004

Summer 1965. In a Winnipeg hospital, Janet Reimer's lifelong dream comes true as she gives birth to twin sons, Bruce and Brian.

But within six months, both boys develop difficulty urinating. The doctors suggest they be circumcised.

On April 27, 1966, Janet drops her boys off for the routine procedure and her dream turns into a nightmare.

The doctors had chosen an unconventional method of circumcision, one in which the skin would be burned. The procedure goes horribly wrong, and Bruce's penis is burned so badly it can't be repaired surgically.

Over the next few months, the Reimers consult with countless doctors. None can offer any hope. Bruce Reimer would have to live with his non-existent penis.

One night, the Reimers see a television profile of an American doctor and his theories on sex and gender. Dr John Money of Johns Hopkins University in Baltimore argues that boys—caught early enough—could be raised to be girls. Nurture and not nature determines a child's gender, the doctor argued.

Janet Reimer thought it was worth exploring. The family went to Baltimore to see Dr Money, who decided that Bruce Reimer was a perfect candidate.

At the age of 21 months, Bruce's testicles were removed. What remained of his penis was left not to interfere with his urinary tract. When Bruce was released from hospital, his parents were told to raise him as a girl. The family was told not to divulge anything to anyone. They went home with a girl they called Brenda.

Janet Reimer did her best to raise Bruce as a girl. She dressed him in skirts and dresses and showed him how to apply makeup. But the transformation was anything but smooth. Bruce Reimer didn't like playing with the other girls—and he didn't move like one either. He got into schoolyard fistfights. The other kids called him names like 'caveman', 'freak', and 'it'.

In an interview with the CBC's *the fifth estate*, Reimer said it got so bad he didn't want to go to school anymore. He felt picked upon and increasingly lonely.

By the time Bruce turned nine, the Reimer family was having serious doubts. Not John Money. He published an article in the *Archives of Sexual Behaviour* pronouncing the experiment a resounding success. It became widely known in medical circles as the Joan/John case.

Money wrote: 'The child's behaviour is so clearly that of an active little girl and so different from the boyish ways of her twin brother.'

The twin brother, Brian, remembered it differently: 'The only difference between him and I was he had longer hair.' 'I tried really, really hard to rear her as a gentle lady,' Janet Reimer said. 'But it didn't happen.'

By the time Bruce was reaching puberty, it became increasingly clear the experiment was not working. He started developing thick shoulders and a thick neck.

At the same time, the Reimers were under pressure from Money to take the final step: allow surgeons to create a vagina.

But Bruce rebelled. He protested that he didn't need surgery and threatened to commit suicide if he was forced to make another trip to Baltimore to see Money. That's when his father broke down and told him everything.

Bruce Reimer said he had one thought at the time: to go to the hospital and track down and shoot the doctor who had botched his circumcision. In the end, he was unable to exact his revenge but turned his anger on himself.

He attempted suicide three times. The third—an overdose of pills—left him in a coma. He recovered and began the long climb towards living a normal life—as a man.

Bruce Reimer left his Brenda identity behind. He cut his hair and started wearing male clothing again. He changed his name to David.

Earlier, the Reimer family had sued the hospital where the botched circumcision was performed. They settled for about $60,000, which was held in trust for David until his 18th birthday. By then, the settlement was worth about $100,000.

Initially, David Reimer only told his story from the shadows—he refused to talk about it if his identity were revealed. That changed in 2000, when American author John Colapinto wrote *As Nature Made Him: The Boy Who Was Raised As a Girl*. A whirlwind of media exposure followed, across Canada and the United States.

Around the same time, research was sounding the death knell for the nurture vs. nature theory. Two studies—released by the Johns Hopkins Children's Center—concluded that it's prenatal exposure to male hormones that turns normal male babies into boys. The studies 'seriously question the current practice of sex-reassigning some of these infants as females . . .'

Janet Reimer said it was a difficult thing for her son to go public with his story, but he wanted to help other children facing a similar fate.

David Reimer underwent four rounds of reconstructive surgery to physically make him a man again. The surgery enabled him to enjoy a normal sex life, but he was unable to father children.

'I'm not going to cry a river of tears over that, because I've got three great kids. I've got a wonderful wife. I've got a good home,' he told CBC News in the wake of the release of the book.

Recently, David Reimer's life had taken another turn. He lost his job and was separated from his wife. His mother said he was still grieving the death two years ago of his twin brother.

David Reimer committed suicide on May 4, 2004. He was 38.

Source: Reprinted by permission of the publisher.

Increasingly, people argue that children who are born with (or who suffer through accidental injury) ambiguous biological sex characteristics should not undergo any form of medical intervention. They should be allowed to live their bodies as suits them best. The Intersex Society of North America (www.isna.org) does recommend that such children should live with a chosen/assigned gender identity. In contrast to David Reimer's experience, however, they also recommend complete honesty and openness about whatever biological ambiguity is present and, above all, no surgical intervention until the children are of an age to make such decisions for themselves. As we will discuss in the next section, we have become much less rigid in our sense of what is an appropriate match between sexed bodies and gendered personalities. We are under less pressure today to make a neat and tidy match between 'male' body parts and 'masculine' personalities. In part, this is because of our better understanding of the incredible variability in the physical manifestation of sexed bodies. It is also because we have become much more tolerant of gender ambiguity. Indeed, we are increasingly aware that ambiguity in gender identification is a much more common phenomenon and, indeed for some, a celebrated way to live.

Against essentializing and dichotomizing gender

Sociologists have cautioned that the analytical use of gender can also suffer from problems of essentialism and dichotomization. There are two aspects of these problems to consider: problems that stem from the continued tie of gender to a dichotomized biology and problems that derive from a form of social analysis that assumes a priori the significance and dichotomization of gender.

Problems of essentialism and dichotomization in the conceptualization of gender can be traced to the continued identification of gender as the social expression of biological traits—in other words, what nurture adds to nature. When it comes to thinking about the role of gender in children's lives, questions of the influence of nature versus nurture come into sharp relief. After all, children may seem, at least in the very early stages of their lives, to reflect more of the former. Consequently, many social science research projects have focused on babies and toddlers as ideal subjects for investigating the allegedly 'natural' expression of gender-identified actions and preferences. Studies of frustration reactions, toy selection, voice recognition, smiling frequency, play behaviour, and so on have become standard fare in research observations of babies and toddlers in an effort to sort out just how much of our gendered behaviour may be biologically hard-wired. But the problem with these investigations is that no matter how soon after birth researchers do their investigations, social influences are already present. Efforts to isolate biological and social influences on gender identity and attributes have been thwarted by this problem: the biological is always socially expressed. From a sociological point of view, there is no denying that as human beings, we have a physical body. But how that body is understood—the way we conceptualize how it works and the values and judgments we subject it to—are very much matters of social knowledge and convention. Adherence to a 'biology is destiny' perspective seems to come in waves (for a critique of the most recent champion, evolutionary psychology, see Kaplan and Rogers 2003). While there continues to be fierce debates on this matter in some disciplines (see, for example, the review of the debate in psychology about the influence of parenting on child development in Collins et al. 2000), a reasonable consensus appears to be building within both the natural and social sciences that any attempt to parse out the independent effects of biological inheritance and social context is doomed to failure. It will be interesting to see where the 'nature via nurture' (Ridley 2003) trends in scientific investigation and argument go. In the meantime, sociologists who study gender have always insisted that the historical and cultural variations in definitions of appropriate female and male behaviour and social activities are strong evidence of the socially constructed character of gender.

Early arguments pointed out that an individual was either masculine or feminine, *usually*. It was the existence of variation from the 'usually' that was thought to provide the most powerful evidence that gender was a social construction. It was useful evidence for the social construction of gender that the pairings of male biology/masculine identity and female biology/feminine identity did not always appear together. One could have male biology and show significant feminine traits and interests. Equally, one could have female biology and show significant masculine traits and interests. It was argued that there were very few personality characteristics, or social roles, that were exclusive to one sex. Drawing on cross-cultural evidence to support this claim, but using evidence from within particular societies as well, sociologists typically argued that feminine and masculine characteristics were distributed within each sex so that although there might be average differences, the range of the distribution from the averages revealed the social variability of gender. There might, for example, be a 'sex difference' in the extent to which children enjoy reading, with girls tending to be more enthusiastic than boys. However, many boys enjoy reading, and many girls prefer to be outside on the monkey bars. So while there might be an aggregate 'sex difference', there is a lot of overlap in the distribution of which gender likes to do what activity.

There was also ample evidence of strong differences in how people generally, and parents particularly, relate to boy and girl children, even at a very early age. Research using babies provided a lot of fun and excellent information about how 'clothes make the man'—or in this case, how clothes make the boy baby or girl baby. Researchers would take a baby and dress it in 'boy' clothes. They would then ask people to observe and describe the baby. People would talk about the baby using more 'masculine' descriptors—sturdy, thoughtful, handsome, determined, aggressive. The researchers would then take the *same baby* and dress it in 'girl' clothes. The descriptors used to talk about the baby when it was wearing girl's clothes were quite different—pretty, shy, worried, contented—and people would be more likely to comment on the clothes themselves: 'Hasn't she got a pretty dress on!' Other studies have noted that boy and girl children are parented differently and are likely to be placed in different socialization settings. For example, watch how parents carry babies in snugglies. Can you detect a gender pattern, with girl babies carried facing inward towards the parent's body and boy babies carried facing outward? (The next time you watch *Family Guy*, notice how Lois carries Stewie!) This closer, more personal contact for girl children has also been observed in child care choices. Child care for girls is more likely to be in more personal settings and smaller groups, whereas boys are more likely to be placed in institutional daycare centres. Of course, all of these observations are of tendencies, not categorical differences, but they do point to the many ways in which being a boy and being a girl are socially orchestrated and constructed from the moment of birth.

Much of this research directs our attention not only to how gender is socially constructed but to the incredible variation that can exist within gender categories. For example, researchers who study gender identification have had to create more and more elaborate schemes to capture how individuals gender-identify. They have also realized that gender identification is not a fixed phenomenon but can change for any particular individual. For example, Eyler et al. (1997) have developed an influential nine-point gender continuum that they offer as a way to help transgendered individuals locate their personal gender identification. The nine points on the continuum are: 1) female; 2) female with maleness; 3) gender-blended, female predominating; 4) other-gendered; 5) ungendered; 6) bi-gendered; 7) gender-blended, male predominating; 8) male with femaleness; and 9) male. They note that any individual gender identification along this continuum should be regarded as potentially temporary, because such identifications may vary over an individual's lifetime.

Even within the social construction argument, however, there have been tendencies to essentialize the category of gender by treating it as always significant, as well as tendencies to regard gender as a single dichotomy with a single definition. More recent approaches have emphasized the need to interrogate the significance of gender (is it an important influence in this case?) and to recognize that there are many variations in definitions of appropriate gender behaviour and activities depending on race, age, religion, class, and many other factors. In short, it has become imperative to recognize the multiplicity of genders—masculinities and femininities. This is no less important when looking at the role of gender in children's lives.

MULTIPLE FEMININITIES AND MASCULINITIES

Nancy liked to play dolls. She liked to play Mother.
And best of all, she liked to play Nurse.

She had a fine doll hospital, complete with BAND-AID Plastic Strips, Spots and
Patches and handy candy pills. But she had no one to play with her.

Her brothers called 'Nurse Nancy!' as they raced past her door.
But they never had time to stop and play. They were always too busy
with big boy games.

Mother stopped in at the hospital sometimes. 'Nurse Nancy,' she said,
when she came one day, 'now that my hurt finger is almost well, this big bandage
is in my way. Can you help me?'

'I have just the thing,' said Nurse Nancy. Down from the shelf she took
a brand-new box. And she put on Mother's finger, in place of the bandage, a brand-new
small pink Plastic Strip. 'There,' she said.

'Thank you,' said Mother. 'That's just fine. Now, I am going to
hurry to the grocery store. Can you look after the house for a few minutes?'
'Yes, I can,' said Nancy proudly.[2]

Nurse Nancy was published in 1952. This short extract from the beginning of the book shows the thinking about gender that was characteristic of the time. It encapsulates many of the main features of gender relations then and to some extent even now. Nancy is a girl of about six. Her play is very gender-appropriate and sums up her adult options pretty well: mother, teacher, nurse. Nancy's space is an interior space— in her room, in the house. Her brothers are preoccupied with 'big boy games', games that keep them outside, uninterested in Nancy's activities and unavailable as playmates. They call out to her; she does not call out to them. Nancy's mother encourages and affirms her daughter's interests in caring and helping activities and anticipates her daughter's domestic role by entrusting Nancy with the care of the house while she runs errands. Nancy's father does not appear in the story. Like most men of the time, he is an absent figure in the daily domestic life of women and children.

While certain ideas about what is appropriate for boys and girls and men and women to do can be very prominent at certain historical times, it is important to realize that rarely is one set of ideas uncontested. Even in the 1950s, the decade that was supposedly one of the most conservative in thinking about appropriate roles and personalities for men and women, there was some variation. In children's literature, there were popular heroines like Dale Evans, who roamed the wide-open spaces of ranching country getting into adventures, with only her horse for company.

> Dale Evans galloped along the desert trail on her beautiful white horse. The air was soft with spring. The sun was warm on the mountains and foothills. The horse's hoofs flew over the sandy trail. He was enjoying the gallop, too. Dale rode around the foot of a hill and came upon a strange sight.[3]

In decades to follow, more and more children's literature started to showcase girls as the main characters, and more often than not, these girls were portrayed as adventurous, clever, and strong. Younger readers encountered the tales of an extraordinary nine-year-old girl named Pippi Longstocking—an unconventional, assertive, and extraordinarily strong girl (she could lift a horse over her head!) who lived without parents in a house with a monkey and that same horse (although sometimes she visited her father, a pirate, on his adventures at sea). Older readers found a compelling heroine in Lyra, the intensely loyal, wise, and fearless central character in Philip Pullman's recent trilogy *His Dark Materials*. Alternative ways to be a girl have become more common fare in children's reading material.

Explorations of masculinity have arrived more recently on the scene, but here too we see in children's literature greater variety presented in what boys like to do and how they engage with the world around them. It is easy to find examples of masculine stereotypes in picture books and stories aimed at school-aged children. The first time we meet nine-year-old Anakin (the future Darth Vader) in the book version of *Star Wars* (Wrede 1999, 64), he exhibits the typical bravado of heroic characters: he tries to woo a woman much older than himself, boasts about his talents as a pilot, and overcomes his fear to rescue the victim of a bully. The story tells us that the constant emotion of Anakin's life is fear; we are also told that he is learning to crush it, to hide it.

But other ways to be male also make an appearance. For example, Charlotte Zolotow's book *William's Doll* opens with three simple but radical lines:

> William wanted a doll.
> He wanted to hug it,
> and cradle it in his arms . . .

And in the now classic Canadian bedtime story *Love You Forever*, it is a son who takes his old and frail mother in his arms at the end of the story, rocking her gently and soothing her fears. Action figures like Spiderman now show a more self-aware and psychologically vulnerable masculine identity (see Mike Graydon's contrast of Superman and Spiderman in chapter 3). Films like *Billy Elliot* show us that even in the heartland of British working-class masculine culture, a boy who wants to be a ballet dancer can be admired and celebrated.

These examples from the books read by us and our children illustrate the idea that gendered identities are varied. At any one time, there are multiple, often competing, gender identities. And certainly over time, constructions of gender identities change. Variations in ideas of femininity and masculinity in children's literature illustrate insights of the second gender shift in sociology, which stress that gender identities have multiple forms that are differently evaluated and normalized in specific social contexts.

CONCLUSION

In this chapter, we have examined some of the ways in which the developments of post-modern society are shaping gender relations in childhood. We have also looked at the consolidation of academic arguments in favour of a more nuanced and dynamic conceptualization of gender. A primary message throughout is that gendered experience is highly varied even at these earlier stages of personal development. To fully understand how children encounter and engage with gender, we need to be aware of the contexts in which they do so. Such contexts involve structural features of the larger society and culture into which they were born, as well as the social institutions within and through which their lives are lived. They also involve the person-to-person and day-to-day encounters with expectations and sanctions regarding appropriate behaviours for girls and boys. As sociologists, we want to be able to identify patterns of continuity in gendered experience, as well as areas of challenge and change.

While we have identified and emphasized the importance of multiple gendered identities, it is true that some have more social legitimacy and power than others. In the next chapter, we use the experiences of adolescence to explore more fully the idea that gendered identities have a hierarchical relation to one another. This hierarchical relation is compounded by the intersection of gendered identities with those of class, race, sexuality, and other dimensions of difference and privilege in our society.

Research Questions

1. Ask your parents to let you look at photographs of them when they were children. Can you tell anything about the gendering of their experience by looking at these photographs? What are they wearing? What are they doing? Who is with them in the photographs—mothers, fathers, siblings? Who is standing close to them? Are they touching/being touched by anyone?
2. Over the course of a day/week, take note of all the statements about children that you encounter—on TV, on the radio, in conversations, on the Internet, in newspapers and magazines. Are the statements about children gendered? What sort of conception of gender is being used in these statements?
3. In this chapter, we have used children's books to help identify variations in what is presented as acceptable behaviour for boys and girls. Can you think of other sources of data that would help you identify multiple forms of masculine and feminine identities within specific social institutions or cultures?

Discussion Questions

1. Do you agree that boys are 'in crisis'? Identify the particular experiences and circumstances that in your view support or refute the idea that boys are in crisis.
2. What aspects of primary schooling are most gendered? Does this vary by age, race, class, ability, language, citizenship? What aspects are gender-neutral?
3. Do you think that children are able to critically engage with the gendered messages they receive via the media?
4. Does the existence of multiple masculinities and femininities suggest a positive change in how children live their gender in today's society?

Further Reading

Fausto-Sterling, Ann. 2005. 'The five sexes revisited', in M.B. Zinn et al., *Gender through the Prism of Difference*, 13–18. New York: Oxford University Press. The authoritative voice on the diversity of sex and gender.

Janovicek, Nancy, and Joy Parr, eds. 2003. *Histories of Canadian Children and Youth*. Don Mills, ON: Oxford University Press. Important collection of material on Canadian childhood and youth over the twentieth century.

Jenkins, Henry, ed. 1998. *The Children's Culture Reader*. New York: New York University Press. Collection of many classic articles on a variety of topics to do with children's culture.

Willms, J. Douglas, ed. 2002. *Vulnerable Children: Findings from Canada's National Longitudinal Survey of Children and Youth*. Edmonton: University of Alberta Press. Research reports from the first longitudinal study of children growing up in Canada.

Films

Little Miss Sunshine. 2006. Beauty pageant with a twist—but still within traditional femininity.

My Brand New Life. 2004. National Film Board documentaries that include young people switching places to see how others live—including boys and girls trying out each others lives.

Toy Story. 1995. Presents a range of masculine identities for boys—and their toys.

Home Alone. 1990. A movie prescient of post-modern childhood?

Websites

www.vifamily.ca
Vanier Institute of the Family. An excellent site reporting research on family life and growing up in Canada. Spring 2000 has a special section on sex roles and stereotypes. Spring 2003 is dedicated to 'Canadian Boys: Growing up Male'.

www.cprn.ca
Canadian Policy Research Network: Children, Youth and Families. A policy-focused Canadian research network with a focus on children and youth.

www.brunel.ac.uk/research/centres/iccfyr
Interdisciplinary Centre for Child and Youth Focused Research brings together European researchers from a variety of disciplines interested in studying the lives of children and youth, including gender issues.

www.unb.ca/crisp
Canadian Research Institute for Social Policy aims to use research to improve the education and care of children and youth in Canada. Many research topics have a gender component.

Chapter 3

Gender Intensification: Adolescence and the Transition to Adulthood

Chapter Objectives

1. To consider gendered aspects of expectations and experiences of adolescence and early adulthood.
2. To emphasize the diversity and fluidity of gendered experience among adolescents and young adults.
3. To introduce hierarchies of gender and the concepts of hegemonic masculinity and emphasized femininity.
4. To appreciate different forms of resistance and challenge to hegemonic gender identities.

INTRODUCTION

If post-modern society is blurring the division between adulthood and childhood (as we suggest in chapter 2), the 'monkey in the middle' is adolescence. Caught between contradictory social pressures—some of which pull back to the dependency of childhood while others push forward to the trappings and liberties of adult life—adolescence is a highly contested and ambiguous experience. Whereas there is a general consensus that it is not a good idea to collapse the boundary between adulthood and childhood, there is considerable debate about the validity of the boundary between adulthood and adolescence. For example, a recent edition of *The Globe and Mail* invited debate on the idea that 'adolescence is obsolete' (25 August 2007, F1). As a society, do we infantilize our adolescents by keeping them from responsibilities and opportunities that they are more than ready for? Or do we push them too far and too fast towards an adult lifestyle that neither suits their developmental state nor honours their right to familial and social support? When we consider possible answers to these questions, are we inclined to answer differently for adolescent boys and adolescent girls? Do we consider the path to adulthood to be the same for girls and boys? Does our perspective on the significance of gender to this journey depend on which aspects of 'adulthood' we are considering—leaving home, getting a job, having your first sexual experience, having a child, identifying your sexual orientation, finishing school, undergoing cosmetic surgery, buying a house?

What it means to be an adolescent is highly dependent on context—the time, place, and social conditions in which one lives. In Canada, adolescents are currently caught between one set of social forces that prolongs their child-like dependence and another set that introduces them to adult-like experiences and issues at younger and younger ages. In the midst of these changes and challenges, adolescents are expected to successfully take on the mantle of adulthood, emerging from their teens and early 20s as socially productive, well-adjusted individuals. In this chapter, we explore several aspects of this time in a person's life, asking to what extent this journey is different for young women and young men and for diverse groups of women and men. We have organized the chapter around three key expectations in this growing-up process: learning how to negotiate social relationships; achieving material independence; and discovering who one is and fashioning an appropriate self-identity. In each case, we present interesting examples of the continued salience of diverse forms of gender, as well as important and fascinating accounts of the 'undoing' of gender as a criterion of social organization and personal experience.

ENTERING THE SOCIAL WORLD OF ADOLESCENCE

Adolescent boys and girls spend a lot of time interacting with each other virtually and in real time—at school, on the bus, on Facebook and MSN, on the phone, at community centres, on sports teams, during social time at movies, dances, or clubs. Learning to negotiate relationships with others, and doing so beyond the watchful eye of parents, teachers, or other adults, is a large part of the adolescent experience. There is a strong undercurrent of growing sexual awareness in many of these encounters and much pressure to 'fit in' to whatever is regarded as 'normal'—who looked at, likes, sent text messages to, walked with, and sat next to whom, gets noticed and talked about. We shall explore later in the chapter the fluidity of gender and sexual identity and the struggle with hegemonic forms of gender identity. First, we want to pay attention to how possibilities for intimate relationships emerge in the social lives of adolescents and some of the ways in which adolescent socializing is constructed as problematic. Adolescent boys and girls are both affected by these general social processes, but not always in the same way.

From parents to peers

As children grow into adolescents, there is a major shift in their patterns of socializing. Two changes are typical. First, adolescents spend more and more time with their friends and comparatively less with their family. Second, adolescent socializing begins to include possibilities for, and realities of, more intimate relationships.

For most boys and girls, the transition into adolescence is marked by how peers become a major part of their social life. When asked to name the people most important to them, the majority of people named by adolescents are peers (Craig et al. 2002, 317). One thing unique in how adolescents spend time with peers, as opposed to the way children do, is that it is more likely to be without parental supervision. Time alone in the company of one's friends provides important moments and opportunities for adolescents to try out ways of speaking and acting that are explorations of identity and of patterns of social interaction. As sociologists have known for a long time, peer relationships are an important socializing agent in the lives of adolescents.

In Canadian culture, intimate pairings are typically heterosexual, and peer relationships are the place where adolescents begin to experiment with mixed-sex friendships and heterosexual relationships. While same-sex peer groups form a significant setting in which boys and girls further explore and develop their relational skills, adolescence is marked by the onset of encounters with the 'opposite sex'. Researchers have noted that it is important to distinguish between mixed-sex peer groups and romantic pairing with the opposite sex when considering 'encounters with the other' in adolescence (Sippola 1999). The meaning of other-sex relationships (and, equally, same-sex relationships) can vary by contextual factors such as stage of sexual development as well as situational and cultural factors. Research from social psychologists points to a wide array of relationships between adolescent girls and boys and indicates that the significance and impact of such relationships can vary according to wider contextual factors. For example, William Bukowski et al. (1999) studied 231 Canadian children in grades 5 to 7 and report that having only 'other-sex friends' is regarded as positive for boys but negative for girls. Nancy Darling and her colleagues (1999) studied a slightly older group of Canadian adolescents (grades 6 to 8) and report that the shift to mixed-sex social networks is associated with positive self-esteem for boys if the interaction is frequent and for girls if the interaction is comfortable. The researchers note that the gender difference in self-esteem is not because same and mixed-sex groups are doing different activities—but, in the context of heteronormativity, can be traced to the more emotionally charged context of mixed-group encounters.

While there is, as the literature suggests, a fairly common shift from single-sex to mixed-sex interactions during adolescence, it is also true that adolescents are positioned to experience this shift in more or less complex ways. There is a growing body of work on intersectional analysis that suggests there are significant differences within and between boys and girls. Two obvious issues here are sexual orientation and ethnicity/race.

Mixed-sex interactions during adolescence are loaded with messages for boys and girls about approved sexual behaviour and partnerships. Everyone—boy, girl, straight, gay—encounters and must deal with the cultural dominance of heterosexuality. Canadian research on growing up queer argues (Adams 1997; O'Brien and Weir 1995) that there is an increasing acceptance of homosexuality among adolescents, although problems with acceptance continue in families, in schools, and indeed on city streets, where adolescent gays and lesbians often face violent responses.

Adolescents from mixed cultural contexts also experience a very complex positioning in terms of encounters with mixed-sex relationships. Amita Handa (2003) tells of the 'tightrope' that young South Asian girls walk between the cultural expectations and practices of their South Asian heritage and those of the dominant white, 'Canadian' culture. Establishing mixed-sex friendships and relationships is experienced through the tensions and contradictions between two (unequal) cultures. Further, as Handa notes, these two cultures are themselves fraught with internal tensions and ambiguities. She describes the controversies that erupted over the attendance of teenagers at *bhangra* dances—which became both an affirmation of South Asian culture and a contestation of it:

> Bhangra music and dances stand in opposition to dominant white culture in the struggle for cultural space. . . . They also assert girls' resistance to parental attempts to control their sexuality. As Salimah explained: 'Most of the girls go to the dances to find guys, Indian guys, 'cause that's the only place to see them. That's the only place where they can do what they want, where they can act the way they feel without parents lurking over them, watching them.' (2003, 116)

Mythili Rajiva (2006) pushes this analysis even further by arguing that it is important to look at variations in racialized identities within the category 'South Asian woman', and in her research she explores the 'boundary events' and 'boundary work' identified by second-generation adolescent girls as pivotal in shaping their experience of 'fitting in' as brown girls in white worlds. As one of Rajiva's respondents recalls:

> 'There are times when I feel slightly different, like my whole group of friends, there's me . . . another Indian girl . . . 10 of us girls and the rest are all White. . . . The guys we hang around with, like they're all White. . . . I feel accepted . . . but I know that there's a difference . . . but I don't think it's a negative thing, I just think it's something that they know I know.' (2006, 175)

From friendship to intimacy

Experimentation with and exploration of gendered relationships happens for adolescents in the process of discovering sexuality. Canadian research shows an increasing level of sexual experience among adolescents. As Vappu Tyyskä (2001, 136) summarizes it, 'sex has now become a natural part of being a teenager.' Approximately half of Canadian teenagers report having had sexual intercourse by the time they are 17. A report from the Public Health Agency of Canada indicates that the average age of first heterosexual intercourse for those aged 15 to 24 is virtually identical for girls (16.8 years) and boys (16.7 years).[1] Studies continue to find, however, common gender differences in how boys and girls rate the intimacy and emotional aspects of relationships. Concerns about 'rainbow parties' and other forms of sexual exploitation of girls raise serious questions about how adolescent girls and boys are encountering and constructing their sexuality. Increasing exposure to (and, one might argue, normalization of) pornography on television, in music videos, and on the Internet presents what some have called 'rape sex' as the form of sexual encounter that women and men should enjoy.

However, (Tyyskä 2001, 132) while these issues are real, studies also find that both boys and girls view romantic relationships positively and share similar concerns about being liked by the 'opposite sex'. There are also indications that current generations of boys and young men have improved relational skills and emotional intelligence. For example, Canadian studies have found that when talking in female–male pairs, and in contrast to adult men, teenage boys do not dominate conversations. Whereas adult men interrupt and challenge their conversation partners, teenage boys do not. Can we interpret this as a sign of progress on the stage of interpersonal gender relationships (or have young men simply not grasped their power to dominate conversation yet)? A wider range of male heroes now populate the movies that young people see and the books they read. In particular, sensitive men are taking leading roles in television series and in movies. Is it not hugely relevant that the most popular children's/teen book of all time has a male hero who relates equally well to his male and female best friends? He combines traditional feminine characteristics of sensitivity and relationality with traditional male characteristics of independence and fearlessness. While he does develop into an athletic teenager, larger and more macho boys still constantly bully him. His appearance includes those quintessential markers of vulnerability—a slight build and eyeglasses. We are referring, of course, to Harry Potter.

In the following insert, Mike Graydon, a PhD student in sociology at Carleton, compares the relational expertise and priorities of two very different sorts of super-heroes—Superman and Spiderman.

Gendering the Hero—A New Man to the Rescue

by Mike Graydon
Sociology PhD Program

Manhood. Masculinity. Such concepts have traditionally been thought of as desti-nations or end points on a socio-biological map drawn centuries ago. Boys are sent down a gendered path to manhood (rife with improper, even emasculating, alternate sidetracks) on a lifetime quest to acquire and reach masculinity. Perhaps it's their apparent diligence, their struggle to stay-the-path that engenders a kind of heroic quality to men and masculinity. Yet the quest of these men-as-heroes forces them to confront hazy myth and fleshy reality along the way, all but ensuring that masculinity is a multiplicity of gendered destinations.

Any perspective on male gender is masked by a symbiotic relationship between an essentialized biological body and a contingent cultural, mythical masculinity—especially given that we view the latter as essential to the former. The quest for masculinity demands that culturally gendered disguises be worn, which then reveal and rework the biological body, according to cultural dictates. Traditionally, heroes don different guises and armour. As a case study, I offer two heroes reflecting different periodizations (paths) and disguises of gender: Superman and Spiderman. In their day jobs, each presents one version of everyday masculinity and one version of a masculinized hero. Superman hides in plain sight as the bespectacled Clark Kent and walks a timeless route to manhood, while Peter Parker as Spiderman walks a newer, emerging path to masculinity.

Peter Parker is hands-down the modern man, embodying an inclusive, feminized take on male gender. Parker is all relationships and responsibility, afraid of disappointing Mary Jane and fretting about Aunt May's jaundiced view of Spider-man. Guilt-ridden over having chosen a path that led to the death of a father-figure uncle, Parker forevermore considers the consequences of Spiderman's actions upon his relationships. For Superman, the people in his life are but bystanders perpetually getting in harm's way. Our hero will save Lois and Jimmy, but Superman's work-first path puts besting Lex Luther atop his to-do list. A grown 'manly man' of action, Superman travels a well-worn path to manhood, unburdened by attachments. Spiderman, taking a newer, unexplored route, remains a perpetual teenage student of relational responsibility.

Each is set on the path to manhood as a means to a different end. Superman, an otherwise unremarkable human, is elevated to 'super-manly' status. To 'make a man' of him, Superman's father sends him to Earth, while 'figure-it-out-along-the-way advice', rather than super strength, is given to Spiderman by his philosophical uncle. Spiderman's 'great power' is the result of circumstance (from the bite of a radioactive spider). Thus for him, power is the gift of happenstance, reflecting the potential of all men to become greater than they are—depending on the path they choose.

En route to a more modern version of masculinity, Spiderman remains a relationally focused, ethically concerned figure. Conversely, Superman grows stronger over his quest, amassing power along the way. The 1940s Superman leapt tall buildings and travelled faster than speeding bullets. With the advent of the 1960s feminist revolution, Superman's powers were expanding as alternate routes to masculinity emerged. Now able to fly, he could fly right through the sun if need be, powerful enough to best any hot-eyed feminist. All the while, Spiderman travelled his tangled web of relationships, always willing to hang around and work it out. This is something only those choosing an alternate path to manhood would do.

If there are multiple paths to manhood and multiple end points of masculinity, clearly men make choices—some willingly, some not—about the route they will take. What are these choices that men must make? Is the relationally focused choice a popular one these days?

Negotiating the negative side of adolescent socializing

As children mature into adolescence, typical concerns and issues also take on a gendered form. For example, adolescent girls develop a highly negative relation to their bodies—describing their healthy-weight bodies as 'too fat' and problematizing their relationship to food (Nelson 2006, 139). They can also develop a competitive relationship to other girls, seeing them as rivals in the body-shaping or boy-getting stakes. Adolescent boys are reluctant to admit to problems and concerns, feeling they need to tough things out or solve things by themselves. Instead of seeing connections with others as a means of solving problems, they look for more individualized solutions. This is one reason why the suicide rate for young males is among the highest in the country. While peers are often a source of pleasure, fun, and solidarity, such relationships can also be highly destructive. As the lyrics from the Billy Talent song 'Nothing to Lose' suggest, peer relations can be a source of pain and personal struggle.

Need more friends with wings
All the angels I know
Put concrete in my veins
I'd always walk home alone
So I became lifeless
Just like my telephone

Never played truth or dare
I'd have to check my mirror
To see if I'm still here
My parents had no clue
That I ate all my lunches
Alone in the bathroom

Teachers said 'it's just a phase'
When I grow up my children
Will probably do the same
Kids just love to tease
Who'd know it put me
underground at seventeen

There's nothing to lose
My notebook will explain
There's nothing to gain
And I can't fight the pain

Billy Talent. 'Nothing to Lose'.

L. Susan Williams (2002) identifies adolescence as a time when individuals are 'trying on' gender identities and exploring gendered relations. She argues that the 'trying on' process is different from the idea of 'doing gender' in that it is especially characterized by experimentation and tentativeness. She uses Connell's concept of gender regimes (those local, contextualized rules and regulations about appropriate gender relations) to investigate how adolescent girls 'try on' a wide range of femininities. She notes, however, that the window for experimentation may be fairly brief. The first year of high school seems to be a moment when options for experimentation narrow considerably and pressure to 'fit in' intensifies. Williams also calls attention to the variability in 'trying on' options depending on the class and race composition of immediate contexts.

The scope for experimenting with or 'trying on' forms of gender relations can be considerably narrowed within social contexts where pressure to 'fit in' and conform to a norm are highly policed—often by adolescents themselves. For example, bullying behaviour among adolescents is often focused on sexual issues and gender relations. Neil Duncan (1999) draws attention to distinguishing features of sexual bullying. He argues that among older children, particularly adolescents, much bullying behaviour targets sexuality and sexual identities:

> I think a lot of what passes for seemingly ordinary bullying does have a certain sexual underpinning, a certain sexual motor behind it, the motivation is perhaps based in a sort of sexual rivalry or sexual competition amongst particularly young boys and young girls who are going through adolescence. (Interview transcript, Australian Broadcasting Corporation, *Lateline*, broadcast 7 February 2001)

This phenomenon is very well observed and narrated in the book by Rachel Simmons (2003) and its companion TV movie *Odd Girl Out* in which the main character is subjected to taunts, gossip, cruel pranks, and cyber-harassment about her appearance, her friendships with boys, and her sexual behaviour. The point is that relational aggression is as pervasive, powerful, and damaging as physical aggression, particularly at a time when adolescents feel exceptionally vulnerable about their sexuality, their changing bodies, and their appearance.

When gender norms and relational conflicts are crossed with racial divisions, the combination can be deadly. The death of Reena Virk is remembered as a particularly vicious instance of targeting a racialized girl who did not 'fit in'. The tragic series of events began on a cold November evening in 1997 when a group of teenagers gathered for a small outdoor party near the Craigflower Bridge, just west of the city of Victoria in British Columbia. Reena Virk, a 14-year-old South Asian teenager who was not normally part of this group, decided to accept an invitation to attend the get-together. With drinking, talking, and smoking, the gathering was unfolding much like such events in communities across Canada. But the night took a fateful turn when late in the evening, a small group of teens—seven girls and one boy—began to swarm around Reena Virk. They began with verbal taunts, but soon the name-calling turned into punching and kicking. Other girls and boys stood and watched as the beating by the eight teens continued with varied kinds of assault. A cigarette was stubbed out on Reena's forehead, and they tried to set her hair on fire. Finally, after persistent pleas by one girl who was disturbed by the violence, the beating stopped, and Reena stumbled away from the group. While she tried to make her way home across the bridge, she was in fact being followed by two of the white teenagers, Kelly Ellard and Warren Glowatski. They dragged her back under the bridge and continued to beat her. Then Kelly forced Reena's head underwater until she stopped struggling. It took more than a week before Reena Virk's death was confirmed. Because the teenagers had formed a pact not to tell others what had happened, Reena was simply recorded as missing, and her family and community went through a horrible ordeal of searching and waiting. Several of the teachers at Shoreline Secondary School had their suspicions, but nothing was done until police divers discovered Reena's partially clothed body washed ashore at the Gorge Inlet, a major waterway on Vancouver Island. While the cause of death was initially identified as drowning, an autopsy revealed that the main cause was 18 kicks to the head.

The media attention to this terrible crime was understandably overwhelming. Indeed, some commentators noted that the events that unfolded in that small BC community had set off a moral panic across Canada. The main thrust of the coverage was that this was a case of horrific girl violence. Academics and psychologists weighed in on how girls' peer relations were becoming as violent as those traditionally exhibited among boys and men. Reena Virk's death was viewed as another example of girl violence on the rise in Canada and in other Western countries, which was accompanied by a sense of bewilderment over this state of affairs. Academic commentators, however, pointed out that Reena's death should be understood as the result of a number of factors, including how race, class, and gender intersected to make Reena the target of peer bullying, abuse, and ultimately murder. A complete understanding of this terrible event required acknowledging the racism and classism that combined with Reena's gender to push her to the social margins. According to Yasmin Jiwani (1997, 2): 'Reena Virk could not "fit in" because she had nothing to fit in to. She was brown in a predominantly white society. She was supposedly overweight in a society which values slimness to the point of anorexia, and she was different in a society which values "sameness" and "uniformity".'

Gendering the risks of sexual relations

Adolescents today have increased access to male and female forms of birth control, and theoretically, sexually active teenagers are better able to manage the possibility of pregnancy. Nevertheless, managing this risk continues to be primarily a young woman's responsibility. In the post-modern context, however, it is not the only risk taken when engaging in sexual activity. In addition to concerns about AIDS and HIV, a lot of attention has been focused on sexually transmitted infections linked to cervical cancer. Recently, there has been tremendous controversy over the Canadian government's plan to support immunization against the human papillomavirus—the most common form of sexually transmitted infection. Two areas of controversy stand out. First, would immunization against the virus be interpreted by adolescents as an encouragement to engage in sexual activity? Second, only girls would be immunized, thus making girls and young women even more responsible for managing the risks of sexual activity.

Key aspects of this debate are set out by Willow Scobie, a recent PhD graduate in sociology from Carleton University.

Young Women and Men and the HPV Vaccine

by Willow Scobie
Sociology PhD, Carleton University (2007)

At the beginning of each academic year, a national charitable organization recruits university students to raise funds on their behalf. Recently, Carleton University and University of Ottawa students set themselves up all over downtown Ottawa with small boxes in order to draw attention to the cause and bring in donations. Each of the students wore an identifying T-shirt and carried a shoulder bag filled with loot. Interestingly, one of the logos on the loot bag bore the name Gardasil, a new vaccination drug produced by the pharmaceutical company Merck. Approved in Canada for girls and young women between the ages of 9 and 26, it is a vaccine designed to offer protection from four types of the human papillomavirus (HPV). It is widely celebrated in many circles as an important advance in sexual health but remains controversial in others.

The human papillomavirus is the world's most common sexually transmitted infection. Although not all types of HPV are sexually transmitted, some of those that are can cause genital warts or may lead to cancer. However, the Health Canada website reports that 'although a high percentage of sexually active people will be infected with HPV, only a small proportion of these would potentially go on to develop cancer' (www.hc-sc.gc.ca/iyh-vsv/diseases-maladies/hpv-vph_e.html).

Nevertheless, the Canadian government has committed funding dollars to support a mass immunization program for girls between the ages of 9 and 13.

Implementation of the immunization program is a provincial/territorial decision, and several jurisdictions have already agreed to support this strategy. 'Nova Scotia, Prince Edward Island, Newfoundland and Labrador and Ontario will begin vaccinating girls against HPV this fall [2007]. British Columbia and Quebec will likely do so beginning in the fall of 2008, and other provinces and territories have not yet decided' (Picard 2007, A9). In Ontario, for example, free vaccine will be offered to young women in grade 8 through a school-based vaccination program to be administered by public health nurses. It is a voluntary program, and consent to receive the vaccine will follow the same procedure as other vaccination programs. Already, a number of Ontario schools are opting out, and there is much controversy about the wisdom of this approach.

According to a report released by the Canadian Women's Health Network entitled *HPV, Vaccines, and Gender: Policy Considerations*, advertisers representing pharmaceutical interests are creating an unnecessary public panic by suggesting that HPV represents an imminent threat (2007). In the case of deaths associated with cervical cancer, the focus should be on the ability of primary care and reproductive health services to address the needs of particular groups of women. Anyone who has a healthy immune system, is well-nourished, and does not smoke will clear an HPV infection from their own bodies, with or without treatment.

An important aspect of this issue concerns the almost exclusive focus on girls and women. Although approval of the vaccine for boys and men is pending, males are conspicuously absent from most discussions surrounding HPV. A vaccination program that includes boys and men would not only contribute to blocking the circulation of the virus to women but also reduce the rates of penile cancer, anal cancer, and genital warts in men. Boys and men not only represent an important link in the health chain as 'carriers' of HPV, but it is also critical that health systems protect boys and men as individuals. By prioritizing the immunization of girls and women, the sexual health of boys and men as individuals and as partners is neglected.

There are clear benefits to slowing or arresting the circulation of sexually transmitted infections. Even if the risk of developing a form of cancer as a result of HPV infection is not an imminent danger to most of those who come in contact with HPV, the prevention of exposure to the virus holds obvious appeal. A number of important questions remain, however.

How does the prioritization of immunizing girls against a sexually transmitted infection fit into broader gender patterns in managing the risks of sexual relations?

Should young men and women be equally implicated in any sexual health strategy? Why/why not?

We have reviewed several dimensions of how gender is and is not operating in the ways that adolescents learn and experiment with social relations, including more intimate and sexual relations. This relational experience is also a significant part of how adolescents explore their own identities and, particularly, how they explore gender identities. We will turn to the issue of negotiating gender identities near the end of the chapter. For the moment, we want to draw your attention to two opposing dynamics in the lives of adolescents and young adults. One is that the negotiation of social relations, intimate relationships, and sexuality is becoming a concern at younger and younger ages. We could say that according to these 'relational' markers, the boundary between adulthood and adolescence is disappearing. But another dynamic is at work in contemporary adolescence that is actually strengthening the boundary between adulthood and adolescence. It is now more difficult for young people to attain the more 'material' markers of adulthood. More and more, young people tend to be older when they acquire the resources that lead to economic independence. We turn now to a discussion of this 'delay' in the movement from the material dependence of adolescence to the material independence of adulthood.

TRANSITIONING TO MATERIAL INDEPENDENCE

The next time you are talking to your mom or dad, ask them how old they were when they left school, when they got their first full-time job, when they moved out into their own apartment, when they bought their first house. Can you imagine yourself doing the same things at the same age? You probably can't, because you live in a time and social context in which individuals are much older by the time they acquire the resources that secure material independence. As the Barenaked Ladies song says, you can't live your life in the baby seat, you've got to stand on your own. However, the trend over the past couple of decades has been to keep more young people in the 'baby seat' for a longer period of time.

> If you think growing up is tough
> Then you've just not grown enough, baby
>
> You can't live your life in the baby seat
> You've got to stand on your own
> Don't admit defeat
> You can't live your life in the baby seat
> You've got to stand on your own
> Don't admit defeat
>
> Barenaked Ladies. 'Baby Seat'.

Several Canadian researchers have contributed to constructing a picture of the remarkable change in the personal circumstances and life situations of Canadians in their late teens and 20s. If we compare those who were this age in 2001 and those who were this age roughly 20 years earlier, the change is dramatic. In 2001, they were more likely to be living at home with their parents and to be registered as full-time students. They were less likely to be married or cohabiting or to have had their first child.[2] Some of these changes are especially striking, and of course they are interrelated. For example, one-third of those aged 16 to 24 in the mid-1970s were enrolled as full-time students. By 2001, half of those in this age group were full-time students. In part because of this change, more than 40 per cent of those in their 20s were living at home in 2001. And along with changes in educational and residential status, there has been a substantial drop in marriages and cohabitations. Whereas in the early 1980s, 27 per cent of men and 46 per cent of women aged 20 to 24 were married or cohabiting, the proportions had dropped to 14 per cent of men and 26 per cent of women by 2001. A similar drop in marriage and cohabitation among the 25 to 29 age group occurred over this period. First-time parents are also much older. In the mid-1970s, women in their 20s accounted for 91 per cent of first-time births. In 2001, this number had fallen to 66 per cent.

Sociologists have been diligent in linking this transformation in the lives of adolescents to large social changes since the mid-1980s. Such changes include the reconfiguration of both labour markets and households. Under neo-liberal changes in relationships between local/global markets, the state, and communities, life has generally become more precarious and uncertain. Such changes have meant that youth must delay entry into the labour market (jobs for them are disappearing) and acquire more credentials in order to compete for the declining supply of good jobs. At the same time, women's expectations of adult life have altered so that jobs and careers are very much a part of future plans. Student debt, insecure income, and career progression mean a delay in having children. Young men's wages have deteriorated relative to those of older men and younger women so that they are no longer capable of serving as breadwinners for dependent families. All of these factors lead to delays in household formation and reinforce the necessity of dual-earner households.

For both genders, there has been a remarkable increase in what some sociologists refer to as 'delayed life transitions'. Although in some cases (such as enrolment in full-time schooling among those in their 20s) gender differences have all but disappeared, there continues to be gender patterns in achieving several of the markers of adulthood. For example, women still tend to be younger than men at their first marriage/cohabitation and the birth of their first child. They are also less likely to be employed full-time at a younger age. Karen Foster, a PhD student in sociology at Carleton, presents further information about the extent to which delayed transitions to paid work are gendered.

Again, it is important to stress that young women and men are not equally placed in relation to the phenomenon of delayed transitions. Extended post-graduate schooling and familial support, though having its own frustrations and difficulties, is the privilege of advantaged individuals. Their transition to material independence may be delayed, but it will happen. Those not so advantaged—from poorer families or suffering various forms of familial disruption and abandonment—could have permanently delayed transitions. Klodawsky et al. (2006) report on the fate of homeless youth in Ottawa. They observe strong gender and racialized patterns of experience

The Earnings Gender Gap for Young Adults

by Karen Foster
Sociology PhD Program

The widespread delay of independence among contemporary young adults has become a hot topic among researchers, journalists, and the general public. Beyond a general tendency towards prolonged transitions to adulthood at the aggregate level, different subgroups, based on intersections of gender, class, ethnicity, geography, and citizenship, tend to reach independent adulthood faster and with more ease than others (Furstenburg et al. 2005). Looking at gender differences alone, North American women coming of age in the 1990s and early 2000s tended to move out, find careers, graduate, marry, and form families at a younger age than the men in their generation (see Furstenburg et al. 2005, 30–4, for details on the US and Beaujot 2004 for Canadian figures). Concomitant with this disparity is the increased presence and success of women in university programs, an increase that prompted Human Resources and Social Development Canada (HRSDC) to push for special policies aimed at 'encouraging young men to pursue post-secondary studies, while ensuring that they do well in high school and are well informed about the job prospects by level of education' (Dubois 2002, 29). These apparent 'advances' for young women, however, have not necessarily translated into increased social mobility and higher incomes.

In fact, recent research using the National Graduate Survey (NGS) from 2000 suggests that there is still a considerable gender gap in earnings among Canadian young adults who graduated from a post-secondary program in 1995 (MacAlpine 2005). This gap could not be fully 'explained away' by other variables, such as occupational field, job tenure, hours worked, and years of education, among others. The study looked at the relationship between salary expectations after graduation and actual salary three years later. Interestingly, descriptive statistics showed a gender gap in expected salary that mirrored the gap in actual salary; the expectations variable also emerged in regression analyses as one of the strongest predictors of later earnings, regardless of gender. Thus, not only were the young women in the survey earning significantly less than their male peers, they also expected to from the outset.

But another finding from the study is particularly salient to this discussion. The gender gap in actual salary was larger among respondents who had begun to form families. Regression models suggested that men's incomes were positively affected by marriage/cohabitation (having children was not significant), while women who were married/cohabiting and/or had children earned less than single, childless women and all men. All of this points to an idea tossed around in the debate about delayed life transitions: that delayed family formation, career attainment, and other markers of adulthood constitute more than widespread laziness or shifts in values— they can also be considered a strategic, pragmatic response (consciously articulated or not) to complex economic realities (Beaujot 2004).

Canadian contributions to research in this area are predominantly quanti-tative. This is no doubt facilitated by the handful of rich, relevant data sets available, such as the NGS, the Youth in Transition Survey, and the National Longitudinal Survey of Children and Youth. Despite these resources, there is a dearth of research dealing with how gender, ethnicity, class, ability, and other variables factor into individual trajectories towards adult independence. This is unfortunate, given evi-dence from the US and the UK in support of an intersectional approach to the issue. In the income study discussed above, other interaction effects suggested that women who identified as visible minorities experienced a further 'reduction' in income relative to other women and all men. Thus, two interrelated gaps exist in the Canadian debate on this topic—ideally, the need for intersectional analyses and in-depth, qualitative research will influence the direction of future research on transitions to adulthood in Canada.

When you think about your future employment prospects, what salary do you expect to earn? Ask other students—male and female—about their salary expectations. Do the male and female students have similar or different expectations?

among homeless youth and that the majority of homeless youth are trying to escape some form of family conflict and violence. Sexual abuse within the family home was especially common among homeless young women and Aboriginal youth. A terribly poignant aspect of the lives of homeless youth is how 'normal' their hopes and ambi-tions are (finish school, get a job) and how impossible it is for them to realize any of these hopes from within the circumstances of homelessness. This creates a horrible catch-22 situation in which young people's wishes to complete school and get a good job are thwarted by not having a stable and suitable home—and finding the stable and suitable home is thwarted by their detachment from school and employment. As Klodawsky et al. comment, helping marginalized youth to transition to adulthood is a complex task, because any form of intervention must recognize the gendered and racialized experiences of homelessness. They conclude (2006, 432) that policies must take seriously the obligation to 'not only provide sufficient funds, but also to direct those monies in such a way that the gendered and racialized contexts within which homeless youth are living manifest qualities of both care and justice.' Helping home-less youth to transition to adulthood requires forms of care that address the personal and psychological consequences of homelessness and its causes.

Sociologists have been very busy trying to find out how young people envision their future and with what importance they view adulthood markers such as education, employment, and family life. Two aspects of this research deserve some discussion.

First, research on contemporary forms of the life course emphasizes how in post-modern societies, paths to adulthood have become more diverse and more varied in their characteristics. Older forms of life course analysis tended to use a narrow range of markers and to see the movement between them as a rather straightforward linear progression. New forms of life course analysis not only recognize greater variation in transition routes, they also pay more attention to how agency and structure interact in shaping the life courses of individuals. Different generations of young people 'come of age' in particular locales and historical circumstances (Marquardt 1998). An interesting longitudinal Canadian study of young women and men who graduated from high school in 1973 uses the term 'structured individualization' to capture the idea that personal biographies reflect choice and preference but that these are always shaped by larger contexts of opportunity and constraint (Anisef and Axelrod 2001). High-school students graduated in 1973 amid significant uncertainties in employment structures and during a profound revolution in women's expectations about careers, marriage, and families. They were one of the earliest cohorts to begin working out what gender equality would really mean, from the kitchens to the boardrooms of the country. A study (Lowe 2001) of youth leaving high school in more recent years stresses the even greater uncertainty facing these young people. Graham Lowe gives a detailed account of the restructuring of young people's employment opportunities over the 1980s and 1990s. He (2001, 30) notes that, as in many other post-industrial societies, the transition from school to employment in Canada has become 'even more risky, protracted and circuitous'. The idea of a job as something that involves continuous employment with a single employer has collapsed as a possibility. There has been a corresponding rise in 'non-standard employment' with negative characteristics that are part of the problem young people face in setting themselves up as independent adults. Young men and women adopt common strategies to deal with this precarious employment situation, but some gender patterns continue to be evident, with young women more likely to find themselves stuck in involuntary part-time work or in various forms of low-income self-employment. Research on employment expectations among 17-year-olds by Victor Thiessen and Jörg Blasius (2002) also shows that young people in Canada continue to have highly gendered expectations regarding their occupational options.

Second, in addition to greater delay and diversity in transitions, researchers are exploring what the future means for young people and how they see themselves as beings 'in transition'. Researchers in Britain and Europe have had interesting debates about young people's perceptions of agency with respect to their future (Irwin 2005; Brannen and Nilsen 2002; 2007; Anderson et al. 2006). Do they live in the present, or do they think of the future? Do they plan? If so, how far ahead? And what do they plan about? Pat O'Connor's research on this topic involved asking young Irish women and men to write their life stories. She found that some aspects of young people's reflections on their lives were highly gendered—such as girls' tendency to reflect on intimate relationships and boys' tendency to reflect on their position in a hierarchy. Equally important, many aspects of the life stories were not at all gendered—including references to jobs, education, travel, and themselves as consumers. She concludes (2006, 120): 'boys and girls were equally likely to take refuge from a daunting future in a focus on an extended present.' Research of this sort is beginning in Canada (Scobie 2007) but has some way to go. A recent, more popular attempt to find out how young Canadian adults think about themselves as beings in the making is Myrna Kostash's (2000) series of interviews with 'the under-35 generation', which includes very entertaining musings on gender matters.

As mentioned earlier, the delay in economic independence, and extension of familial dependence, for post-modern adolescents clashes with what is otherwise happening to them as physical, emotional, and social beings. Sexual maturity and identity formation do not wait for bank balances, job offers, or a home of one's own. We turn now to examine how in the context of push–pull forces, young people engage in the important task of discovering who they are, including very important explorations of sexual orientation and gender identity.

BECOMING ONESELF

Becoming oneself, knowing oneself, is a huge expectation of adolescents. As parents of teenagers, Andrea and Janet know what a roller-coaster ride it is—from the highs of self-confidence, surety, and enthusiasm to the lows of isolation, uncertainty, and self-doubt. Recall the Billy Talent lyrics 'Nothing to Lose', and compare them with the following lyrics from Prozzak's 'Be As'. The two sets of lyrics capture some of the extremes in the roller-coaster ride.

Be as white as you want to
Be as black as you want to
Be as brown as you want to
Don't let anybody stop you

Be as straight as you want to
Be as gay as you want to
You can wait if you want to
We all need something to hold on to

And if there is a way that you and
I could both be free
Have a little understanding and
we will be

Be as shy as you want to
Be as loud as you want to
Be as small as you want to
Don't let anybody stop you

Be as thin as you want to
Be as fat as you want to
Be as short as you want to
We all need someone to hold on to

Prozzak. 'Be As'.

Source: Written by James McCollum and Jason Levine. Published by Sony/ATV Music Publishing Canada, (SOCAN)/Memilo Music, (SOCAN)/Mentalcase Music, (SOCAN). All rights reserved. Used by permission.

There is a huge emotional, personal, relational, and institutional distance between the message that as an adolescent you can be as 'you want to' and the sometimes very painful realization that not all forms of being are equally welcomed or even tolerated. On the one hand, youth are encouraged to find themselves, be true to who they are, and be free of constraining labels and divisions. On the other, 'being yourself' can be a lonely and socially isolating experience, leading to a sense of despair with 'nothing to lose'. Much of adolescence is a struggle with these mixed messages and an effort to find a way to be oneself. Mixed messages around gender and sexuality are part of this picture. In this final section of the chapter, we deal with a powerful social force that narrows gender options and choices in the exploration of the self. We also present paths of resistance, avoidance, and creativity that celebrate openness and multiplicity in the place of gender as a component of the self.

Developments in the conceptualization of gender reflect the way we live our lives as sexual and social beings. In particular, we are now less likely to associate a specific form of sexuality or sexual orientation with a specific gender identity. There is recognition that both sexuality and gender identity can have multiple forms. These forms are not necessarily fixed for any particular individual, nor is there a fixed relationship between a specific gender identity and a specific sexuality. However, in the midst of the multiplicity and fluidity of sexual and gender identities, there is also the spectre of hegemony. Becoming oneself—developing a sexual and gender identity—inevitably involves confronting the contours and power of hegemonic gender and sexual identities. We discuss here aspects of how young people encounter hegemonic forms of gender and sexuality and the ways in which these forms are challenged and resisted. These hegemonic forms and the encounters with them are also heavily shaped by other fault lines that specify gendered experiences.

Hegemonic masculinity

We begin by considering the relationships *between* multiple femininities and masculinities. While at any one time, and within any specific culture, there may be multiple ideas of what it means to be masculine and feminine, not all ideas have the same power or legitimacy. The relational quality of gender often involves relations of power and dominance. Relations of power and dominance are built into particular versions of masculinity—defining them not only against femininity but also against contending versions of masculinity.

Although early feminist work tended to paint a portrait of all men's lives as privileged, more recent work focused on intersectionality points out that some men suffer from oppression and disadvantage relative to other men and even some women. Male scholars began to develop an area of study that has become a burgeoning field within the social sciences and has come to be referred to as the field of 'men and masculinities'. Key scholars in this area include Kaufman (2002), Frank (1997; with Evans 2003), and Abdel-Shehid (2005) in Canada; Hearn (1998), Morgan (2001), Whitehead (2002), and Seidler (1997) in Britain; Kimmel (2000) and Messner (1997) in the United States; and Connell (2000) in Australia.

One of the most critical concepts to emerge from this field is 'hegemonic masculinity'. '[T]he hegemonic definition of manhood is "a man *in* power, a man *with* power, and a man *of* power" ' (Kimmel 1994, 125). The term is adapted from the work of Antonio Gramsci and has been particularly well developed in the work of Connell (1987; 1995; 2000). Hegemonic masculinity is defined as 'the most honored or desired' form of masculinity (Connell 2000, 10), one that usually aligns itself with traditional masculine qualities of 'being strong, successful, capable, reliable, in control'. Further, as Connell points out, hegemonic masculinity is perhaps most strongly identified 'as the opposite of femininity' (Connell 2000, 31); however, it is also defined against other forms of masculinity. Other forms of masculinity, then, have come to be viewed as *subordinated* (especially gay masculinities), *marginalized* (exploited or oppressed groups such as ethnic minorities), and *complicit* (those organized around the complicit acceptance of what has come to be termed the 'patriarchal dividend') (Connell 1995; 2000).

Because femininity is never a dominant player in the gender relationship, there is no 'hegemonic femininity'. There are, however, forms of femininity that support and comply with hegemonic masculinity—and Connell identifies them as 'emphasized femininity'. There is, argues Connell, 'a kind of "fit" between hegemonic masculinity and emphasized femininity' (1987, 185). Starting in childhood and intensifying over adolescence and into early adulthood, boys and girls are introduced to hegemonic masculinity and emphasized femininity. They may be introduced to other forms of gendered identity as well, but every child must negotiate the dominant forms of gendered identity in their society. We shall discuss how girls encounter hegemonic masculinity and emphasized femininity in a moment, but first we look at boys and young men.

Boys and young men, Connell suggests, are 'made an offer' regarding their place in the gender hierarchy during their adolescent years. Part of what adolescent boys have to do at this time is begin to position themselves vis-à-vis the privileged gender position their culture places them in. Will they accept the offer—or will they challenge and redefine it? The plurality of masculinities produced in contemporary society are outcomes of this engagement with hegemonic male identity. Of course, not all boys are 'made an offer', because ethnic and class variations in the positioning of masculine identities also feature in what identities boys are presented with and the means they have at their disposal to engage with them. As Connell notes (2000, 163), the making of gender identity among adolescents is 'far from the simple learning of norms suggested by "sex-role" socialization. It is a process with multiple pathways, shaped by class and ethnicity, producing diverse outcomes.' Rule-breaking—in and out of school—is one way by which boys (particularly classed and racialized boys) actively construct their masculine identity. Indeed, Connell (2000, 163) argues that this is one of the main reasons why boys have difficulty at school. For boys with few others resources, rule-breaking becomes a major means of demonstrating peer loyalty and achieving social recognition. The classic sociological study of the marginalization of working-class boys in British schools (Willis 1977) concludes that working-class boys settle for working-class jobs as an affirmation of their masculinity. More recently, a Norwegian study identified rule-breaking as a 'collective way to produce masculinity' among early adolescent boys and as a strategy that included drawing both gender and ethnic boundaries around the peer group (Haavind 2003).

Hegemonic masculinity is embodied. This means that male bodies are shaped, touched, exercised, clothed, and pushed to limits in an encounter with hegemonic masculinity. The hegemonic form of masculinity also has a sexual identity. It is heterosexual and heterosexist. In Canada, a good expression of embodied hegemonic masculinity is found in competitive hockey. As Canadian folk singer Lynn Myles laments in her song 'Hockey Night in Canada', 'Boys always seem to get their way. . . . It's Hockey Night in Canada every day it seems'. In their book on Hockey Night in Canada, Richard Gruneau and David Whitson (1993) critically assess the role of hockey—and particularly competitive hockey—in solidifying and reproducing hegemonic masculinity. They argue that since many boys work out—or in L. Susan Williams's (2002) phrase 'try on'—masculine identities via sports and are strongly encouraged to do so by parents, teachers, and others, the predominance of specific male identities in sport is a matter of concern. For many Canadian boys, the dream of playing in the National Hockey League comes with a lot of gender, as well as class and race, baggage. The whole gamut of experiences—including teams, coaches, trainers, locker rooms, tournaments, trophies, most valuable player awards, stars of the game, and 'playing through the pain'—may indeed make 'boys into men'—but what kinds of men and at what cost?

In elaborating on their analysis of gender and sport, Gruneau and Whitson state:

> Gender relations involve not just relations between men and women but also hierarchies among men and different ways of being male. There are clearly many ways of being male.... Yet pride of place in the eyes of many men still goes to the games that seem to most clearly differentiate men from women—games featuring force, aggressiveness and the opportunity to dominate an opponent physically. It is precisely this capacity to dominate that is at the core of many men's traditional ideals of masculinity, and hence at the core of a hegemonic masculinity that remains dominant so long as its exemplars are celebrated as heroes in our culture. (1993, 195–6)

Richard Giulianotti (2005, 94) draws attention to 'femophobia'—the fear of appearing effeminate—as a strong ingredient in some (not all) men's sporting culture. Perhaps this is part of the explanation for the way women are often positioned in hyper-masculine sporting events. They frequently appear as 'emphasized femininity'—that is, cheering from the sidelines, often scantily clad.

As detailed in the insert below by PhD student Kevin Walby, sport is not the only venue in which one can encounter pressure to follow normative ideas and behaviours of masculinity. He also talks about ways to keep sexuality and gender options open.

Thrown in All Directions

by Kevin Walby
Sociology PhD Program

I am not sure whether it would be proper for you to call me an adult yet—or ever. Sometimes it is difficult to pinpoint exactly when you've arrived at 'adulthood'. Being thrown in all directions—this is how we become the people we become. At the start, it was my parents doing most of the throwing. Then came those crucial years at the end of high school when I felt I could branch out, do what I wanted, not what my parents asked or forced me to do. As I branched out, I realized there are more webs to get stuck in, more pressures. Let me explain.

I played college football for a few years out of high school, back in Saskatchewan. Right then, exactly the time I felt I could begin to be free with my body and explore beyond the confines of heterosexuality, I was stuck in a locker room with a group of tough athletic fellows. These young men were quick to judge anyone who did not fit the prevailing notion of 'normal'. There were cold tubs in the locker room after games where we would sit in giant buckets of ice to lessen the swelling of our injured torsos and limbs. It was a veiled pleasure of mine to be nude in the tubs with my teammates, whom I honoured for their strength and tenacity on the playing field but at the same time worshipped simply for their taut musculatures. Expectations existed about our bodily appearances. Unwritten rules governed what we could and could not do with our bodies. My desires were prohibited. Homosociality could turn into nothing more for my teammates. What a pickle for me! On one hand idolizing and emulating the toughness of these men, many of whom were older, on the other hand trying to confront the assumptions concerning sexuality that were evident all around.

At the same time, I played guitar in a punk band. I never felt accepted in the punk scene either. Didn't sew patches on or rip holes in my jeans. No piercings or tattoos. The confusing part was that I couldn't understand how punks held the same ideas about sexuality as jocks did. The underlying theme encountered in football and in the punk scene is this: ambiguity is not much accepted during the years of becoming adult, if ever. People want to feel secure, which means they will exclude others from their group to achieve self-assurance. The more spheres of life I've been thrown into, the more difficult it has been to manage people's views of who I am becoming.

I felt scattered. I thought maybe I was flawed. My desires never seemed to be appropriate. Then through sociology, I realized that there is a lot of social exclusion that goes on around gender, sexuality, and appearance. I ended up doing a doctorate in sociology, provinces removed from the prairie soil I grew up on. As a graduate student, I am aware of expectations for me to become professional, dapper, and grown-up. I feel the burden to conform in disparaging glances. Some of my fellow graduate students have become those football players quick to judge others interested in the world of pleasure beyond heterosexuality. They've become those punks who ran the scene, excluding everyone operating outside their idea of what an insider should talk like, look like. Normative conceptions of adulthood pop up in all spheres of life.

If becoming adult means settling down into some fixed notion of self, that's not what I want. I do not want to conform. Sociological knowledge remains a critical lens through which I can view and challenge conventional, gendered ideas concerning adulthood.

What are the similarities and differences in the pressures on young men and young women to conform to sexual norms?

Are young women and young men equally able to resist peoples' expectations about gender performance?

Are norms about gender and sexuality useful in any way?

Emphasized femininity

For girls, one of the confrontations with emphasized femininity (and with it hegemonic masculinity) involves a struggle over and with their bodies. As with hegemonic masculinity, emphasized femininity is also embodied. Early encouragement of girl children to use their bodies for sport and adventure is overtaken in teenage and early adult years by the message that their bodies are for display—especially for viewing by a male gaze. The media and cultural worlds that surround girls continue to be full of blatant sexualized display of particular kinds of female bodies (e.g., Lil' Bratz dolls, cultural and media icons such as Posh Spice, Lindsay Lohan, Britney Spears, and Paris Hilton). Those bodies have become intentionally shaped—sometimes to the point of being misshapen—to highlight lips and breasts. Even supposedly positive female heroines do not escape the requirement to enhance and display sexualized body parts— witness the transformation of Pocahontas into 'Pocahooters', whose breast enlargement was accompanied by other transformations (she was whitened and given an anglophone accent) to make this female character more acceptable as a Hollywood commodity (Jhappan and Stasiulis 2005). It is interesting to note, in contrast, that a popular television show starring a girl with the body type that most girls have is titled *Ugly Betty*.

Many scholars have pointed to how the early years of childhood present a fairly wide array of identities and practices to young girls. Being a 'tomboy' or an athletic girl is, we would argue, just as acceptable an identity for a girl as the more traditional or 'girlie girl' identity that embraces anything pink and mainstream ideals about feminine beauty and more domestically defined pursuits such as cooking, decorating, and shopping. The teen years are a different matter. Writers such as Lyn Mikel Brown (2003) and Carol Gilligan (1992) as well as Mary Pipher (1995; see also Shandler 1999; Dellasega 2002) have highlighted how at the transition between girlhood and adulthood, girls are much more likely to plunge downward into depression and low self-esteem. Pipher, who regularly conducts speaking tours in the United States and Canada, contends that we live in a looks-obsessed, media-saturated, 'girl poisoning' culture wherein teenage girls are immersed in a 'junk' culture filled with inducements to shop, consume, be sexual and self-absorbed. She argues that in early adolescence, girls face overwhelming and mounting pressure to be thin, attractive, sexual, and popular while also feeling compelled to place less priority on grades, sports, and other achievements.

In the following insert, Riva Soucie, a PhD student in sociology at Carleton, talks about the ways girls and young women are encouraged to regard their bodies as improvement projects. She challenges the close association of femininity and corporeality and particular ideals of female embodiment.

The discussion by Riva, and the earlier one by Kevin, problematize a number of aspects of hegemonic masculinity and emphasized femininity and show how, as academics and as people, one can begin to challenge and resist dominant forms of gender and sexual identity. We now move on to tackle this issue directly, for it is a crucial part of how contemporary adolescents are addressing the place of gender in their sense of who they are.

Learning to Leave It Alone

by Riva Soucie
Sociology PhD Program

As a tween, teen, and emerging adult woman, I learned not only what is 'wrong' with my body but also how to fix it. For a teenager, hairy legs and armpits are unsightly. Shaving is an easy fix. Chewed fingernails were childish, so I grew them out. My hair was too dark, so I dyed it red. In university, the stakes were higher. Pubic hair wasn't sexy, so I learned to wax. I wanted a flatter stomach, so I ate only crackers and prunes for four months. My friends envied 'celebrity smiles', so I had my teeth shaped.

Postmodernists claim that women can take back their bodies by performing body modification in novel and meaningful ways. That looking 'unfeminine'— through tattoos, body piercing, jet black hair, and dark makeup—can be a way of resisting the cultural imperatives to hyper-feminize the female body.

But it is ironic that women are praised for resisting the imperatives to shave, wax, dye, snip, cut, tuck, lift, and diet by piercing, tattooing, more dyeing, and even overeating. Some forms of modification are seen as resistance, while others are seen as compliance.

Maybe it's time to stop associating femininity so closely with corporeality. After all, women are more than bodies; we are also a collection of actions, relationships, and continuously changing cultural practices. Susan Bordo[3] argues that the expectation that we must *decide* about our bodies, or even that we *can*, ignores the fact that our decisions are made in the context of biology, culture, and social location.

Centralizing the female body in discussions and practices of female identity and everyday life means that, for many women, the most obvious choice is to be obsessed with their bodies. But one courageous, novel, and challenging way to deal with any body is to treat it as only one part of our overall identities and every-day lives.

Do you worry that it is impossible to perfect the 'right look' for your body? Do you feel a lot of pressure to look a certain way? Or are you pulled in different directions—expected to look sexy one evening, casual in class, classy at work, understated around your parents, older around men, younger with your family?

Or do you enjoy 'looking different' on purpose? Is resisting the pressure a bit of a challenge for you? And maybe a way to define yourself?

Of course, maybe you don't think about your looks as much as the other parts of your life, like school, work, or friends. How do you feel about all the pressure to work on your body all the time? Or maybe you're a guy who feels pressure to be muscular, fit, and tall, with a full head of hair. Do you think men feel the same kinds of pressure as women to 'make themselves over'?

Challenging the norm, creating new options

When sociologists talk about the social construction of gender, they are generally referring to the social processes and normative expectations associated with being a boy or being a girl and how these processes and expectations are produced and reproduced in society. The question arises then as to what happens when people do not fit into one gender or the other. Over the past few decades, there has been increasing awareness and, in some sectors of the population, wholehearted acceptance of the different ways in which women and men want to enact their lives. The acceptance of gay marriage in Canada, as well as the ability of gay fathers and lesbian mothers to form families, is one example of the increasing acceptance of diversity in gendered practices and identities in Canadian society.

In terms of gender and sexuality, we can identify two types of resistance and challenge. In one type, people cannot accept the biological body they were born with and the gender identity they lived as a young child. We are referring to transsexual or transgendered individuals. There are different kinds of transgendered individuals, and they make a range of choices on how to reconfigure their lives as men or women. In general, however, we could say that this type of resistance works across current gender categories and definitions. In the other type, people resist any specific or static assignment of gender and/or sexuality. They consciously choose to live a more androgenous life—mixing and matching the feminine and masculine or trying to define a self outside of gender labels. This type of resistance is more disruptive and thought of as an attempt to 'undo' gender. We briefly discuss both strategies.

Working across gender

There are many examples of transgendered individuals who leave behind their identity as one gender and live a new life as the other gender. The 'leaving behind' can be accomplished in a number of ways. The more straightforward manner is to adopt the dress, occupational interests, and lifestyle of the opposite gender. One famous example from the mid-twentieth century is Billy Tipton, a saxophone and piano player who made a career out of leading jazz bands in the 1940s and early 1950s in the American southwest and northwest. Tipton reportedly lived a glamorous life that included several marriages and a wide range of friends. His last wife was a former stripper named Kitty with whom he adopted three sons. It was only when he was rushed to the hospital at the age of 74 that his secret transsexual life was uncovered. His youngest son watched as a paramedic attempted to resuscitate his father and, in the process, revealed the startling fact that the dying Billy Tipton was, in fact, a woman.

A more permanent 'leaving behind' of an unwanted gender/sex identity involves a reconfiguration of the body through a process called sex reassignment surgery. An example within sociology itself is the Australian sociologist R.W. Connell, one of the pre-eminent sociologists in the world and the most trusted voice on issues of gender, men, and masculinities. At the age of 62, the esteemed R.W. Connell underwent a sex change and is now Raewyn Connell. With hardly a mention within the sociological community, this scholar, previously known as a male, now continues, in a differently sexed/gendered body, to teach, write, lecture, and chair her Department of Sociology.

Tipton and Connell exemplify grown men who faced the ambiguity of dealing with a body that did not fit their sense of themselves as gendered beings. While both men must have faced many challenges in their gender struggle, we do not know much about what it was like for them to grow up as teenagers and young adults. Did they face embodied ambiguity at that time as well? Because all teenagers are confronted with issues of socially 'fitting in' and finding out who they are in the midst of dramatic changes in their body, the added issue of gender ambiguity can be overwhelming—personally and socially. Some teenagers experience this ambiguity so severely that they too undergo sex reassignment surgery. The youngest ever transsexual is a British boy who underwent a sex change at the age of 12.[4]

The scholarship and activist work that began to emerge in the mid-1990s emphasizes the courage it takes to decide to change one's gender identity, and in some cases, one's body as well. One of the best known contributors to this issue is Kate Bornstein. Formerly Al Bornstein, who underwent a male-to-female sex-change operation in 1986, Kate Bornstein set about to write in ways that drew attention to the limitations of a binary gender system. In her acclaimed books *Gender Outlaw: On Men, Women, and the Rest of Us* (1995) and *My Gender Workbook: How to Become a Real Man, a Real Woman, the Real You, or Something Entirely Different* (1998), Bornstein writes about the inherent oppression of a binary gender system in which individuals are forced to choose, and conform to, one of only two gender options. She identifies herself as a lesbian feminist writer, actor, and performance artist. In *Gender Outlaw*, she writes about the complexities of living at the boundaries of gender and the personal toll exacted by living a 'non-traditional gender identity':

> I know I'm not a man—about that much I'm very clear, and I've come to the conclusion that I'm probably not a woman either, or at least not according to a lot of people's rules on this sort of thing. The trouble is we're living a world that insists that we be one or the other—a world that doesn't tell us exactly what one or the other *is*. . . . All my life, my non-traditional gender identity had been my biggest secret, my deepest shame. It's not that I didn't want to talk about this with someone; it's just that I never saw anything in the culture that encouraged me to talk about my feelings that I was the wrong gender. When I was growing up, people who lived cross-gendered lives were pressured into hiding deep within the darkest closets they could find. . . . Going through a gender change is not the easiest thing in the world to do, but I went through it because I was so tired of all the lies and secrets. (1995, 8)

Bornstein's work anticipates a current interest in moving beyond gender—so as to 'undo' the imperative of choice between being masculine or being feminine.

Undoing gender: Working beyond gender

un·do·ing *n*

1. the ruin, downfall, or destruction of somebody or something, or something that causes this
2. the opening, unfastening, untying, or unwrapping of something
3. the canceling or reversing of the effect of an action[5]

There are two lines of thinking that have become particularly salient in thinking about how to challenge gender by undoing it. The first can be traced to Candace West and Don Zimmerman's (1987) 'doing gender' approach, which has become very well known within sociology. The second is the work of Judith Butler as rooted in her earlier work on gender performativity theory (1990) and particularly her more recent book *Undoing Gender* (2004). Both of these approaches share an interest in theoretical conceptions of an ungendered subject and argue for the need to move beyond gender binaries and hierarchical gender arrangements. While sharing a similar intent in their thinking, these two approaches differ in their theoretical underpinnings.

On the one hand, West and Zimmerman's work, along with the large body of literature that draws on it, is rooted in sociological thinking and particularly in symbolic interactionism and ethnomethodology. West and Zimmerman focused their work on how 'participants in interaction organize their various and manifold activities to reflect or express gender' (1987, 4). Despite seeing gender as an active creation, they were not inclined to acknowledge that it could cease to be created. More recent developments of this theoretical approach have begun to focus on just this possibility—the 'undoing' of gender. For example, American sociologist Francine Deutch (2007) has put forward a powerful argument that we need to reframe questions around 'doing gender' to interrogate more closely how we can 'undo' gender. Specifically, she argues that more sociological research should focus on '(1) when and how social interactions become less gendered, (2) whether gender can be irrelevant in interaction, (3) whether gendered interactions always underwrite inequality, (4) how the institutional and interactional levels work together to produce change, and (5) interaction as the site of change' (2007, 106).

Unlike Deutch's, Butler's work is located in post-structuralist and psychoanalytic theories. Similarly, however, Butler also sees possibilities for change and would 'undo gender'. She points to how social norms and institutional structures create and reinforce acceptable gendered practices and behaviours while also limiting the possibilities for alternative ways for women and men to live out their lives. It is only when one starts to break down binary thinking around gender (i.e., man versus woman; masculinity versus femininity) that one can really envision a way to undo gender and to live in more liberatory ways. Butler is not always an accessible theorist for undergraduate students. Nevertheless, her book *Undoing Gender*, a collection of essays on 'the experience of becoming undone in both good and bad ways' (2004, 1) has been well received by students and seasoned scholars alike for what it offers to thinking creatively about doing and undoing gender. Butler makes a compelling argument that relates to the examples of transgenderism discussed above. Specifically, she argues that gendered norms can ultimately force us to live a life that is not worth living. Emphasizing the positive aspects of undoing gender, she writes:

> Sometimes a normative conception of gender can undo one's personhood, undermining the capacity to persevere in a liveable life. Other times, the experience of a normative restriction becoming undone can undo a prior conception of who one is only to inaugurate a relatively newer one that has greater liveability as its aim. (2004, 1)

These two theoretical approaches, as briefly described above, can help us to think about how to move beyond gender dualism. While it may not always be possible to act in ways that can be considered ungendered, given the extent to which structures, institutions, and ideologies are gendered, it is also important to recognize that some individuals go to great lengths to live a life in which gender is not a defining feature. We are thus drawing attention to individual and collective agency to enact the undoing of gender in social life. Nevertheless, important questions need to be asked in thinking about the necessity of gender and the possibility of moving beyond its reach. Can transgendered subjects such as the ones we described above (i.e., Billy Tipton, Raewyn Connell, and Kate Bornstein) be seen as examples of challenging gender, or do their actions reinforce gendered categories? If individuals cross to the other gender (either through crossdressing or through surgery), are they challenging gender or only further reinstating it? Can there be such a thing as a third gender? Is it liberating enough to think of living according to a fluid continuum of gender identities rather than in a binary opposition between male and female? What would this look like? Would it be something you would promote, or would you be opposed to it? Or do we need to think about liberation as a gender-free zone? These are challenging questions that we know will generate much discussion and debate in your classroom and between you and your peers.

Girls and young women also find ways of resisting and create alternative identities and practices that work to counter or dismantle dominant cultural ideals of emphasized femininity. Renuka Chaturvedi, a PhD student at Carleton University, points to her own unique strategies for confounding the pressure to conform to traditional ideals of femininity or girlhood as she made the transition into adulthood. Her focus is on living fluidity and multiplicity—and thereby escaping dichotomized gendered identities altogether.

Transitions to Adulthood—Fluidity and Creativity

by Renuka Chaturvedi
Sociology PhD Program

There is no single transition to adulthood. We tend to think of our lives as a series of stages, stages in which we rest for some time until we pass through and reach the next stage. We have markers that indicate to us when we have passed through one stage and on to another. Eventually we become adults. Thought of in this way, 'adulthood' becomes a state of being (generally thought to occur around age 30) that we all eventually reach and in which we live out the remainder our lives. In my experience, this is a myth. Adulthood has not been a state of being but a continual process of becoming. I become more 'adult' via my practices that more and more begin to coalesce with the dictates of adulthood. I wash my floors, and I make sure my dishes are done. I invest money, I consider buying property. I start to live my life in terms of a future I plan for, not only for the moment in which I find myself. These are various ways I increasingly practise adulthood. And because throughout my life I make transitions upon transitions, I have experienced adulthood as a fluid, ever-evolving state.

Some of the most significant transitions I make in the move from young adulthood concern my gender identity and how to occupy the space of Woman. As far back as I can remember, I had rejected all things traditionally associated with femininity. This means I would wear neither dresses nor makeup, that I smoked a pipe. I spat and swore. And people didn't consider me feminine, because I wasn't playing out femininity as it is traditionally practised. So I would be given the usual titles, 'tomboy', 'boyish'. The masculine monikers angered me. Because I did not fit feminine, I was automatically assigned the identity of masculine. Under a binary conception of gender, what is not feminine is masculine. And so by not playing out femininity, I felt as though I was denied the identity of female. And it was then that I realized that gender identity is a lot like celibacy. Sometimes it gets thrust upon you whether you like it or not.

But as I began to study social constructivism in university, I realized that like adulthood, gender is not an inert state of being. Rather, gender is something we play out; gender is a set of practices. And for this reason, gender is fluid. Gender has no objective form that exists outside the way we practise it. So gender is something we can define for ourselves, and these definitions are as legitimate as the definitions handed to us by social mores. And so in my transitions to adulthood, I am embracing my transgressions of gender.

Peer groups have played a large role in taking this very academic point and making me comfortable with living out a more androgynous version of gender. I have found individuals who normalize subversive gender practices, who inspire me and teach me that moving away from traditional gender roles does not make me a man, does not mean that I want to be a man. Rather, I am becoming comfortable with a gender identity comprised of practices considered masculine *and* feminine. One way I take up masculine and feminine practices is through the way I present my physical self. So, for example, almost everyday I wear men's cargo pants and T-shirts. But I also keep my hair very long. I don't wear makeup, but I have a colourful scarf tied around my neck. At the gym, I don't hesitate to build muscle mass in my upper body in addition to my legs. When I merge masculine and feminine practices but still choose to identify solely as female, calling myself a woman becomes a political statement, because I am reclaiming a subordinated gender status within a reworked version of that gender, a version that is self-determined and in that way much more powerful. And while being a girl does not appeal to me, being a woman certainly does. However I may practise it.

How important is it to you to be considered feminine? Masculine?

What might your reactions be if someone were to consider you as something other than your chosen gender identity?

Can you imagine yourself living a gender-free identity—as neither masculine nor feminine?

CONCLUSION

Encounters with gender intensify over the adolescent and young adult years as individuals take more responsibility for their own identity and for their social relationships. Physical, including sexual, maturity and increasing independence add drama,
anxiety, and excitement to the negotiation of gender as both a potential identity and
a social practice. The second shift in sociological thinking about gender provides a
more expansive and flexible set of conceptual resources to cope with the open-ended,
fluid, and variable experiences of gender that adolescents encounter.

In spite of greater avenues for transgressive gender strategies, however, Canadian
adolescents grow up in a cultural context that continues to be defined by hegemonic
masculinity and its companion, emphasized femininity. Boys and young men are differently placed in terms of the 'patriarchal dividend'. It is primarily reserved for those
who are white, able-bodied, and heterosexual. Hegemonic masculinity defines itself
against other subordinate forms of masculinity (identified by intersections of class,
race, sexual orientation, dis/ability) as much as it defines itself against femininity.

While girls and young women have made great strides in expanding what they
are expected or allowed to be and do, there remains the problem of realizing these
gains in adulthood. Yes, girls are outperforming boys at school, but they are not
carrying this advantage into the worlds of higher education and employment.
Articles in the October 2007 issue of *University Affairs* illustrate the extremes of these
educational and employment issues. On the one hand, Daniel Drolet's article 'Minding the Gender Gap' asks (2007, 9) why '[b]oys seem to underachieve academically
relative to girls'. On the other hand, Cynthia Dusseault reports in her article (2007, 34)
on a study at the University of British Columbia that shows 'three times more men
than women achieve full professor status 15 years after being hired.' We shall explore
in the next two chapters how gender inequality continues to shape the adult lives of
women and men.

The growing disconnect between education and employment for young women
and men is part of a larger phenomenon involving delays in the transition to adulthood for both genders. Sociological research in Canada in this area is unequivocal:
major changes have happened in how those in their late teens and early 20s live their
lives. Interestingly, this phenomenon has also encouraged sociologists to rethink the
idea of transitions to adulthood, regarding them now as more variable, open, multi-
faceted, and less linear. The phenomenon of boomerang sons and daughters—those
who leave home only to return again—is becoming more common as the means to
achieve independence become more difficult to obtain and sustain. These patterns
are defined by intersections of gender and other fault lines of inequality, but it is
important to note that on some dimensions, gender differences are disappearing.
Explorations of self and personal relationships cannot be put on hold until transitions
to material independence are settled. It is a significant characteristic of the current
generation of 20-somethings that many explore who they are—including discovering
their sexual orientation and gender identity—outside of institutions of marriage, parenthood, and the workplace.

Research Questions

1. Construct a gender profile of teen magazines. What types of magazines are directed at girls—at boys? What topics do the magazines cover? What products do they advertise? Who is shown in the magazines—what is their skin colour, body type, size, look? How are relationships between boys and girls, men and women, presented in the magazines? Can you detect presentations of—or challenges to—hegemonic masculinity? Emphasized femininity?

2. Have a look at 'advice to teens' books written over the past few decades. Can you identify changes in how teens are spoken to and the advice that is offered? Are messages directed at boys and girls separately? Can you detect differences in expectations for boys and girls? Does this pattern change over time?

3. Can you think of a good case study that would illustrate efforts to 'undo' gender? How would you go about collecting information on this case study?

Discussion Questions

1. How prevalent is the phenomenon of hegemonic masculinity in Canada? What impact does it have on your daily life?

2. Does the fact that Canadian youth are experiencing a delay in the transition to adulthood add to or reduce inequalities between young women and men?

3. Can we 'undo' gender? What would this look like?

4. What inequalities within gender (for example, by class, race, ethnicity, dis/ability, sexual orientation) are most significant when one thinks about differences in how adolescents experience high school? Are there high-school experiences in which gender does not matter?

Further Reading

Adams, Mary Louise. 2005. 'Death to the prancing prince': Effeminacy, sport discourses, and the salvation of men's dancing', *Body and Society* 11, 63–86. Considers the imposition of and challenge to hegemonic masculinity in dance.

Bibby, Reginald. 2001. *Canada's Teens Today, Yesterday, and Tomorrow*. Toronto: Stoddart. Reports on successive surveys of the attitudes, ideas, and priorities of Canadian teens.

Connell, R. 2000. *The Men and the Boys*. Cambridge: Polity. A classic contribution to masculinity studies, including discussions of strategies for change.

Handa, Amita. 2003. *Of Silk Saris and Miniskirts: South Asian Girls Walk the Tightrope of Culture*. Toronto: Women's Press. Sociological research on how South Asian high-school girls negotiate the complex interconnections of gender and race.

Tyyskä, Vappu. 2001. *Long and Winding Road: Adolescents and Youth in Canada Today*. Toronto: Canadian Scholars' Press. A comprehensive sociological discussion of many aspects of adolescent and youth experience.

Films

Generation XXL. 2007. A Gemini Award-nominated film that follows the lives of four Nova Scotia teens—two boys and two girls—as they struggle with their oversized bodies (www.generationxxl.ca).

Vagina Monologues. 1996. The film version of Eve Ensler's one-woman show about the female body, which became a sensational worldwide phenomenon, performed by many women around the globe.

About a Boy. 2002. A film based on Nick Hornby's novel of the same title that explores relational intelligence and other masculine challenges.

Girls Studies Collection. 2007. Four National Film Board films: *Becoming 13*, *It's a Girl's World*, *Shadya*, and *This Is My Body: A Film by High School Girls*.

Websites

http://schools.tdsb.on.ca/triangle
Website for the only high-school program in Canada (introduced in 1999) specifically for gay, lesbian, bisexual, and transgendered youth.

www.fazeteen.com
The on-line version of a Canadian teen magazine launched in 2000, dealing with many teen issues including gender.

www.youth.society.uvic.ca
Website of the Centre for Youth and Society at the University of Victoria, an interdisciplinary centre conducting research on, for example, adolescent dating relationships and transitions to adulthood.

Chapter 4

Diverse Paths: Gender, Work, and Family

Chapter Objectives

1. To introduce the changing forms of paid work that contest the simplicity of one single model of paid work (i.e., the standard employment model or the 'male model' of work) and to look inside and beyond this dominant model of work and how it has hidden inequities based on gender and ethnicity.
2. To explore changing family formations in Canada and ask you to consider what kinds of families Canadian adults will form in the years to come.
3. To unpack the complexity and diversity of unpaid work as a category of work, activity, and identity in Canadian households, highlighting key issues in the study of paid and unpaid work.
4. To explore some of the reasons why 'divisions of labour' persist in Canadian households—that is, why women and men do different kinds of work—and to reflect on how and why this is changing, urging you to think about what your own households will (or do) look like in this regard.
5. To engage you in 'so what' questions: why is the study of paid and unpaid work in the lives of Canadian men and women important? Does it really matter if there are gender differences in paid and unpaid work? More specifically, what difference does difference make? Which differences turn into disadvantages?

INTRODUCTION

We begin this chapter with two sociological stories and visit two mothers in different countries and in different time periods.

It is 1969, and we are in London, England, where we meet Ann Oakley, a mother of two young children who is undertaking her PhD part-time and is married to a British university professor. On this particular day, while dusting in her husband's office at home, she comes across a book by sociologist Robert Blauner entitled *Alienation and Freedom.* She puts down her duster and begins to read. When she comes to the part where Blauner writes about alienation and gender, she has to sit down. She reads: 'Women workers are less alienated than men because their primary source of fulfillment does not come from work, but rather from caring for children.' Reading these words, Oakley is confused, then astounded. She looks around the room that she has just cleaned, and then she walks into the kitchen and sees the dishes she still has to clear away after lunch, and there is dinner to be made, and her two children are just waking up from afternoon naps, one is calling out for her, the other is crying loudly. She wonders aloud: 'Why is this not work? Why is housework not considered work?' This thought not only enrages her but preoccupies her for weeks, until she goes to see her thesis supervisor at the University of London. She says to him: 'I want to do my doctoral dissertation on housework.' His reply is that housework is not a proper sociological topic to study. Oakley, not dissuaded, persists in her quest and searches until she finds a doctoral supervisor who will permit her to write her dissertation on the sociology of housework. She completes her PhD a few years later and publishes two books, both of which have become classics within sociology: *The Sociology of Housework* (1974a) and *Housewife* (1974b).[1]

It is 1991, 32 years later, and we are in a small town in Saskatchewan, where we meet Carol Lees, a full-time mother of three. She opens her front door to a census-taker from Statistics Canada. Lees takes a moment to look through the form and notices that her full-time occupation of 'mother' or 'household manager' is not included on the form. She politely refuses to fill out the census form, telling the census-taker that she is unable to comply since it would mean declaring that as an unpaid homemaker, she doesn't 'work'. The census worker walks away dumbfounded. Weeks later, Lees receives a letter from Statistics Canada's chief statistician in Ottawa, threatening the full weight of the law, including fines and jail time, if she does not fill out the census form. Lees holds firmly to her position, and she works with others, such as the organization Mothers-Are-Women (MAW), to create the Canadian Alliance for Home Managers, which is focused on the valuing of unpaid work. Widespread media coverage is generated, and three questions about unpaid labour are added to the Canadian census in 1996. This sets up an international precedent in the recognition of unpaid labour in public statistics. Her rationale for her actions is summed up in statements she made later: 'People who work, both paid and unpaid, need to be valued,' Lees explains. 'The census is a key instrument on which government policy is based. If you're not represented on the census, then you don't have a voice . . . and policy isn't developed on your behalf' (Luxton and Vosko 1998, 50).

These two stories share several themes. The first is a long social and political narrative about how housework, child care, and the domestic sphere were not, for many years, taken seriously within sociology. Indeed, if domestic work was mentioned at all in academic studies, it was most likely only in the discipline of home economics. Dorothy Smith (1987) came to identify such gaps between women's experiences and academic understandings of that experience as 'fault lines'. The second is a more recent narrative about how even though feminist scholars have been advocating, with grad-ual success, a place for domestic labour and care work in sociology, their effort has fallen largely on deaf ears in policy circles. It has been difficult to convince policy-makers that unpaid work deserves the same status, value, and measurable quality as paid work. More recently, however, thanks to the initiative of women like Carol Lees and many other activists and scholars, these concerns have become central within sociology as well as within policy discussions. The third and final theme is that the above stories all revolve around female protagonists, which raises the question: where are the men in these stories?

This chapter focuses on issues of paid and unpaid work for women and men during their adult 'productive' years. We highlight the importance of studying house-work and unpaid work, the issue of why it is not valued, and the changing role of women and men in relation to this fact. We review several key themes that help us to understand the life choices of and opportunities for women and men as they carve out their adult lives. How, where, and why does gender matter in the structuring of choices, opportunities, and demands placed on women and men in relation to paid and unpaid work during their working years?

This chapter also introduces some of the debates that have challenged the 'fiction' of the separation of public and private spheres, and we outline the significance of this challenge through the main areas of 'work' and 'family'. We trace both what is hap-pening 'on the ground' and how the discipline of sociology has studied and framed the domestic practices, identities, and space of social life. While much has changed in women's and men's lives during the 'productive' years of adulthood, profound differ-ences and disadvantages continue to exist in the career and family paths of women and men. The impact of motherhood and other caring responsibilities on women's lives remains substantial, and we interrogate continuing debates about how this should and could be socially addressed. We also bring men's perspectives into the chapter, arguing that these are *gender* issues, not only *women's* issues. Issues of intersectional-ity along the lines of class, ethnicity, age, sexuality, and geographical location are also central to our discussion of this area of study.

Throughout the chapter, as well as in the study questions, we urge you to think about these issues in your own life, now and in the future, and to reflect on how your own life is different from, or the same as, those of your grandparents' and parents' generations.

PAID WORK

A male model of work

When we think about paid work, we often think about the typical 9-to-5 job: people leave home early, have an hour off at lunchtime and two coffee breaks, and then return home. This is what researchers have identified as the *standard employment relationship* in which a worker has continuous full-time employment. If we are speaking about Canada historically—in the times of your great-grandparents, grandparents, and even your parents—this full-time job would likely have been with the same on-site employer for all or most of their working lives, either as a traditional eight-hour workday or as shift work (Fudge and Vosko 2001). This model of work has also been described as '48 hours for 48 weeks of 48 years' (Coote, Harman, and Hewitt 1990, 49) or a 'male model of employment' (Brannen and Moss 1991).

The word 'male' appears in this description of paid work for several reasons. First, the model of continuous unbroken commitment to the labour market has histori-cally been available mainly to men. For both of our fathers, their work patterns were consistent with the dominant norm of white male employment in Canada after the Second World War. While Andrea's father worked for more than 35 years for a pulp and paper mill company, Janet's father spent all of his working life as first a draughts-man and then a salesman for an Ontario steel company.

This model of paid work, however, began to wane in the late 1970s when other forms of employment, largely filled by women, became more common (Fudge and Vosko 2001). Such employment has been termed *non-standard employment* (Krahn 1991; 1995), *contingent employment* (Polivka and Nardone 1989), *precarious employ-ment* (Vosko, Zukewich, and Cranford 2003; Vosko 2000), or *temporary employment* (Galarneau 2005). Whatever the name, this kind of work includes part-time employ-ment, temporary employment (e.g., short contracts, casual or seasonal work), and self-employment. Moreover, what all of these jobs share are low wages, insecure work-ing conditions, and limited access to social benefits and statutory entitlements (such as employment insurance, maternity leave, and parental leave). What is notable as well is the gendered processes involved. For example, in 2002, women accounted for more than six in 10 of those employed in part-time temporary jobs or part-time self-employment, and for nearly three-quarters of part-time permanent employees (Vosko, Zukewich, and Cranford 2003).

With regard to casual work, contract work, seasonal employment, and employ-ment from a temporary agency, such jobs have increased almost twice as rapidly as permanent employment in recent years and accounted for almost one-fifth of over-all growth in paid employment between 1997 and 2003. In her book on women and self-employment entitled *Risky Business*, Karen Hughes notes that since the mid-1970s, self-employment has accounted for one-quarter of all job growth in Canada (Hughes 2006). The rise in part-time work has been equally dramatic. Throughout the first half of the 1990s, part-time work was the major source of employment growth, a growth that still continues. In the decade between 1990 and 2002, the number of those employed part-time increased by about 30 per cent, while the number of full-time jobs increased by only 15 per cent.

In addition to the patterns of waged work described above, it is also important to point out that alongside the dominant standard employment relationship, and subordinate models that have emerged beside it, many other patterns of paid work exist. These work patterns, described below, were dominated by women who were not dependent, by choice or by necessity, on a male wage.

Inside the 'male' model of work

During the 1950s and early 1960s the traditional family was the norm. Young men and women married early and had rather large families relatively quickly. Divorce was rare and unmarried childbearing practically unheard of. Young women worked before they were married and some continued working until their first child was born, but almost all mothers of infants left the labor force for an extended period and many did not return. Women earned much less than men because they had less education and training, because they almost all worked in 'women's jobs', and because they either had just started working or would soon leave. (Waite and Nielsen 2001, 23)

It is a common misconception that there was a time in the past when women did not work for wages and only men did. Yet such a view raises a question: who are we including and who are we excluding? Not only is it a gendered way of seeing work, but it is a lens that is focused only on white, middle-class households. The ways of thinking described in the quote above also appeared in sociological descriptions of the 1950s and 1960s North American family. It is not that such descriptions are wrong; rather, they are incomplete.

Talcott Parsons, a prominent American sociologist from the 1960s, most famously promoted the notion of distinct, but complementary, spheres of home and work and corresponding gender divisions of labour, with women taking on unpaid work in the 'private' sphere and men taking on paid work in the 'public' sphere (Parsons 1967; Parsons and Bales 1955). This dichotomy between paid and unpaid work, and a household model with men as breadwinners and women as homemakers, characterized to some extent the early stages of industrial capitalism when the reorganization of production physically separated the home from the workplace. Later, it thrived in suburban middle-class North America when, as well depicted in films and documentaries focusing on the 1950s and 1960s, men got into their large cars and drove to the city every day, while women stayed home to care for young children. Spatially, practically, and ideologically, these spheres of home and work did indeed seem separate.

It was within this context that the notion of the 'family wage' was popularized; it represented a man's working wage, adequate to support his wife and children. The concept of the family wage assumed that a woman would not want or need paid work herself, and it was reinforced by social norms about gender roles as well as by men's trade unions, which sought to exclude women from the paid labour force (Walby 1986).

While scholarly and public assumptions about the male wage and home/work dichotomies persisted for many years, there were always several weaknesses with these assumptions. First, women, especially women in low-income households as well as African-Canadian and immigrant women, had always worked for wages. Cross-cultural research has clearly demonstrated that many working-class households have always required more than the male wage; thus, women contributed to the maintenance of the household either by intensifying domestic and self-provisioning work inside the home or by earning money through the informal economy. In Canada, the work of Canadian historians Bettina Bradbury and Joy Parr depicts how during periods of early industrialization in the late 1800s and early 1900s, working-class wives took on varied kinds of wage labour within and between households in order to make ends meet; they did extra sewing, took in washing, cleaned other people's houses, raised poultry and pigs, and took in boarders (Bradbury 1984; 1993; Parr 1990). In widening the concepts of work and home to include self-provisioning work, these accounts add to the evidence detailed by family scholars on the intricate intersections between the theoretical concepts and the physical sites of home and work. That is, it is important to recognize that historically, women have always found ways to add to the family economy through household provisioning work. Drawing on her own family history, Andrea remembers how her grandmother, who ran a farm with her husband, contributed to family income by selling homemade butter and buttermilk. Her mother took on unpaid self-provisioning work by sewing all of the family clothing and making endless meals from beef reared on the family farm and pickled vegetables from the same farm.

Andrea and the Male Model of Work

I grew up with the male model of work. Its taken-for-granted and hegemonic quality hung over my seaside town like a constant fog. Through the years of the 1960s and 1970s, I lived in a small town in northern New Brunswick, in a large wooden house on the Baie de Chaleur, a small bay on the coast of the Atlantic Ocean. My house, which both my grandfather and father grew up in, sat on Main Street in the working-class, Catholic side of town. That house, my neighbourhood, and the whole town moved slowly and unquestioningly along gender-divided lines. In our house, my father rose early six days a week, went to work at the paper mill, called in by the screeching 8 a.m. whistle signalling the start to the men's morning shift. Along with hundreds of other men who had forgone a university education to remain in this town, he would enter the mill through a front gate that was usually staffed by the mill's only female employee. He would have his work card punched and then work eight to 12 hours in the paper-making plant. At both ends of my town, in the south and the east, there were similar scenes of men, fathers of the girls I went to school with, entering their long shifts at the nickel mines and the coal smelter. My father worked at the paper mill for more than 35 years, with his time split between being a labourer and then a foreman/superintendent. He received about five weeks of vacation each year, and we were well-treated with a generous dental plan and university scholarships, as well as lobsters in the summer and a large fir tree each Christmas. My father earned a wage, which my mother ingeniously stretched to feed, house, and clothe six children.

Did women in my town work outside the home? Of course they did. Nevertheless, the dominant, normatively accepted narrative was that of the male breadwinner bringing in a family wage. The underside of this narrative was that it was assumed and expected that women would not compete with men for jobs and that women would not need, or desire, to work outside the home. For a woman to live a counter-narrative, without negative community judgment, she generally had to meet one of the following conditions: she was young and unmarried; she was a teacher or nurse with school-aged children; she worked in the family business; she was single or divorced; or family finances were so tight that extra income was needed to 'make ends meet'.

Some of the self-provisioning in Janet's family happened intergenerationally, with her grandfather and her grandmother distributing various foods to their children's families both to help with family meals and to share in cultural traditions. After a stint of baking, her grandmother would distribute Finnish coffee bread and buns. If the hunting season went well, her grandfather would show up at the front door with packages of butchered moose meat that went into the freezer and was brought out over the winter for Sunday roasts. Early on, before store-bought items became affordable and readily available, Janet's mother would make many of her own clothes. Other sewing jobs provisioned the house with curtains, cushions, and bedspreads. There were days of jam-making in the fall, with all the female relatives pitching in to stir the pots, sterilize the bottles, and melt wax to seal the tops. And there was short-bread-baking at Christmas, when each of her mother's sisters would bake more of her particular specialty than her family needed, and then they would all meet to swap the surplus of their goodies.

Janet: My Mother's Experience as a Working Mom

My main memory of my mother, Peggy, is as a working mom. After graduating from the technical high school in the Soo and throughout her early married years in the late 1940s and early 1950s, she worked full-time as a bookkeeper for the local public utility company. I've got pictures of her from those years, heading out to her downtown job, gloves and hat on, hair nicely curled, matching purse and shoes, her spring coat buttoned up. A thoroughly modern woman. She knew how to drive, but she took the bus to work—driving to work was a luxury reserved for my father. I'm not exactly sure how much time my mother was at home full-time when my brother and I were small, but it can't have been too long. I remember her working part-time doing the books for a local real estate agent when I was still in early elementary school.

By the time I was 10, my Dad was promoted to a job in Toronto, and after our move to the big city, my mother was again working full-time—this time for the Royal Bank. She was an 'assistant accountant'. The bank was not far from our house, and she'd sometimes meet my brother and me at home for lunch. She was rarely at home when we returned from school but would come in soon after and start getting supper ready. My Mom loved her job, enjoyed the vicarious access it gave her to exciting worlds of high finance and exotic travel, made great and lasting friendships among 'the girls' at the bank, and was proud of her ability to find me summer employment as a teller. The stresses of having a full-time job as well as the home responsibilities of cooking, cleaning, shopping, doing laundry, and monitoring what my brother and I were up to sometimes got too much for her. At those moments, she would string together the most inventive and colourful collection of swear words I'd ever heard—and we'd get the message that we had to help more around the house!

After about 10 years, my father's job was moved back to our hometown. My mother had to quit her banking job—although she wanted to, she was not able to get a transfer to the Royal Bank back home. After the move back, she tried to get a job in other banks, but her age was against her, and people with university degrees were now being hired for the position she had left. The whole banking industry was in transition, and the person-to-person service work that my mother had done was being downsized. She never really worked outside the home again—except occasionally and seasonally for a tax firm and as a volunteer in the box office of the local arts festival.

Not being able to return to banking, and especially losing her independent source of income and social network outside the home, was devastating for my mother. However, her experience is typical of a generation of women for whom their husband's employment determined where the family lived and when they moved on. Employment was always important to my mother, but in our family it was never seen as requiring as much consideration and accommodation as my father's job. Decision-making about our family's moves never gave much attention to my mother's job or career interests—she was just expected to start again, to find something new. That she always did so, or tried to do so, tells me that in spite of the stresses and strains, being a working mom meant something very significant to her.

Just as more men are taking primary caring roles within the family, so too are women's careers becoming more prominent in couples' decisions about where to live and when they move on. How have your mother and father made decisions about their jobs? When your family moved, was it for your father's job or your mother's? Do you know of any couples who are trying to manage, and give equal consideration to, two careers? How are they doing this?

The false distinction between home and work is well captured in the concept of the 'household work strategy', which, as defined by British sociologist Ray Pahl, is 'how households allocate their collective effort to getting all the work that they define has, or feel needs, to be done' (Pahl 1984, 113). The household work strategy of each household blurs the distinction between home and work because it combines three basic forms of work that can be done at various sites, including the household, the workplace, and within other households. These forms of work include domestic work, various forms of work in the informal or voluntary economy, and paid employment in the formal economy. While Pahl developed his concept of the household work strategy within a British context, similar ideas have been developed in Canada in the work of Meg Luxton and Bonnie Fox through the articulation of family households as sites of 'social reproduction' (Fox and Luxton 2001), which refers to 'the activities required to ensure day-to-day and generational survival' (Luxton 1998, 2).

Interconnections between home and work, paid and unpaid work

For many years, sociologists studied work and family as though they were separate, but complementary, spheres. This tendency to treat home and work dichotomously has meant that the interconnections between the two spheres, and between paid and

Andrea: My Mother's Unpaid Work

My main memory of my mother is as a mom working in the home. There is a running joke in my family about how my mother's life was divided into two parts. First, there were the years when she worked at the Bank of Nova Scotia on Main Street in my small Maritime town. She had spending money, and she enjoyed the luxury of living away from her parents' farm and renting a small house on the beach with several other women. There are a few black and white photos of her in those days—pretty, glamorous, in high heels, smoking cigarettes, laughing with friends.

Then, there was my mother's life after she left her job at the bank. Like many women of her generation, she quit her job when she got married and quickly settled into creating a home and raising children. My mother had three children in three years, followed by three more over the next 10 years. If she ever had a desire to return to paid work, I never heard her express it, partly because the expression of such desires would have been viewed with surprise or incomprehension. There were children living at home for 22 years, and by the time my youngest brother went to university, she was in her mid-50s. Through all those years, my mother's life was filled to the brim with unpaid work. Piecing together a life out of a labourer's salary, she filled her days with the never-ending family chores of cooking all meals 'from scratch', housecleaning, washing clothes in an old-fashioned wringer-washer in our basement, hanging out loads and loads of laundry, and driving us to various activities when required. There were no appliances like dishwashers, modern washing machines, food processors, or blenders. Making meals for a family of eight was almost a full-time job in itself. She sewed most of our clothes (even our winter coats), pickled summer vegetables from my grand-mother's garden for the winter, served beef and fish in an infinite variety of ways from cattle reared by my grandfather and fish caught by friends of my father who were seasonal fishermen. She volunteered at church and school events, diligently brought our old clothes to what were called the 'low-rental houses' just down the street from the paper mill, and worked tirelessly to accommodate the countless relatives who drove down from Ontario to visit their New Brunswick homestead each summer.

My understanding of my mother's work has changed. In the years before I came to feminism, my description of my mother was that she worked before marriage and then stopped working. After reading early feminist work on domestic labour, I suddenly realized that my mother had indeed worked throughout her life—in the years when she worked at the bank and then in the years when she worked in our home and community.

How does child care and housework differ today from the case studies drawn from the 1960s and 1970s described here? What do you think the lives of stay-at-home mothers are like today compared to that of Andrea's mother? Do you think housework and child care should be paid work?

unpaid work, particularly crucial to an understanding of women's adult lives, was neglected as a focus of analysis for many years. This situation began to change during the 1980s when feminist scholars began to call for recognition of the integration of the private and public work worlds for women. In the United States, notable examples can be found in the work of scholars such as Patricia Zavella, who penned a book about the home and employment lives of Chicano women in the Santa Clara Valley of New Mexico (Zavella 1987). Another scholar, Louise Lamphere, wrote about working-class immigrant women over two generations in New England industrial towns (Lamphere 1989). In Canada, feminist scholars of work and family in varied regions and sectors of the Canadian economy (Connelly and Macdonald 1983; Luxton 1980; Armstrong and Armstrong 1984; Duffy, Mandell, and Pupo 1989) underlined how women's experiences of work and family were intricately linked in ways that differed from the experiences of men. Yet it also gradually became clear that little was known about men's experiences of balancing home and work responsibilities. That is, while attention was being given to making women's lives visible within sociology, a different kind of gender-blindness around men's lives was appearing inadvertently.

Early critiques emphasized the tendency within sociology to use different explanatory models when examining women's and men's relations to employment. Feldberg and Glenn (1984) drew attention to the tendency of researchers to use a 'gender model' to analyze women's employment and a 'job model' to analyze men's, a distinction that stressed the differences, and underplayed the similarities, between women's and men's relations to employment. Janet's research in the 1980s and 1990s (1986; 1994) revealed that much of what had been identified as occupational 'gender' segregation in employment was a highly structured interrelationship of household and employment circumstances that defined men's as well as women's employment. Her case studies of two gender-skewed jobs in London, England, (telephonist and postal worker) showed strong relationships between the household responsibilities and employment circumstances of both men and women in each job. Whereas it had been common to think that only women's employment was conditioned by their household and family position, this also seemed to be the case for men. For example, jobs that provided lots of opportunities for overtime work were valued by men with young families and female partners who were either temporarily not employed or employed part-time. Of course, there continued to be high levels of gender inequality in employment. But sociologists were beginning to look at the relationships between household and employment structuring (rather than their presumed separation) for explanations of both women's and men's relative positions and rewards.

By the late 1980s and early 1990s, it had become clear that the issue of work and family was not simply a women's issue and that leaving men out was further solidifying the binary distinction between paid and unpaid work that sociologists were seeking to dissolve. While a few scholars picked up on the importance of examining men, work, and family in the early 1980s, this crucial focus became part of mainstream sociological studies on work and family in the 1990s and in the new millennium. Indeed, research on men as fathers, domestic partners, and carers has become a burgeoning literature. We will address this issue later in the chapter.

Outside of the male model of employment:
Gender, ethnicity, and paid work

Women have also been excluded from the frame of the 'male model' in that the financial remuneration women receive for their paid work has consistently been less than that accorded to men. According to a 2003 Statistics Canada report, women's average hourly wages remain lower than men's in all occupations. The greatest male–female wage gap, however, occurs in 'blue-collar' occupations, where women earned 68 to 72 cents for every dollar earned by men; these sectors include trades, transport and equipment operations, processing, manufacturing and utilities, and primary industries (such as mining). On the other hand, women's earnings are more comparable to those of their male counterparts (88 to 97 cents for every dollar earned by men) in natural and applied sciences, social sciences, education, government, religion, the arts, culture, health, recreation, and sport (Statistics Canada 2003a).

While women's participation in paid work was of a sparse, intermittent, or (as examined below) invisible nature in the past, the past several decades have witnessed dramatic growth in the proportion of women in the paid workforce. In Canada, 57 per cent of all Canadian women aged 15 and over had jobs in 2003, up from 42 per cent in 1976. There have been particularly sharp increases in the employment rate of women with children. Women with children, however, are still less likely to be employed than women without children (see figure 4.1) (Statistics Canada 2003b).

While women earn less than men in paid employment, the situation is even more aggravated for immigrants, especially for women who are both members of

Figure 4.1   Employment Rates of Women Aged 15–54 by Age of Youngest Child at Home

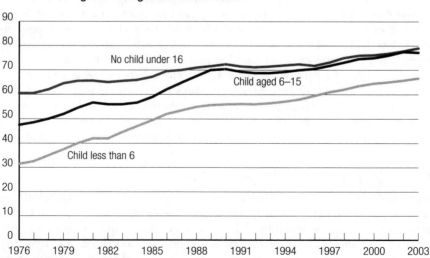

Source: Adapted from Statistics Canada, *The Canadian Labour Market at a Glance 2003*, cat. 71–222, chart 10, at
<http://www.statcan.ca/english/freepub/71-222-XIE/2004000/chart-b10.htm>.

Table 4.1   Employed Persons Working Part-Time, by Age, 2002

	Women (%)	Men (%)
Workers aged:		
15–24	52.9	38.2
25–44	21.2	4.9
45–64	32.1	6.9
65 and over	59.4	35.3
Total	27.7	10.9
Total employed part-time (000s)	1,983.7	900.0
% of all part-time employment	68.8	31.2

Source: Statistics Canada. 2003. *Women and Men in Canada: A Statistical Glance.*

visible minorities and recently arrived immigrants (Palameta 2003). In 2000, recent immigrants (in Canada for less than seven years) employed full-time in low-education jobs had weekly earnings at least 20 per cent lower than their Canadian-born counterparts. Indeed, the gap reached 30 per cent among 35- to 54-year-olds (Galarneau and Morissette 2004). Meanwhile, for recent immigrants with a university degree and employed between 1991 and 2001, at least one in four had a job requiring no more than a high-school education. It is worth noting that these disadvantages are particularly lasting for women. That is, for many immigrant women working full-time in low-education jobs, the earnings gap remains even 10 years after their arrival in Canada (Frenette and Morissette 2003).

In addition, women's employment remains overwhelmingly concentrated in part-time work. Part-time work is especially common among women aged 25 to 44. Just over one in five workers in this group worked part-time in 2002, while only a small minority of adult men (5 per cent) did. Women's part-time work is concentrated in health care and social assistance, retail trade, and educational services. Many women between 25 and 44 are attracted to part-time service sector jobs because of their responsibility for children as well as care of the elderly (see table 4.1). According to Statistics Canada, 20 per cent of Canadian women worked part-time because of personal or family responsibilities in 2002. In sharp contrast, only 2 per cent of male part-time workers cited these responsibilities as reasons why they did not work full-time. We now turn to a discussion of some of these responsibilities in a section on unpaid work.

WOMEN AND MEN AND UNPAID WORK

After Canadians put in a long day working for pay, they usually return 'home'. Yet what is home and family for Canadians today? During their adult and productive years, how do Canadians spend their days? In this section of our chapter, we examine the ways in which Canadian women and men form households and how they take on the unpaid work that sustains these households and families. Moreover, we unpack some of the complexity and diversity found in the category, and practice, of unpaid work.

Canadian families

During midlife, many women and men form households independent of their family of origin—either as individuals, as couples (heterosexual or same-sex), as families (of whatever configuration), or as collectives of friends. Issues of balancing work life and home life come to matter greatly at this time. Although husband–wife families are still the norm in Canadian society, they are much smaller than they were a few decades ago. For example, in 1961, 16 per cent of Canadian families were made up of six or more persons, compared with only 2.6 per cent in 2002. Meanwhile, the number of people living alone increased substantially during that time to the extent that while individuals living alone made up only 9 per cent of all households in 1961, they constituted 26 per cent by 2001.

It might be surprising for you to learn that in Canada, heterosexual marriages are still the dominant form of Canadian family. In 2002, for example, married couples headed about 84 per cent of Canadian families. On the other hand, the number of young people getting married has been declining steadily. Following the Second World War and the marriage boom of the 1950s, fully half of women aged 20 to 24 were married. That proportion had fallen to about 11 per cent by 2002. As for men, three-quarters of men in their early 20s were single in 1951, compared to 95 per cent 50 years later.

While marriage is still the most common form of household in Canada, the average age for first marriages is rising steadily for both brides and grooms. In 2000, first-time brides averaged nearly 32 years of age, while grooms were, on average, 34. Only two decades earlier, women and men were 26 and nearly 29 years old, respectively, when they got married. Why have these changes occurred? As you can probably guess, factors such as greater economic opportunities for women and the growing popularity of common-law unions have contributed to the postponement of first marriages. Thus, the marriage rate in Canada is steadily declining. In 2001, the proportion of married-couple families was 70 per cent, down from 83 per cent in 1981, while common-law partnerships increased to 14 per cent from 6 per cent.

Several other changes are important to this discussion of changing Canadian families. One is the increasing number of lone-parent families in Canada. About one in four Canadian families with children (approximately 1.4 million families) were headed by a lone parent in 2002. This represents a 58 per cent increase from 1986, whereas two-parent families only increased by 10 per cent over the same period. In 2001, women headed 81 per cent of lone-parent families, whereas men headed only one-fifth of lone-parent families.

Divorce has risen—but also fallen—over the past few decades. The proportion of marriages ending in divorce before the 30th wedding anniversary increased slightly from 36 per cent in 1998 to 38 per cent in 2000. While this might seem high, the numbers have actually decreased since 1995 when the divorce rate was 40 per cent and since 1987 when the rate was even higher, 51 per cent. While the divorce rate has altered over time, it is still reasonable for couples to fully expect their marriages to last 'for all the days of their lives'.

The links between divorce and economic dependency have also been well highlighted over the past decade, in international as well as Canadian research. American research by Kristin Anderson (2007) points to how the odds of leaving a violent relationship are affected by some indicators of structural gender inequality, particularly economic dependency. Most notably, women's overwhelming responsibility for all or most of the domestic labour leaves them most vulnerable at later points in their lives when they have probably forgone earnings as well as the right to benefits and a pension.

Finally, it is important to note that not all families include children. In 1999, the fertility rate for Canadian women aged 20 to 24 was 100 births for every 1,000 women, whereas in 1972, it was 130 for every 1,000. Some, but not all, of this decrease can be attributed to postponed childbearing. The age at which women have a first child increased from approximately 26 in 1975 to almost 29 in 1999. The number of children women have is also decreasing, from an average of four children per woman in the mid-1960s to 1.5 children in 1996.[2] The drop in fertility can also be explained partly by lower rates of marriage and trends towards later marriage and/or common-law marriages, since single people are much less likely to have children than those who are married (Stobert and Kemeny 2003). In Canada, sociologist Jean Veevers conducted research with voluntarily childless couples and women during the 1970s and 1980s (Veveers 1980). Apart from her work, this issue has been virtually ignored in contemporary Canadian gender studies. Recently, however, Riva Soucie, a PhD student in sociology at Carleton University, has begun new research in the area of gender and childlessness.

Reflections on Childlessness

by Riva Soucie
Sociology PhD Program

I became interested in studying voluntary childlessness partly because I am in my late 20s, an age at which women are typically expected to become mothers. Even with advances in reproductive technologies, biology still plays some part in the pressure to procreate by a certain age. But culture and social structure play an even bigger part in why women my age are constantly pressed to think about motherhood.

Recently, I have begun to resent this pressure. I resent being seen by some people as 'potentially pregnant' or merely as a 'walking womb'. As one of my friends said recently, 'I am more than an ongoing baby-bearing project.' I resent that deciding about whether or not to have children is seen as 'the most important choice a woman will ever make'. For some women—as for many men—reproductive decisions are *not* central in their lives—they may think about other things far more. Not all women are necessarily suited to be mothers, not all of us *want* to become mothers, and some of us don't even want to have to think about it. Liberation from having to 'think about it' all the time is one of the greatest achievements of safe, accessible birth control.

For other women, reproductive choices are highly constrained, so decisions depend on culture, religion, class, age, and circumstance. It seems unfair to place *all* the responsibility for choices about motherhood on the women who must make them—often in undesirable contexts.

I am fortunate, I suppose. My family and friends are supportive of my choices—whatever they are. And I have come of age in an era when women *can* make reproductive choices. I know many women from older generations who say, 'I never considered *not* having kids. It's just what you did.' But now it is both possible and accepted to delay or abstain altogether from childbearing. It is also okay to create meaningful, caring relationships in other ways—through adoption, friendships, committed partnerships, or paid work or volunteerism.

Of course, many women in North America structure their lives in ways that do not centralize caring at all. Thinking about whether or not to become a mother is a decision that is an important part of some—but not all—women's lives. It is important to consider women as individuals whose reproductive decisions are made in the contexts of personal preferences, social constraints, and cultural expectations.

What about you? Are you a woman who has never felt the desire to be a mother . . . or would like to but aren't sure how to 'fit it in' between school, work, family, and friends . . . or maybe you have a disability and feel that others don't want you to be a mother . . . maybe you aren't married and would like to be a mother but are afraid of stigma and lack of support . . . or are you married and feeling pressure to have children? Maybe your decisions about reproduction are complicated by non-heterosexual sexual orientation, infertility, or other constraints. Perhaps you're a man who would like to become a father. Have you considered how women are implicated in this desire?

Women's decisions about mothering are complex and contextual. It is important to support both mothering *and* childlessness.

Whatever the reasons, the decision to opt for childlessness—intentional or otherwise—must be included in discussions about family and gender, paid and unpaid work. We now turn our attention to the latter.

DEFINING AND UNDERSTANDING UNPAID WORK

As we made clear in the opening vignette at the beginning of this chapter, the life and work that occurred within households was largely absent from sociology until the 1970s. With each passing decade, it has come to occupy an important place within several areas of sociological research and studies, including the sociologies dealing with families and households, gender, production and reproduction, paid work, and consumption, as well as in emergent sociologies of emotions, of space and place.

Unlike paid work, the definition and meanings of unpaid work are difficult to pin down. Unpaid work is largely invisible or unnoticed, difficult to measure, and has many subjective meanings that vary according to context. For example, child care can be both paid and unpaid and can be seen as leisure or work, as both love and labour. It changes over time, with the number and ages of children in each household, and each aspect of child care encompasses varied dimensions of pleasure or burden. The same thing can be said about housework, which some do for pay while others do reluctantly. All households, furthermore, have differing standards, routines, and approaches as to how it gets done.

While there are many ways of categorizing unpaid work, many sociologists agree that several dominant categories capture the unpaid work done by most Canadians. These categories include: housework, child care, community activities, and subsistence activities, as well as care of the elderly and volunteer work. We will deal with some of these categories below.

Housework

While housework and child care are often conflated into one category of domestic labour, sociological researchers have become increasingly adamant that they are separate categories of work and experience (Fox 1998; 2001). Several general points can be made about the work that occurs within households. First, housework is not a universal and homogeneous category. Its detailed composition varies among countries, regions, and classes and according to such factors as available technologies, number of children, income level, and availability and access to domestic services (e.g., house-cleaning services). Second, housework has changed greatly over the past 50 years (Luxton 1980; Cowan 1983). While labour-saving devices have made some aspects of housework less onerous (e.g., washing clothes and dishes), growing consumption patterns within households and greater activity levels of children have led to new kinds of housework that entail household management, organization, and planning. Finally, it is worth pointing out, as Olivia Harris did more than a quarter-century ago, that the degree to which housework is oppressive or burdensome differs greatly and is influenced by various forms of cooperation and collectivity among households (Harris 1981). This point is particularly relevant in developing nations, where housework can very much resemble housework in the early part of the twentieth century in Canada, since many low-income households do not have access to water and electricity and are thus forced to do housework in ways that are time-consuming and extremely labour-intensive.

Who does housework? It is now a well-recognized, cross-cultural fact that women still take on the lion's share of housework. According to Statistics Canada, in 2001 about 21 per cent of women aged 15 and over devoted 30 hours or more to unpaid household work a week, compared to 8 per cent for men (Statistics Canada 2003a). Other Canadian data reveal that women, more than men, have become 'time poor'. For example, Statistics Canada's analysis of the General Social Survey 1998 reveals that in families where both spouses work full-time, women are still responsible for daily housework such as meal preparation, meal clean-up, housecleaning, and laundry (Marshall 1993; Palameta 2003). Furthermore, while Canadian households are increasingly buying household cleaning services (one-tenth of husband–wife households in 2000), a key factor determining the decision to buy domestic help is the wife's share of the household income. According to a report from Statistics Canada:

> Buying domestic help is not just a matter of having sufficient household income. It also matters whose income it is. Consider two husband–wife households, identical

in every respect except that the husband makes 75% of the income in one household while the wife makes 75% in the other. . . . [T]he second household will be roughly twice as likely to pay for home services. (Palameta 2003, 15)

What these Canadian data reveal most poignantly is how women's greater financial contribution to the household provides her with a greater rationale for easing her unusually large share of domestic labour. In 1989, American sociologist Arlie Hochschild wrote in a bestselling book that working women are coming home to take on a *second shift* of work (Hochschild 1989). Canadian women with income clout are demonstrating that they are now attempting to avoid this situation by putting some of their income towards housework relief.

Child care
In households with children, the care and upbringing of these children constitutes a large part of adults' daily lives. While we are conceiving of housework and child care as two separate categories of unpaid work, they are obviously closely linked. Both kinds of work are usually performed for other household members and thus may be viewed as family-based work. Moreover, some tasks (e.g., cooking and cleaning) may constitute *both* housework and child care activities. Finally, it is important to recognize that both housework and caring activities may have monotonous and routine aspects as well as rewarding and creative dimensions.

Several noteworthy distinctions can, however, be drawn between housework and child care. First, there is a greater degree of flexibility in doing housework than with child care responsibilities; this is particularly the case with infants and young children for whom continuous care must be undertaken by household members or must be arranged and organized to be undertaken by others. Second, improved technology may have had an impact on household tasks (e.g., cooking) but has had little impact on caring activities, which are heavily reliant on human input.

Who does child care? Historically and cross-culturally, women overwhelmingly have taken on the work and responsibility of caring for children. Indeed, many researchers have argued that, more than any other single life event, the arrival of children most profoundly marks long-term systemic inequalities between women and men.

This is not to say that fathering and mothering have been static over time. Throughout the previous millennium, they have been radically altered by changing state policies on balancing employment and child rearing, by shifting labour market configurations in relation to gender (e.g., full-time and part-time work, flexible working hours), by diverse ideologies, and by mothers' and fathers' varied choices in relation to all of these factors. Mothering has been particularly affected by rising employment rates for women, especially for mothers of young children, throughout all Western industrialized countries. Yet while women have become workers and earners and sometimes breadwinners, they still remain as primary carers. Men, on the other hand, have moved from being primary breadwinners but have retained a secondary role in caregiving. While many have argued that today's fathers are more involved in their children's lives than fathers of previous generations, with significant increases in the time allotted to their involvement as well as a greater gender balance in the performance of child care tasks, there nevertheless remains an outstanding stability in mothers' *responsibility* for children and for domestic and community life. This pattern of gendered responsibilities has not shifted even when women have equal participation in paid employment.

While the overwhelming majority of men have not come to share in the responsibilities for raising children, there has nevertheless been somewhat of a revolutionary change in fathers' involvement in Canada and other Western countries. A good indication of men's increasing involvement in child care is clearly revealed in two sets of statistics. The first set concerns fathers at home on a long-term basis, while the second has to do with fathers taking parental leave. With regard to the former, the most recent data from Statistics Canada suggest that the number of stay-at-home fathers (about 111,000 of them in 2002) has increased 25 per cent in the past 10 years, while the number of stay-at-home mothers has decreased by approximately the same figure (Statistics Canada 2002). The second set of statistics relates to the recent extension of parental leave in Canada (from six months to one year) and the increased use of parental leave by fathers to care for infants. A recent study by Statistics Canada reported that in 2002, parental benefits taken up by fathers had increased five-fold from just two years earlier (Marshall 2003; Pérusse 2003).

The sandwich generation

Another aspect of care for many families has led to application of the term 'sandwich generation' to many middle-aged Canadians. According to Statistics Canada, 'a sandwiched person is defined as looking after children 15 and under while providing care to a senior' (Williams 2004, 11). At the beginning of this new century, the overall number of people in the sandwich generation was still relatively small; nevertheless, family analysts predict that the ranks will grow steadily. This is partly due to an aging 'baby boomer' population as well as to delayed marriage, the postponing of children, decreased fertility rates, and increased life expectancy. Recent figures from Statistics Canada indicate that approximately one-quarter of Canadians between the ages of 45 and 64 with unmarried children in the home are also caring for a senior family member. Given that a large majority of these caregivers are also in the paid labour force, this added shift of care work can affect hours spent on the job, income, and pensions. While historically, the care of the elderly was a family responsibility that often fell to middle-aged women, the striking difference at the beginning of the twenty-first century is that the majority of women taking on these responsibilities are also employed. While Canada has seen increased provision of largely private services for the care of the very young, much less attention has been paid to the care of Canada's older persons. Just as gender differences continue to exist in child care and domestic work, such divisions persist in elder care and women are more likely than men to be 'sandwiched', devoting nearly three times as much time to elder care per month as men do (Williams 2004).

Community responsibility or inter-household work

Another category of work—essentially an extension of both housework and child care—has only recently come to be considered in sociological studies on unpaid work.

In her work, Andrea has used the term 'community responsibility' to refer to the extra-domestic, community-based aspect of work involved in home and child care responsibilities. That is, the responsibility for domestic life and for children involves a wide set of relationships *between* households as well as *between* the social institutions of families/households, schools, the state, and the workplace. Within and between households and other social institutions, parents share responsibility for their children with others who take on caring practices—caregivers, other parents, neighbours, relatives, child care experts, nurses and doctors, schoolteachers, librarians, music teachers, sports coaches, and so on. Each stage of child rearing introduces its own sets of issues, according to the particular needs and demands of each child. For all of these issues and decision-making processes—from a child's pre-school to university years—*other people* are often consulted, and relationships are thus built on the basis of a shared interest in particular children. Community responsibility is beautifully captured by political theorist Selma Sevenhuijsen, who writes that caring implies 'not just the meeting of children's needs but also the *ability to "see" or "hear" needs, to take responsibility for them, negotiate if and how they should be met and by whom*' (Sevenhuijsen 1998, 15, emphasis added). The unpaid work of child care and domestic work more widely thus involves not only a domestically based set of tasks and responsibilities but also community-based, inter-household, and inter-institutional responsibilities. This work of parents *and others* appears in varied guises in a wide body of feminist research. Concepts such as 'kin work' (di Leonardo 1987; Stack 1974), 'servicing work' (Balbo 1987), 'motherwork' (Collins 1994), 'household service work' (Sharma 1986), and 'relationship work' (Dollahite, Hawkins, and Brotherson 1997) each describe domestic work as much wider—spatially, theoretically, and practically—than simply housework and child care.

This idea of community responsibility is also explored in the work of scholars working in Third World settings, who point to complex webs of social relations within which domestic labour and parenting is enacted (Goetz 1995; 1997; Moser 1993; Scheper-Hughes 1992). Moreover, black feminist scholars highlight how community networks and inter-household relations are integral elements of black motherhood (Collins 1994; 2000). Patricia Hill Collins, for example, points to the way that 'the institution of Black motherhood consists of a series of constantly negotiated relationships that African-American women experience with one another, with black children and with the larger African-American community' (Collins 2000, 180). Similarly, Nova Scotia author and filmmaker Sylvia Hamilton has illuminated community responsibility and inter-household work in the lives of African-Canadian women living in Nova Scotia (as well depicted in the documentary film *Black Mother, Black Daughter*). Finally, Micaela di Leonardo provides one of the most colourful descriptions of community responsibility in her definition of 'kin work' as:

> . . . the conception, maintenance, and ritual celebration of cross-household ties, including visits, letters, telephone calls, presents and cards to kin; the organisation of holiday gatherings; the creation and maintenance of quasi-kin relations; decisions to neglect or to intensify particular ties; the mental work of reflection about all these activities. . . . (1987, 442–3)

While community or inter-household responsibility can vary in the way it is enacted and experienced across class, ethnicity, sexuality, and cultural lines, feminist researchers who have written about similar and parallel kinds of domestically based work—such as 'kin work' or 'household service work'—have consistently agreed that this work remains significantly gendered.

Subsistence work

A fourth category of unpaid work is 'self-provisioning', which is the production and consumption of goods and services undertaken by household members for themselves (Gershuny and Pahl 1979; Pahl 1984; Wallace 2002; Wallace and Pahl 1985). In general terms, self-provisioning includes vegetable-growing, household maintenance and repair, car maintenance, the production of food and beverages (e.g., jam, wine), and sewing or knitting clothes. These tasks go beyond the routine tasks of daily household mainte-nance and take in the wider notion of what British sociologists term a 'household work strategy', which is how household members allocate their time and labour to make ends meet. In Canada, contemporary households are less likely to self-provision and more likely to buy these services. Nevertheless, low-income families and households on a tight budget often take on such tasks themselves. Moreover, environmental concerns as well as the desire to live in more cooperative and sustainable ways have led some Canadians to engage in such self-provisioning activities as growing their own organic vegetables, raising livestock, and taking on environment-friendly and/or low-cost household main-tenance projects. Self-provisioning is more prevalent in developing countries, where subsistence work is a key aspect of the family's household work strategy and performed mainly by women. Typical subsistence activities include the cultivation of vegetables for family use, fetching wood and water, and the care of livestock.

As revealed in Andrea's research on stay-at-home fathers, some men who give up a formal investment in the labour force may replace employment with self-provision-ing work, which allows them to contribute economically to the household economy as well as display masculine practices, both to themselves and to their wider community. That is, stay-at-home dads may take on 'male self-provisioning activities' (Mingione 1988, 560), which include 'building, renovation . . . carpentry, electrical repairs and plumbing, furniture making, decorating, constructing doors and window frames, agri-cultural cultivation for own use, repairing vehicles' (Mingione 1988, 560–1). While some of these activities can be viewed as masculine hobbies, which these men would probably have picked up from their fathers or male peers, they also contribute to the household's larger work strategy, and they display or justify men's masculinity, which seems to alleviate some of the discomfort men feel with giving up breadwinning.

In addition to all the above kinds of unpaid work, other kinds also take up the time and energy of Canadians. Such work can include volunteering for activities asso-ciated with one's children (e.g., helping out in the classroom, chaperoning field trips, coaching children's sports) as well as volunteer work for formal non-profit organiza-tions. Data from the 2000 National Survey of Giving, Volunteering, and Participating (NSGVP) indicates that women are largely the ones who perform volunteer work. Another kind of work is family members' unpaid work in family businesses. In Canada, unpaid family work is particularly common in the family businesses of immi-grant families and on family farms.

In summary, both Canadian women and Canadian men engage in a considerable amount of unpaid work. Yet it is now a well-recognized cross-cultural and historical fact that women take on the lion's share of unpaid work—whether it be housework, child care, inter-household work, subsistence work, informal caring, or volunteer work (Bianchi et al. 2000; Coltrane and Adams 2001; O'Brien 2005). In 2001 in Canada, about 21 per cent of women aged 15 and over devoted 30 hours or more to unpaid household work a week, compared to 8 per cent for men (Statistics Canada 2003a). Moreover, Canadian statistics from the General Social Survey 1998 indicated that while women and men averaged a total of 7.2 hours a day engaged in paid and unpaid work, there was a distinct gender division of labour, with women spending an average of 2.8 hours a day on paid work and 4.4 hours on unpaid work. Men's situation, on the other hand, represented an almost perfect reversal of these numbers (see figure 4.2).

Since the mid-1980s, many studies have laid out the contours of unpaid work and how gender differences persist within the varied kinds of work. The question we turn to now is why these differences have remained and where and how they are changing.

Figure 4.2   Average Time Spent on Paid and Unpaid Work Activities by the Population Aged 15 and Over, 1998

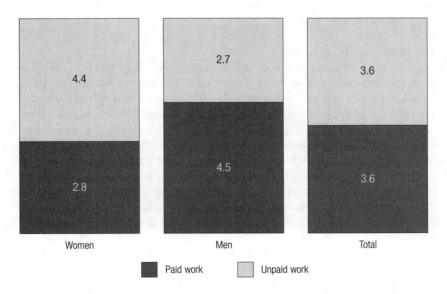

Source: Adapted from Statistics Canada, *General Social Survey*, cat. 12F0080XIE, released 9 November 1999.

GENDER DIFFERENCES IN HOUSEWORK AND CHILD CARE

Beginning in the late 1970s, Canadian scholars began to study housework and child care and to engage in a field of study that has come to be called 'gender divisions of domestic labour'. Within this field, Canadian academic studies have collected three major types of data on the division of domestic work: *time* (e.g., Meissner et al. 1975; Zuzanek 2001), *tasks* (e.g., Blain 1994; Marshall 1993), and *responsibility* (e.g., Doucet 2004; 2006; Luxton 1980). All three of these areas of study have revealed constant movement and change but with women still putting in more time, taking on more tasks and, most importantly, the *responsibility* for housework and child care. Using a combination of large-scale surveys and in-depth interviews (e.g., Duxbury et al. 2004; Fast and Keating 2001), such studies have indicated that although men have increasingly come to appreciate the importance of work–family balance, most of the balancing or juggling of home and work continues to fall on women.

In highlighting the persistent connection between women and the time, tasks, and responsibilities associated with domestic life and care work, and the fact that they bear the weight of balancing work and family life, many researchers have also put considerable thought into the question of *why* gender differences persist in paid and unpaid work and why the progress towards gender equality or symmetry has been slow. That is, why do women and men perform different kinds of work? Why do women continue to take on a larger share of the unpaid work during their adult lives? To address these questions, we highlight a number of important factors that have recurred over the past 30 years of scholarship on gender and unpaid work. These factors include: gender as a social structure; gender ideologies; links with the labour market; state policies; constraints on men as fathers; constraints on women as mothers; processes of 'doing gender'; and gendered social networks and social support for caring responsibilities.

Gender as a social structure

To explain the first factor that will assist us in understanding gender differences in the gender division of unpaid work, we return to a discussion laid out in chapter 1 about how gender acts as a social structure in the patterning of work and family lives. While there are now ample theoretical treatments of gender as a social structure, our view is that R. Connell's gender relations approach is a useful one for summarizing our overall theoretical perspective on gender relations in that it seeks to 'understand the different dimensions of structures of gender, the relations between bodies and society and the patterning or configuration of gender' (Connell 2000, 24–5). Connell posits a four-fold model of gender relations—incorporating relations of power, production, emotions, and symbolism—that has been developed over the past two decades (Connell 1987; 1995; 2000). The approach also focuses on gender as structure and agency, thus recognizing the local and global structures within which households and families are located while noting the potential for change by groups of individuals.

Framed within this gender relations perspective, we note the gendered power relations that exist in a society like Canada where women and men still face different sets of opportunities and where gender divisions of labour, responsibilities, and expectations persist both in home life and in employment. Thus, in examining the 'choices' and actions of women and men as they negotiate who stays at home and who works, how housework is divided, and who takes responsibility for varied aspects of domestic life and child rearing, we are reminded that such actions, decisions, and 'strategies' must be situated in a wide set of social relations in which women's and men's lives are structured differently. As detailed in chapter 1, men and women face differing constraints and opportunities in the workplace and in social life more widely. For example, 'glass ceilings' are still in place for women who try to move up in male-dominated professions (such as the upper echelons of the corporate world), while men glide more easily on glass escalators that enable them to move to the top of female-dominated professions (such as nursing or education). Gender relations matter profoundly in social institutions (work, family, state policies, communities, the courts, education, the media), and all these social institutions are implicated in thinking through how it is that gender continues to matter in domestic life and how these relations might begin to change. As well stated by American sociologist Barbara Risman, 'We cannot simply attend to socializing children differently, nor creating moral accountability for men to share family work, nor fighting for flexible, family-friendly workplaces. We must attend to all simultaneously' (Risman 2004, 441).

Gender ideologies

A second factor that helps to understand gender difference in domestic life is the existence of gender ideologies. We agree with British sociologist David Morgan, who has argued that ideology is 'one of the most troublesome words in the sociological lexicon' (Morgan 1992, 36, drawing on Williams 1983). In order to present a relatively clear and accessible definition of the term, we draw on the work of our Carleton University colleagues Trevor Purvis and Alan Hunt, who in a well-known article on ideology and discourse argue that ideology works in a taken-for-granted way, much like 'common sense' or tacit knowledge. They write: 'It is precisely the "spontaneous" quality of common sense, its transparency, its "naturalness", its refusal to examine the premises on which it is grounded, its resistance to correction, its quality of being recognizable which makes common sense. At one and the same time, "lived", "spontaneous" and unconscious.' (Purvis and Hunt 1993, 479).

Building from this succinct definition of ideologies, our view is that 'gender ideologies' can be loosely defined as a taken-for-granted set of social beliefs about men's and women's roles and relationships in both private and public spheres. Gender ideologies can recur in a number of domains of lived experience, including masculinities and femininities and motherhood and fatherhood, as well as ideologies of marriage and family life. With regard to unpaid work, there has been both consistency and change in gender ideologies. For decades, researchers in many countries reported on the differing definitions of understandings of a 'good mother' and a 'good father'. A 'good mother' was defined as a woman whose chief responsibility was caring for her children and running a household, while a 'good father' was the family provider and chief breadwinner. Dominant and even *hegemonic* for many decades and as recently as the 1990s, these ideal stereotypes also worked to sustain gender divisions of labour within the workplace and the household and were supported by and closely related to views on maternal employment. That is, throughout the 1970s and 1980s, British, American, and Canadian studies cited solid disapproval of working women—particularly mothers of pre-school children—on the part of most men and women.

Ideology also plays out in media representations of mothers and fathers. Many scholars have argued that the mainstream media put forth popular cultural representations portraying the 'new father' as more involved and nurturing than previous generations were. Recent research by Glenda Wall and Stephanie Arnold, however, argues differently (2007). Based on an analysis of a year-long newspaper series on family issues in *The Globe and Mail*, their findings suggest that media representations of father involvement are still focused on fathers not as equal or shared partners in caregiving but as part-time, secondary parents in relation to the role played by mothers.

The issue of ideology further complicates the issue of equality in the home. On the one hand, it has been well established that women in dual-earner households continue to perform the large bulk of household work in terms of time, tasks, and responsibilities. Yet on the other hand, throughout the 1980s and 1990s, researchers constantly puzzled over why so few women expressed little overt dissatisfaction and criticism of the unequal division of domestic labour (e.g., Berk 1985; Hochschild 1989). That is, if the division of labour within households is indeed unfair, then why have women not pushed for more change? Why have they exhibited an apparent acceptance of their greater share of child care and housework? How are these inequalities tolerated and perpetuated in the context of daily household interactions? In dealing with this issue, we are recognizing that just as it is important to examine why men have not changed quickly, it is equally critical to examine women's resistance to challenging traditional gender roles within the household. There are several possible explanations for this, and we shall examine some of them in this chapter. What we wish to highlight here is how gender ideologies, and the taken-for-granted assumption that caring is more 'naturally' women's work or part of women's identity, partly account for how and why women continue to take on a larger share of housework and child care in Canadian households. That is, traditionally, there are deep tracks of socialization for women to become wives and mothers, and this often translates into women's feelings of fulfillment when they undertake these unpaid duties. As one British sociologist described it more than two decades ago:

> While researching the relationship between women's paid work and the 'caring capacity of the community', I became convinced that despite women's increased participation in paid work, the ideology of housework and caring was so strong that women continue to work their dual roles largely irrespective of their changing material circumstances. (Ungerson 1983, 32)

Further evidence can be found much more recently in Andrea's research on stay-at-home fathers. She was continually amazed at how fathers, irrespective of the number of years at home (which ranged from one to 12 years) still felt the weight of ideological conceptions of men as earners and women as caregivers. One father interviewed by Andrea expressed this latter point particularly well when he pointed to how mothers' responsibilities are framed in terms of a long history of societal expectations and that 'women might feel a little more inclined about their responsibilities as mothers' while he, on the other hand, had to 'take care of myself as a guy':

I'd like to think I'm a little less inclined to come into my kids' whimsies as much as my wife is. They'll say—'Can we go swimming? Can we go fishing?' And I'll say— 'No we'll go at a different time.' Whereas my wife would kind of think about it, and say—'Let's not do that but let's think of an alternative. Let's do this or that.' . . . I think she is more inclined to want to please the kids. And I think that I have learned that I have to take care of myself as a guy, as a dad, as a person, that I have to look out for my own limits, and my own sort of state and not really feel guilty about that. And I think that is partially, probably a trend that men and women are different in the sense that women might feel a little more inclined about their responsibilities as mothers. You can't ignore the fact that you've got a much bigger history of women doing this kind of job than men. And so, you have to contend with the fact that this is an issue that she has struggled with. It is that—'Am I shirking my god-given responsibilities, the thing that my mother did and my mother's mother and everything that has been expected of me?' *Women are expected to raise their kids*. (Doucet 2006, 109–10)

This same father, Tom, who was a stay-at-home father of three children for seven years, also underlined how men still feel governed by gender ideologies of the 'good father' as a family breadwinner. He spoke at length about his 'big struggle':

It is actually a big struggle for me. . . . But each time I think of working full time, each time I think about that whole thing, I get a little bit of a heavy stomach because I think about being away that much from the house and the home and it gives me a feeling. So I have this overwhelming, probably from my own background—a sense of men are supposed to go out and work, men are supposed to be generating income, men are supposed to be sitting around at parties answering questions when people say what are you doing for a living and saying something other than I am at home, I sweep floors and squeeze blueberry shit out of diapers. That is a very big struggle, and I don't think being a man at home you can ignore that. . . . There is a traditional sense behind me, there is this traditional feeling like—Gee, shouldn't I be earning a living? Shouldn't I make money doing something sitting around the water cooler with people talking shop or something like that? (Doucet 2006, 194–5)

Another father, Jesse, stay-at-home father of one daughter for three years, spoke in a similar way about his 'background' and his 'struggle'. He noted that these perceptions are 'so ingrained' through men's upbringing that they 'can weigh on you' and that there is a gendered quality to these feelings ('it's a guy thing'):

These things are so ingrained in us. . . . It can weigh on you, those kind of things. Sometimes I do wonder if people have that sort of perception of me as a stay-at-home father. I am still not sure if there is a widespread acceptance of it. I think some people still wonder 'Why is the father at home? Like he can't earn as much as his partner or something?' I struggle with that, because it is also my own internalized kind of condition too that I have this struggle. You know, my background, working-class, a strong work ethic. *And it's a guy thing*. (Doucet 2006, 195)

Gender ideologies, along with normative stereotypes of motherhood and father-hood and attitudes towards maternal employment in Canada and elsewhere, have proved very resistant to change. Moreover, they exist in a dialectical relationship with government policy and labour market structures so that ideology legitimates policy and structure, which in turn reinforces ideological conceptions.

Links with the labour market

One simple answer for gender differences in unpaid work is that they link up with gen-der differences in paid work. That is, household patterns of women and men are influ-enced by the structure of the labour market and the nature of women's participation within it. As discussed earlier in this chapter, while women's participation in paid employment has risen steadily in all countries, women's employment, especially moth-ers' employment, has been largely characterized by a strong part-time component.

The answer to the question 'Why do women work part-time?' is multi-faceted. Nevertheless, one overwhelming reason for this choice is women's caregiving respon-sibilities. These responsibilities include the care of children but also care of the elderly. For many decades, many women with children have been attracted to part-time serv-ice sector jobs because although these jobs involve no formal recognition of parental responsibilities such as provision for child care, they often offer conditions that accept and reinforce women's major responsibility for child care. Such conditions include part-time hours, evening jobs, home-based work, and casual and temporary employ-ment. The price that women with children pay for these conditions is low earnings, poor prospects, less security, and minimal training and promotion opportunities.

In the 1990s and 2000s, greater attention has been given to men's practices and identities as fathers and how they too experience work–family conflicts. As pointed out below in our discussion on men as fathers, research now indicates that against a back-drop of rising employment for women, levels of parity in certain educational sectors, and higher rates of male unemployment, men are also exploring how to be involved partners and parents and how to have adult lives focused on more than breadwinning.

State policies

What role should the state play in assisting with gender divisions of labour in unpaid work? Put differently, should child care and parental employment be viewed as indi-vidual matters to be dealt with by households or as matters of public concern to which tax dollars should be directed? In Canada, domestic work and child care have histor-ically been considered private matters. Thus, families needed to decide themselves how they would care for their children and how they would pay for this care. Until recently, parents also had to devise their own solutions to the issue of caring for infants, since maternity leave benefits, with provincial variations, allowed women only a few months' leave from paid work to care for their newborns. Thus, even though women's and mothers' employment has risen with each passing decade, suc-cessive Canadian governments have maintained the view that the care of children is essentially a private matter to be left in the hands of parents.

Researchers in Canada have long looked across the sea to countries like Sweden, where work–family issues have been framed as issues of public concern. For several decades, Sweden has provided affordable and high-quality child care to working parents and generous parental leave policies so that women and men can spend at least the first year at home with their infants. Parental leave is available to both women and men, and indeed a period of one to two months is reserved exclusively for fathers to encourage them to take at least part of the leave.

Regarding state polices that support or hinder equal division of unpaid labour, two are seen to be of critical importance: child care policies and parental leave policies. How do these policies play out in Canada?

Child care policies

Given the ample evidence that women feel a strong responsibility for children, access to affordable, quality child care has been widely recognized as an important support for working mothers. During the 1980s and 1990s, several international research studies highlighted how critically important child care was to women's ability to pursue a career and feel comfortable with it while raising children. Canada's approach to child care has come under heavy scrutiny in the early years of this millennium. According to a study by the Organisation for Economic Co-operation and Development (OECD), Canada's approach to child care provides 'basic babysitting, but not much else' for working parents and 'disregards the importance of early education' (Doherty, Friendly, and Beach 2003; OECD 2004). As a nation, Canada also invests less than half of what other developed nations devote to early childhood education and has enough regulated child care spaces for less than 20 per cent of children under six with working parents. This compares to the United Kingdom, where 60 per cent of young children are in regulated care, while in Denmark the figure is 78 per cent.

Quebec is unique in that the provincial government introduced a public child care system based on daycare centres and private homes in 1997, which initially cost parents $5 per child per day (increased to $7 a day in 2003). Quebec currently accounts for about 40 per cent of the regulated child care centres in Canada. Criticisms of Quebec's system have led to measures to improve the quality of care, nutrition, and worker–child ratios (CBC 2004; Jenson 2002). Moreover, according to recent research by Patrizia Albanese, Quebec's $7-per-day child care program has had positive impacts on family and community life in economically disadvantaged communities in Quebec (Albanese 2006).

Through Andrea's work on stay-at-home fathers, we have come to the view that the decision of Canadian parents to have one parent stay at home is part of a strategy to balance work and home for both parents in a country where daycare has never been seen as a viable option for many parents. Such options are differently configured in countries with large investments in child care such as Norway and Sweden, where parents have many choices for balancing work and home because of universal high-quality child care, generous parental leave, and options for working part-time while children are young. While a national daycare plan has made repeated appearances during federal election campaigns in Canada, it merely slips off the political agenda when governments are sworn in. Liberal governments have been more likely to at least consider the issue, while the Conservative Party has been much more inclined to see child care remain a private issue in which Canadians are left to make their own 'choices'. In our view, these choices are very limited ones, because child care remains expensive and, in some communities, unavailable for many working parents. The stress of inadequate child care can and does force some parents, usually women, to reconsider their career choices.

Parental leave policies

While academics and policy-makers have heavily critiqued Canada's approach to child care, there has been much praise for its approach to parental leave. In contrast to its poor record in child care provision, one of Canada's greatest strengths in family policy is its Employment Insurance Act of 2001, which provides paid parental leave for almost a year. While 15 (and in some provinces, 18) weeks are reserved strictly for maternity benefits, either fathers or mothers may take the following 35 weeks. Drawing again on OECD commentary, this policy is regarded as a 'very important contribution to both equal opportunity for women and infant well-being and development' (OECD 2004, 5).

In principle, parental leave is aimed at men as well as women, but in reality, it is used mainly by women. Indeed, according to Canadian data, only 10 to 11 per cent of the partners of women who used the parental leave scheme took part of the leave in 2003 and 2004. Data for 2005 indicate that the rate has risen to 14.5 per cent. However, the length of parental leave taken by men is clearly quite limited, since women take on average a full 11 months of the leave. While we can highlight these gender differences in the take-up of leave, we should also emphasize the positive point that Canadian fathers' use of parental leave jumped dramatically when it was extended from six months to one year. Statistics Canada reported that in 2002, parental benefits taken up by fathers increased by five-fold over what it had been just two years earlier (Marshall 2003; Pérusse 2003). Quebec's approach to parental leave is unique in that it allows for greater flexibility in the time of take-up, higher replacement rates, and up to five weeks reserved as 'daddy days' that can be used only by the father. Early indications are that nearly 40 per cent of Québécois fathers are taking these weeks. Even though the Quebec plan is more generous, with more take-up by men, gender differences are still noticeable: mothers take most or all of the first year of parental leave. As for why men take no parental leave or less leave than women do, this situation may relate to issues discussed below in our section on men as fathers.

Constraints on men as fathers

Beginning in the 1980s, scholarship on fatherhood has gone from a relatively ignored topic (relative to motherhood) to a 'hot topic' in the 1990s (Marsiglio 1993, 88) to a burgeoning field of theoretical and empirical research in the twenty-first century. The proliferation of research on fathering has arisen partly out of the profound social changes in women's and men's lives over the past few decades. Within North America and much of Europe, men's declining wages, increasing male unemployment, sustained growth in women's labour force participation, and changing ideologies associated with men's and women's roles and identities have all increased the emphasis on understanding the changing social institutions of mothering and fathering. At the same time, increased social alarm on the part of certain sections of the population over issues of fatherless families, combined with an interest in issues of enhanced personal development for involved fathers, has led researchers of all political and theoretical stripes to turn their critical gaze to understanding fatherhood.

It is no longer possible to speak of fathering or fatherhood as monolithic concepts or experiences. Just as Adrienne Rich pointed out that mothering differs as experience and institution (Rich 1986), the same applies to our understandings of fathering and fatherhood, with the former being more closely related to how fathers perceive, live out, and enact the practices of fathering while doing so within the larger political, social, cultural, symbolical, ideological, and discursive institution of fatherhood. Both fathering and fatherhood vary, as rich bodies of research increasingly point to a diversity across class, ethnicity, sexualities, age, culture, dis/ability, and household form. Fathering occurs for fathers who are stay-at-home fathers, sole-custody or joint-custody fathers, and incarcerated fathers, and research is also scrutinizing such concepts as 'deadbeat dads' and unmarried or non-residential fathers (Waller 2002).

Until recently, consideration of the ways in which men are constrained in their roles as fathers and as potentially equal participants in housework has been a much less common thread in sociological literature. An investigation of the social and economic constraints that structure the individual and social experience of fatherhood can shed new light on the problem of the slow transformation of gender roles within the household. The fathering literature has thus drawn attention to key obstacles to greater fatherhood involvement. We have explored many of these obstacles throughout this chapter, including gender ideologies and discourses, the role of work in fathers' lives, and state policies. We now turn to two additional obstacles: maternal gate-keeping on the part of female partners and the processes of 'doing gender'.

Mothers as experts

Many researchers have written about how mothers start out as child rearing *experts*, largely because of pregnancy, breastfeeding, and maternity leave. Such research on men and women's transition to parenthood has demonstrated that with the birth of a couple's first child, gender roles become more clearly differentiated. Indeed, many researchers have argued that, more than any other single life event, the arrival of a child most profoundly marks long-term systemic inequalities between women and men. At this transition point, women tend to assume greater responsibility within the home, and men generally increase their workload outside the home. Embodied differences, most obvious during pregnancy and childbirth, channel men and women into distinct gender roles, with women taking a primary role and men relegated to a secondary position (Fox 1998; 2001).

For many years, the notion of women and their skill as mothers was reflected in the fact that when sociologists and social psychologists wrote about parenting—in the 1950s and 1960s, for example—they meant mothering; most studies on infants and young children were about 'the absolute need of infants and toddlers for the continuous care of their mothers' (Bowlby 1953, 18). Early research on parenting, in both the child development and the family sociology literature, tended to view the mother not only as the primary caregiver but also as the main agent of socialization and the most dependable source of information about parenting and child development within the family; fathers were generally considered only through mothers' reports (e.g., Newson and Newson 1968). This relative exclusion of fathers extended to the practices of providers of health care and community services for parents. Even in this new millennium, as revealed in research on new fathers in Canada, many fathers still feel excluded by health care providers and throughout the birthing process (Bader and Doucet 2005).

Again, in her work on stay-at-home fathers, Andrea found that the influence of mothers on fathers and mothers' involvement in housework and child care was extremely strong. She has argued that parenting is a 'mother-led dance' whereby women lead and men follow and rely very much on mothers' cues as to how and when to be involved (Doucet 2006). These observations are not novel; rather, they confirm two decades of research on mothering and fathering that has argued for the central importance of women's attitudes and feelings 'as the single most important influence on a father's involvement with his child' (Barnett and Baruch 1987, 61). What is novel, however, is that mothers' central role in child rearing remains evident even in households where fathers are actively involved. Some of the reasons for this can be further understood through the well-known concept in sociology known as 'doing gender'.

Doing gender

A 'relational' or 'interactional' approach to gender roles within households can help us to understand why gender specialization within domestic life persists and why women in particular are resistant to change. Rooted in ethnomethodological analyses of gender relations, a relational or interactional approach to domestic labour focuses on how couples create and maintain gendered distinctions in domestic life and in gendered identities through their daily interactions. As stated by Linda Thompson and Alexis Walker nearly two decades ago: 'Women and men participate together to construct the meaning of gender and distinguish themselves from each other *as* women or *as* men' (1989, 865). This approach has frequently been referred to as 'doing gender'. It has several features worth mentioning. First, men and women seem to collaborate to sustain the belief that men and women are 'fairly' sharing child care and housework, whereas in actual fact, women do considerably more than men. Men, on the one hand, readily see their contributions to housework and child care as a sign that they are sharing the work, while women, on the other hand, may accept as especially valuable the performance of tasks that, for example, their fathers probably did not do. In addition, acknowledging the 'pressures' in each other's lives can make the division of labour appear fair to partners even if they are not sharing the work equally.

Second, even in dual-earner households where women are clearly discontented with their double workload, they nevertheless often exhibit loyalty to their partners and refrain from revealing deficiencies in the marriage. Many women excuse and justify their male partners' minimal involvement in housework and child care. The fact that their husbands/partners are more involved than their own fathers were years before, or compared to other men they know, leads women to be grateful for men's help, however minimal. Understanding women's roles within the household within a 'relational' or 'interactional' approach allows us to understand why women may give little attention to inequalities in the domestic sphere and exaggerate the extent of

Shared Baby Care: Janet and Partner Attempt a Gender-Neutral Division of Labour—Even at 3 a.m.!

When my son was born, I intended to breastfeed him. However, breastfeeding seemed to be one of the great divides between new fathers and new mothers—she has the equipment for it and he doesn't! Too often I'd seen well-intentioned new dads become more and more marginalized from newborn care because breast-feeding created such a strong mother–child bond. This divide did not sit well with my partner and me, as we were committed to shared parenting. How could we truly share parenting of our newborn if only one us was experiencing those intimate moments of nurturing? Also, I have to confess I was not happy with the thought that I would be up at all hours while my partner luxuriated in a good and full night's sleep. Share the pleasure, share the pain! And so we settled on a very specific division of labour for every daytime and nighttime feed. Our son's belly button became the dividing line between our respective tasks. I would deal with belly button up requirements (feeding), and my partner would deal with belly button down requirements (diaper-changing). Since both were needed at every feed, both of us were involved in our baby's care 24 hours a day.

Those special moments when it's early morning, the world is quiet, your baby is clean, well-fed, and drifting off to sleep in your arms, and you feel there could be no greater happiness—are part of how we both remember our son's babyhood. We were all there together, all the time. Yes, there was still a semblance of a gendered division of tasks in that I was the only one who ever breastfed our baby. But there was also gender-neutrality in the sense that we each had hands-on responsibility for our baby's care 24/7. This shared responsibility created an equality in the care of our baby that also meant our son was equally comfortable being cared for by either one of us. That our son's earliest experiences are of receiving the necessities of life from both his father and his mother equally means a lot to both of us.

How we personally negotiate the place of gender in the shaping of our every day/every night activities is a key aspect of gender politics. Is there a situation in your own experience in which you have tried to challenge gendered norms and forge more equitable relationships and daily practices between yourself and the 'other sex' (be they siblings, partners, or classmates)?

How would you do 'shared parenting'? Would it be the same as a 'gender-neutral' division of care? How else might gender-neutral baby care be organized?

'sharing' to avoid household conflict. These are the complex *gender strategies* (Hochschild 1989) that couples employ whereby sustained beliefs about fairly shared divisions of domestic labour impede progress towards any substantial change.

It is noteworthy, too, that 'doing gender' can include the very decision to have children or not. Being a mother is often very much tied up with traditional notions about womanhood. But women (and men) who choose not to or who cannot have children highlight alternative ways to 'do gender'. Other women may 'do gender' differently by becoming mothers in alternative contexts—through lesbian relationships, collective parenting arrangements, adoption, or intentional single parenthood.

WHY DO DIFFERENCES MATTER?

In examining gender differences in paid and unpaid work, as well as how ethnicity and class intersect with gender, the question of 'Why does this matter?' can often arise. Indeed, the question is invariably asked by at least one student each year when we teach the sociology of gender: *what difference does it make that women do most of the unpaid work in society?* What do women want with men? Is it equality? Is it sameness? These are vexing issues for people who study domestic life and unpaid work, because equality is difficult to define in spaces where people conduct their everyday lives. We urge you to discuss these issues with your friends and classmates, as well as with your parents and even grandparents, because there are both individual and generational differences (as well as differences in terms of class, ethnicity, and culture) around these issues.

These are not new dilemmas. Issues of equality and difference have, in fact, run through feminist theory for centuries, going back perhaps most notably to one of the first full-length books advocating women's equality with men, Mary Wollstonecraft's *Vindication of the Rights of Woman* (Wollstonecraft 1992 [1792]). In the past few decades, equality and difference have constantly interspersed, both politically and theoretically. They recurred, for example, throughout the 1970s with debates in the United States over the Equal Rights Amendment, in the 1980s with the publication of Carol Gilligan's *In a Different Voice* (1982), and then through the late 1980s and the1990s with Italian, Dutch, and French feminists pulling out complex strands of variations in the thinking around equality and differences (Bock and James 1992; Bono and Kemp 1991; Cavarero 1993). There have been no simple or neat answers in this theoretical debate or to the dilemmas raised. The theoretical and political conversation has nevertheless persisted, because it builds on ongoing debates over whether and how women and men are different or the same, the interplay between the social and the embodied, and how equality might be achieved in spite of or through the incorporation of differences.

Gender differences in paid and unpaid work:
What difference does difference make?

One way of exploring the question 'What difference does it make?' in paid and unpaid work is to link claims for equality with differences and disadvantages. Drawing particularly on the work of feminist legal scholar Deborah Rhode, it is clear that the issue of concern is not difference per se but rather 'the disadvantages that follow from it' (Rhode 1990, 204). As phrased by Rhode: 'The critical issue should not be difference, *but the difference difference makes*' (Rhode 1989, 313, emphasis added). What difference *does* difference make? We would argue that it matters in several ways. First, it matters that women do most of the unpaid work and caring. Ample scholarship has highlighted the economic, social, political, and personal costs to women of the gender imbalance in the 'costs of caring' (Folbre 1994; 2001; Ruddick 1995) for the very young, the very old, the sick, and the disabled in all societies. American journalist Ann Crittenden describes the gender disparity in care and the costs to women particularly well in her bestselling book *The Price of Motherhood: Why the Most Important Job in the World is Still the Least Valued.* She writes:

> The entire society benefits from well-raised children, without sharing more than a fraction of the costs of producing them. And that free ride on female labor is enforced by every major institution, starting with the workplace. (2001, 86)

In addition to this 'free ride' of unpaid labour that society reaps from women, weighting the balance of unpaid labour on the side of women has been very costly in terms of paid work opportunities for many women (Bianchi et al. 2000; Cohen 2004). These costs can include occupational downgrading; loss of earnings, pensions, and benefits; economic vulnerability in cases of divorce; and long-term poverty for women (Arber and Ginn 2004; James, Edwards, and Wong 2003).

It is also important to point out that gender differences in unpaid work can also make a difference to men. The losses for men as a result of not being involved with their children have received much attention in the 1990s and 2000s, but the attention actually goes back to several feminist 'classics', perhaps most notably Dorothy Dinnerstein's *The Mermaid and the Minotaur* (1977) and Nancy Chodorow's *The Reproduction of Mothering* (1978). Dinnerstein, for example, outlined the fundamental imbalances that occur in a society when *one* gender does the metaphoric 'rocking of the cradle' while the *other* gender 'rules the world'. She argued that the 'division of responsibility, opportunity, and privilege that prevails between male and female humans, and the patterns of psychological interdependence that are implicit in this division . . . stems from a core fact that has so far been universal: the fact of primary female responsibility for the care of infants and young children' (Dinnerstein 1977, 4). Meanwhile, Chodorow's oft-cited work on mothering, written 30 years ago, pointed to the losses for men and for society that female-dominated parenting engendered: 'the very fact of being mothered by a woman generates in men conflicts over masculinity, a psychology of male dominance, and a need to be superior to women' (Chodorow 1978, 214). A few years later, in 1983, feminist philosopher Sara Ruddick argued that men's greater participation in the daily dramas of care would create revolutionary change in society as well as in social conscience. She wrote: 'It is now argued that the most revolutionary change we can make in the institution of motherhood is to include men in every aspect of child care. . . . Again and again, family power dramas are repeated in psychic, interpersonal, and professional dramas, while they are institutionalized in economic, political, and international life. Radically recasting the power-gender roles in these dramas might just revolutionize social conscience' (Ruddick 1983, 89).

While feminists have been calling for men's involvement in housework, child care, and informal caring partly to ease the gendered costs of caring and as one of the routes towards greater gender equality, men have also been busy documenting the personal and relational losses that they incur from not being fully involved in caring. Most of these claims are found in the burgeoning literature on fatherhood, which has drawn attention to the costs of stress and work–family conflict, the burden of being breadwinners, and the lack of opportunities to develop close emotional and relational attachments for men who are distant or absent fathers (Bumpus, Crouter, and McHale 1999; Milkie and Peltola 1999; Pruett 2000). Alternatively, scholars have pointed to the important generative effects for fathers who are highly involved with their children (Hawkins et al. 1993; Hawkins and Dollahite 1996; Snarey 1993). As well summarized in a recent Canadian overview of fathering research, '[i]t is clear from the research that father involvement has enormous implications for men on their own path of adult development, for their wives and partners in the co-parenting relationship and, most importantly, for their children in terms of social, emotional and cognitive development' (Allen and Daly 2002).

A third point about the difference that difference makes is that these differences have to be widened to ask: *which* women and *which* men are disadvantaged? Aboriginal men and men of ethnic minorities, particularly recent immigrants, are disadvantaged in paid work in comparison to males and females who are white and middle-class. Yet Aboriginal women and ethnic minority women are doubly disadvantaged because they face inequalities in the labour market while still taking on extra shifts of unpaid work.

CONCLUSION

What do you think families and households will look like in 10 years time? In 20 years? This is something that we would encourage you to discuss in your classroom, in your tutorials, and with your friends and parents. In concluding this chapter, we would like to highlight some key issues that will demand academic and policy attention in the years ahead.

Men as carers within families

While men continue to do less child care and elder care than women do, there has been dramatic change in the past 30 years with regard to men's involvement in household life and labour. One indication of this change is the gradual increase in the numbers of stay-at-home fathers—25 per cent over the past 10 years in Canada, while the number of stay-at-home mothers has decreased by approximately the same figure (Statistics Canada 2002). Today, Canadian fathers account for about 10 per cent of all stay-at-home parents. Meanwhile, the number of families with stay-at-home mothers has declined over recent decades as single-earner, two-parent families have become less common. Single-father households have also consistently been on the rise. In 2002, there were approximately 96,000 male lone-parents in Canada—16 per cent of all lone-parents—compared to approximately 480,000 female lone-parents (Statistics Canada 2002). Joint-custody decisions by courts have also been rapidly rising, up from 10 per cent of all decisions in 1986 to 62 per cent in 2002 (Statistics Canada 2003a). This translates into at least some degree of shared parenting between women and men.

With changing gender ideologies, there is a steadily increasing expectation on the part of women that men will be involved fathers. This expectation combines with changing state and employment policies that accept and even encourage active fathering, as well as a rise in programs specifically directed to fathers by community organizations across Canada. Our view is that fathering will likely continue to become a greater part of men's identities. And our hope is that personal preference and inclination, rather than gender, will be key factors motivating women and men in their decisions about how they will juggle their adult responsibilities as carers and as workers.

Women as earners

During the past 40 years, there has been a significant increase in women's and men's employment in industrialized countries. The tensions and stresses that can pose for women can be overwhelming. In the past few years, much media attention has focused on the varied challenges mothers face in balancing paid work and child care. A recurring story in these debates has been the mommy 'opt-out', which, as reported in *The New York Times Magazine* (Belkin 2003), *Time* magazine (Wallis 2004), and *The Globe and Mail* (Pearce 2006), refers to how North American mothers—especially older, highly educated new mothers—are increasingly 'opting out' of employment when they have children. Against these front-page news stories, however, is an alternative social narrative about mothers 'opting in' based on long-term data on mothers' employment in both the United States and Canada (Cootnz 2006; Bouchey 2005). Recent data indicate that women are now primary breadwinners in nearly one-third of Canadian dual-earner families (Sussman and Bonnell 2006).

The gains achieved by feminism, combined with social trends, changing attitudes, and labour market projections, strongly suggest that we will not witness a reversion to the Parsonian model of complementary gender roles within the household and workplace. Mothers of young children will continue to enter the labour market, and dual-earner households will continue to strike a difficult balance between work and home responsibilities. Increasingly, women may choose to have only one child or not to have children at all, which makes the issue of balancing paid and unpaid work somewhat more manageable.

Of course, not all women in the workforce are mothers. Employers place increasing demands on such women to work after-hours and on holidays when unpaid work demands are high for women with children. This shift in effect simply downloads responsibility for child care and household work onto women who do not have these responsibilities.

Balancing paid and unpaid work

The issues involved in challenging work and family will remain compelling for Canadian policy-makers, scholars, and families. At a conceptual level, one central issue is the place of paid work in the lives of men and women and the balance that must be struck between home and work so that men, women, and children may reap the benefits. Should continuous full-time employment with career advancement as first priority be the norm for men and women for '48 hours for 48 weeks of 48 years'? (Coote, Harman, and Hewitt 1990, 49). Or should work be restructured so that employment careers can be successfully pursued along different pathways? At the empirical level, we need more research into the kinds of working conditions that would help men and women to continue to lead lives that are productive and valuable for society while at the same time allowing them to do the caring work that society equally needs. Such research would entail examining such working conditions as job sharing, career breaks, and flexible working hours.

For most scholars who write about work and family life, there is no doubt that our society needs quality services for children to attend while parents are at work or engaged in other activities. Yet institutional child care cannot be seen as the only solution to the totality of society's child care dilemma. There are, for example, several groups of children whose needs may not best be met by institutional child care. These groups include children with disabilities or special needs, infants, sick children, and school-aged children after school hours. As well, households have differing perceptions and values with regard to appropriate child care arrangements and may want part-time or more flexible arrangements.

In addition to the provision of some level of publicly provided child care, there are two general approaches as to how society's overall child care needs may be met. The first approach entails paying others to perform domestic services such as child care and housework. Parallel to the rise in women's employment in industrialized countries has been a significant increase in the number of nannies, mother's helpers, domestic helpers, and childminders working for middle- or upper-middle-class families with ample economic resources to employ lesser-paid women to perform these tasks (Bakan and Stasiulis 1997; Coltrane 2003; Stasiulis and Bakan 2003). Paying others to perform domestic services such as child care and housework ultimately means passing on women's traditional domain from one group of women to another, thus hardening the boundaries that exist around gender and caring. The end result is that work and homemaking remain as devalued 'women's work', with an ever-broadening lower tier of women paid meagre wages to perform a 'modified housewife' role while other women do work that is more socially 'valuable'. As eloquently phrased by one author, this model seems to trap us into 'endlessly remaking the world in the same image: some people in the public sphere, the world of power, of importance, and some people in the private sphere, rocking the cradle but never really ruling the world' (Rothman 1989).

The second approach to child care, which promises to supersede the problem discussed above, entails a reformulation of gender roles so that both men and women are able to share in child care and housework. A combination of institutional services and support for men's and women's participation in the domestic sphere would allow both men and women to strike a better balance between the demands of their home and work lives. Moreover, there would be an implicit recognition that 'caring' work is important to individuals, communities, and the re-creation of caring societies.

The future of families and households

There is no doubt that family lives in Canada are changing. Looking back to our parents and grandparents and forward through the lives of our children, it is clear that the lives that women and men inhabit together or separately, with others or on their own, vary with each passing generation in their form as well as in the norms that judge them. Your own family formation will likely be completely different from that of your grandparents and parents. Over the course of your own lifetime, many of you will do one or many of the following: cohabit, marry, separate, divorce, parent one or more children with a partner or on your own, or choose not to have children. All of your own decisions about the ways in which you organize your family life will be affected, in turn, by larger processes, both local and global. These processes include rising labour force participation by women, increasing participation by men in the domestic sphere, families with fewer or no children, as well as the institutional and social challenges posed by an aging society.

Families continue to change and evolve, and multiple family forms now exist as choices for Canadian women and men. These new forms, which American sociologist Judith Stacey has named the 'postmodern family', include single-parent families (both single-father and single-mother families), blended families, two-household families with joint custody of children, cohabiting couples, lesbian and gay families, stay-at-home father families, and varied kinds of two-income families (Stacey 1990). This movement towards what David Cheal has called a 'convergence to diversity' and the 'destandardisation of the family' (Cheal 1991) exists in parallel with non-standard employment models. This evolving diversity, complexity, and plurality in both paid and unpaid work will continue to pose exciting theoretical and methodological challenges to sociologists engaged in the study of work and family life (Cheal 1991; 1999; Lewis 2003).

According to a recent book, *Canada's Changing Families*, edited by McQuillan and Ravenera (2006), the most significant trends that have dramatically affected Canadian families in the early years of this new millennium are: high rates of separation and divorce; smaller families and declining fertility; the increased popularity of alternative family arrangements such as cohabitation; the increasing involvement of women in full-time paid labour; and global and local changes occurring in the economy and the larger society, which have brought new pressures to bear on families.

While all of these changes are occurring, it is always important to note how they are experienced by, and their impact on, different groups of Canadians. Disadvantages continue to exist for immigrant women as well as for Aboriginal women in Canada. For example, labour force activity varies greatly by Aboriginal status; recent research highlights how registered Indians are more likely to be unemployed than other Aboriginals and non-Aboriginals as a result of lower educational attainment, child rearing responsibilities, and lone parenthood (White, Gyimah, and Maxim 2003). As we have emphasized throughout this book, as sociologists we always need to ask questions about the families we are studying: *Which* women are we talking about? *Which* men? In what socio-economic and ideological conditions? In what part of Canada and in what historical time frame? With what desires, options, opportunities, and constraints?

Research Questions

1. Look at the division of labour in your own home and in your parents (or guardian's) home. What did/does the work consist of? Who did/does what and why? What tasks were/are fought over, and what tasks were/are decided upon easily? Was/is the division of labour gender-divided? If so, have you ever thought what would have to be

done to change it? If there was/is an unequal division of labour, what are the notice-able consequences of this? What difference does difference make?

2. Conduct an exercise in 'participant observation' in your community: Look around your community, and notice the division of child care all around you. Look into coffee shop windows, walk in parks and by schoolyards. Who is caring for the children? Are they alone or with others? Is it nannies? Mothers? Fathers? Child care workers? What stands out for you? If you notice fathers with their children, how old are the children? Might he be on parental leave? Or is he a stay-at-home father? What is he doing with the child/children? Is he conversing with other parents or standing on the sidelines? What kind of jobs do men and women have in your community? How is the care of children done? By men? By women? By daycare workers? By nannies? By grand-parents? What are your reflections? Locate yourself in your thinking: is this a new line of thinking for you, or are you engaged in care work yourself, and thus do you con-stantly think about these issues?

Discussion Questions

1. Look back to the generations of your parents and grandparents, and reflect on how they structured their paid and unpaid work. What challenges and opportunities did women and men face? How was paid and unpaid work structured by gender, eth-nicity, and class?
2. Why is the standard employment model often considered to be a 'male' work model?
3. What types of unpaid work do you engage in? Do you consider them to be 'work'? Why or why not?
4. Why do scholars consider it important that men take on a fair share of society's unpaid work?

Further Reading

Bezanson, Kathryn, Meg Luxton, and Katherine Side, eds. 2004. 'Never done: The challenge of unpaid work', *Atlantis: A Women's Studies Journal*, 28, 2. Addresses a range of key issues on the politics of paid and unpaid work.

Doucet, Andrea. 2006. *Do Men Mother? Fathering, Care, and Domestic Responsibility*. Toronto: University of Toronto Press. Involves an extensive qualitative research pro-ject with more than 100 Canadian fathers who are primary caregivers and explores issues of men and masculinities, space and embodiment, and the intricacies of gen-der relations in everyday life.

Luxton, Meg, and June Corman. 2001. *Getting by in Hard Times: Gendered Labour at Home and on the Job*. Toronto: University of Toronto Press. Examines how the extensive polit-ical and economic changes of the 1980s and 1990s—globalization, economic restruc-turing, cutbacks, and layoffs—affected the lives of white working-class families in Canada.

Vosko, Leah. 2000. *Temporary Work: The Gendered Rise of a Precarious Employment Rela-tionship*. Toronto: University of Toronto Press. Addresses gender relations, temporary employment in Canada, and changing employment relations in a global context.

Films

9 to 5. 1980. A film revolutionary for its time, touches on issues such as sexual harassment, gender discrimination, and the difficulties faced by mothers working for pay.

Rock n Roll Mamas. September 2007 release. Exploration of what it means to be a mother struggling to maintain a creative identity.

The Motherhood Manifesto. 2006. Produced and distributed by momsrising.org, analyzes America's 'crisis of caring' but also relevant to Canadian families.

Black Mother, Black Daughter. 1989. National Film Board of Canada documentary that explores the lives of several generations of black women in Nova Scotia, including their contributions to home, church, and community.

Websites

www.fira.ca
Canadian project focused on understanding and supporting diverse groups of fathers in Canada.

www.mothersarewomen.com
Canadian organization of feminist mothers.

www.genderwork.ca
Gender and Work Database at York University, Toronto.

www.familypride.org
Working to secure equality for GLBT families.

Chapter 5

Making Change: Gender, Careers, and Citizenship

Another world is not only possible, she is on her way.
On a quiet day, if I listen very carefully, I can hear her breathing.[1]

Chapter Objectives

1. To illustrate how social contexts shape careers in complex ways, including gendering and racializing career paths.
2. To consider gender as performative in women's work lives.
3. To introduce globalized production as a key force in shaping gender inequalities.
4. To explain why citizenship is an integral component of understanding employment practices and career paths equitably.
5. To depict career equity concerns from an intersectional perspective.
6. To present and evaluate solutions to gender inequality in the social organization of work.

INTRODUCTION

Melca Salvador travelled from the Philippines to Canada in 1995 to clean house for and look after the children of a Canadian mother. Salvador was admitted to Canada under specific conditions defined by the Live-In Caregiver Program (LICP), which allowed her to work here but denied her eligibility for citizenship before she had completed her first two-year contract. Although Salvador had not realized it at the time, she was pregnant when she got here, which meant that her son was born with Canadian citizenship. Her employer fired her for being pregnant, and this prevented her from fulfilling the program's 24-month work criterion for staying in Canada (Hwang 2003). She faced an impossible choice. The impoverishment of her home country made the life chances for her son very limited there; alternatively, Salvador would have to leave her son with strangers if he were to stay in Canada and she were to follow the immigration laws and leave.

Both Salvador and her employer are making choices structured by social constructions of race and gender. The responsibilities of cleaning houses and looking after children are designated as feminine. Because it is feminized work, the performance of these duties is devalued to the extent that well-educated Canadian women often find more profitable things to do with their time than to directly look after a household. Abigail Bakan and Daiva Stasiulis's research on domestic workers in Canada shows that it is usually a woman of the household who oversees the work of the domestic worker (1995). The inequality of economic and social opportunities experienced by women with different citizenship status finds expression in many domestic labour contexts as a direct power relation between the women. This example illustrates the complexities of the process of developing gender solidarity. The more powerful woman in the household could participate fully in the exploitation of the less power-ful hired woman, the women could unite their voices in challenging the devaluing of care-giving work, one could support the other in challenging racially constructed immigration laws, or, most likely, they could negotiate a complex and personal com-bination of responses. Understanding the commonalities between them as women and workers, as well as their differences as Canadian citizen and imported temporary worker from the Philippines, is an essential first step if an inclusive politics of gender liberation is going to be possible.

Ironically, Salvador's situation was created by a Canadian society that imagines itself to be organized locally and democratically, but when a woman is placed in a sit-uation where she must choose between having a job to support herself, obeying the law, and seeing her child grow up, we need to examine and question the regulations and processes that produce such an impossible choice. We must also examine the advantages, freedoms, and opportunities that Salvador's situation offers to her female employer. What are the implications of such inequalities between women for gender politics? Are political solidarities possible across such divides? As we take a closer look at women's work lives in Canada throughout this chapter, you will come to realize that gender inequalities and injustices in the work lives of Canadians are frequently linked to such profound distortions of human organization that the scope of the problem is a global one and the solutions must work through all levels of social organ-ization, from households to international relations. Following chapter 4, which explored issues of work and family strategies for Canadian women and men, this chapter widens that discussion to look at the intricacies of gender inequalities between and within genders as well as the wider global structuring of the choices, opportuni-ties, and conflicts faced by both genders in contemporary Canadian society.

Despite the advancement of claims to equality of opportunity on the basis of race, gender, class, and other markers of difference, the work lives of Canadians are deeply stratified and becoming more so for certain segments of the population. 'Strat-ified' means that the population is divided into layers or strata by a complex series of social and economic structures that bestow advantages and disadvantages on groups within the population. The opening example illustrates the significant disadvantages experienced by women working in the LICP. As detailed in chapter 4, those disad-vantages are shaped by social structures that assign child care responsibilities to women and a culture that devalues the work of caregiving. You will read later how racist immigration policies in Canada restrict the freedoms and opportunities of women from some countries. Sociological analysis of the social structures, policies, and personal relations that created Melca Salvador's impossible decision reveals a hierarchy structured by gender, race, country of origin, citizenship and immigration status. The construction of this hierarchy is a power-based process whereby work done by men becomes most valuable because it is done by men, work done by white women is moderately devalued (as is the work of Third World men), and the work of Third World women tends to be even more deeply devalued.

Women's career paths are shaped by processes of identity formation, by gendered contexts of what is valued and how social responsibilities are understood, by racialized and gendered policy constructions, and by an economic climate of neoliberal globalization. If you think that the work world is now characterized by much greater equality of opportunity than was experienced by your own mother, grandmother, and great-grandmother, that may or may not be true depending on the economic, educational, and ethnic backgrounds of that chain of women antecedents. This chapter confirms, as pointed out in chapter 1, that there are areas of social and political life in which women are still 'invisible, absent, and devalued' and further highlights how this occurs specifically as a result of the policies and institutions of the Canadian state.

The chapter begins with a consideration of how caring as a gender order affects the social patterns of work in Canada. It is evident when we look at who does what forms of work that there are intersecting hierarchies, one of which devalues caring work, another that ranks men over women, and a third that values whites over non-whites. We then move on to consider the social constructions of these hierarchies as manifested in the employment patterns of women in the academic workforce, in nursing, in law, and in 'non-traditional' jobs. These patterns indicate the need for an intersectional analysis. Third, we address the gendered consequences of globalization. The emphasis is on the ways that colonization, immigration, and citizenship have shaped not just the work patterns of the least advantaged women in Canada but also their geographic locations and family lives.

Fourth, and finally, we consider routes to improvement. The most powerful sociological traditions are those that move beyond analyzing problems to create visions of a better society and theorize processes for fulfilling such visions. It was certainly the intention of many Canadian feminist theorists, who looked at issues of women and work, to help create practical changes. So we outline and assess the strategies and processes for overcoming the hierarchies and inequalities of the deeply stratified work world of Canada today. Such goals for gender equality are part of a broader context of struggles for liberation, self-definition, sustainability, and global justice.

CARING AS A GENDER ORDER

As described in chapter 1, first-shift theories of gender inequality gave considerable attention to the linkages between gender roles and work roles. These insights, however, also laid important groundwork for challenging 'malestream' perspectives on what was defined and characterized as work and for addressing the issue of career inequalities between women as well as between women and men.

More recent analyses continue to note that the gender stratification of employment remains a compelling subject for analysis. The gender gap in the numbers of women in employment compared to men has been closing, but there are other factors to consider. As outlined in chapter 4, most women in Canada work for pay for at least part of their lives. The women most likely to be paid workers are those aged 25 to 44, among whom 77 per cent were employed in 2006, but 65 per cent of those aged 45 to 54 are also employed (Statistics Canada 2007, table 282-0002). This is a somewhat smaller proportion than that of men. Data from 2006 show that 87 per cent of 25- to 44-year-old men and 85 per cent of 45- to 54-year-old men worked for pay. The figure drops to 63 per cent for men aged 55 to 64, presumably because many of them take retirement in those years (Statistics Canada Labour Force Survey 2006). In case this seems unremarkable to you, consider that Canadian women's participation rate in the paid economy was roughly 23.5 per cent between 1946 and 1955, but only 11 per cent of them were married (in 1951). Marriage gradually became less of a factor, and by 1961, 22 per cent of married women were participating in paid labour (Porter 2003, 38, 60). Meanwhile, 84 per cent of men (and 90 per cent of married men) were in the paid labour force in 1951, dropping to 78 per cent of all men and 87 per cent of married men in 1961. You can see that gender no longer determines who works for pay to the same extent that it once did, but within the workforce, employment segregations persist.

Gender is one of the factors shaping what jobs most people hold, and recent statistics suggest that caring persists as a gender order. For example, in 2004, 87 per cent of nurses and health-related therapists were female, while 55 per cent of doctors and dentists were (Lindsay and Almey 2006, 13). Doctors and dentists are situated in more profitable, authoritative, and autonomous brackets within the health care field, and this pattern echoes the overall exclusion of women from top jobs (Clement, Myles, and Lochhead 1994; Krahn, Lowe, and Hughes 2006). More broadly, 75 per cent of all clerks and administrators were women, and while only 30 per cent of men were teachers, nurses, health practitioners, clerks, administrators, salespeople, or service workers, 67 per cent of employed women in Canada worked in these traditionally female occupations (Lindsay and Almey 2006, 13). These outcomes can be seen as connected to parenting practices, education processes, media presentations, government policies, and religious doctrines that continue to create gender roles and label caregiving as feminine.

While individuals do not necessarily embrace such traditional socialization patterns, systemic barriers alongside processes of reward and rejection help to perpetuate these differences and inequalities. Many widespread assumptions and processes can be included within the analytic category of 'systemic barriers'. Sometimes they consist of written rules that literally block women's access, such as restrictions that once kept women from attending university, married women from working for pay, or First Nations people from being able to hold government offices. Other systemic barriers consist of a series of assumptions with accompanying lack of services, such as the combination of the notion that girls are delicate and a lack of female dressing rooms, which kept girls off hockey rinks for many years.

What about your own thinking: can you imagine a brother making a living as a professional athlete more easily than you can a sister? Do you have any qualms about seeing a male teacher working with very young students? Who or what formed those gender assumptions in your thinking? Did or do you babysit to earn some spending money? What about your friends—male versus female? You have choices about how you think of gender and employment, but thinking freely is probably also going to bring you to interesting and possibly challenging encounters with social structures.

Perhaps the most troublesome structural barrier for women attempting to move into higher-paid and time-demanding careers is the persistent lack of regulated child care in Canada. This issue has been the focus of a great deal of activist women's effort and agitation since at least the 1980s. Nevertheless, while the passage of a national child care bill had considerable momentum at three separate times in the 1980s and 1990s, there has been little change in Canada's weak child care system. In 2002, only 10 per cent of the children of Canada's working parents were in regulated care (Hamilton 2005, 58). By itself, that situation would not create a gendering of employment income, but within the reality that men have the opportunity to earn higher wages in their working hours than women do, women in most heterosexual families put their careers on hold or treat them as secondary during the early child-rearing years. Studying the social construction of gender in employment adds clarity to that wage inequality. Over recent years, the province of Quebec has developed a high-quality, affordable child care program, so it will be interesting to see whether it helps over time to balance career progress between the genders in that province relative to the other provinces.

Although 70 per cent of women in Canada still work in traditionally 'feminine' career areas and men still predominate in other fields (many of which involve superior financial rewards), this pattern is not static. It is continually being reconstituted in slightly differing ways. In the upcoming section on traditional solutions to gender inequality, we will discuss how one set of structural barriers to gender integration in employment was addressed through policy in the 1970s, only to be replaced by new economic and political constructions. Jane Gaskell has directed our attention to the gendered ways in which skill is recognized or denied. She answered the 'chicken-or-egg' question of whether jobs were lower-paid because women held them or whether women rather than men held certain jobs because they paid less (1986). Her examples of 'skilled trade' workers versus clerical workers demonstrated that there is a power struggle over what is defined as a skill. Historically, men have used their power more successfully to limit competition for their jobs and keep the pay rate higher (Gaskell 1986). Current examples of devalued 'feminine' skills can be found now in the high-tech sector. The emotional labour necessary for soothing irate customers over the telephone and sufficiently allaying dissatisfaction to hold on to a sale (all within a strictly limited time frame) requires highly developed skills involving voice intonation, patience, reframing, and other sophisticated communication strategies that must be deployed by the employee in an instantaneous and spontaneous manner (Buchanan 2006, 189–93). Production of the computer software that organizes on-screen information about the product being sold and assists in the processing of orders is also highly skilled work, requiring great attention to detail and knowledge of computer programming. Programming work frequently involves time pressures, but as work that is gendered 'masculine', it is usually done in a more comfortable environment than a call centre,[2] the remuneration is much higher, there is more personal freedom at work, and the job has greater prestige. Attempting to understand how these gendered evaluations of job skills occur and, by implication, how they could be adjusted to better reflect work's value reveals the limits of gender order theories and pushes our inquiry to how ability is a socially defined construct.

SOCIAL CONSTRUCTION OF GENDERED EMPLOYMENT

Many social forces contribute to the creation of a gendered division of labour and to valuing work along gendered lines. In this section, we begin with consideration of a few factors in timing and location of work that artificially create distinctions between paid and unpaid work. We then take examples of non-traditional employment to reveal the social and personal structures that help to construct gender categorizations. We briefly address the role of the state, which is often not neutral in this process, and use the example of unemployment insurance programs to see how government institutions have favoured various forms of the breadwinner/homemaker domestic pattern over other domestic arrangements. Then, before shifting towards a look at the gendered consequences of globalization in the next section of the chapter, we note that when we consider ethnicity and citizenship as well, other significant hierarchies in the economic and social value of work are revealed.

Beyond the gender order that designates caring as a feminine characteristic, there are entrenched social patterns and legal supports that in combination sustain and recreate the gender divisions of employment in Canada. Some of the persistent inequalities experienced even by women in elite positions are inequalities that arise from the social contexts in which these positions are embedded. One of the most salient features of the social context that results in the gendering of careers is the persistent and increasingly false assumption that households consist of a male breadwinner married to a female homemaker. While there has been a slow dismantling of these normative assumptions of women as caregivers and men as breadwinners, it still holds ideological weight. As demonstrated in the discussion of stay-at-home fathers in chapter 4, men still feel pressure to be earning, even in households where women are primary or sole breadwinners. Women, conversely, still feel pressured to take on a disproportionate amount of unpaid care work, even when they are working full-time for pay.

Have you ever wondered why so many jobs are organized around an employee having to arrive at a particular place at a particular time and to remain there over an extended period of time even though such demands no longer make sense in terms of better accomplishing the tasks that need to be done? Why, for example, are school days for elementary children socially constructed to end more than an hour before the average workday? A presumed separation between home life and work life still characterizes most work environments (except for self-employment, which is becoming increasingly common). A greater degree of flexibility about work hours would make it easier for parents to share household and parenting responsibilities, avoid time wasted in traffic, and have time with their families without in any way lessening the quality or quantity of paid work accomplished. Other feminist suggestions point out that parents of young children would be less stressed (and therefore more productive) if there were child care facilities on-site at their workplaces and they were given the opportunity to check on their children throughout the workday.

A combination of ideology and social policy constructs gendered employment. The gendered division of work not only categorizes tasks 'masculine' or 'feminine', it also fits jobs into a hierarchal structure in which greater value is attributed to the masculine than to the feminine. Sociologists refer to this as a pattern of vertical gender segregation—the pattern that jobs numerically dominated by women tend to be jobs of lower status and reward than those dominated by men (Krahn, Lowe, and Hughes 2006, 190). Since the distinction between 'male' jobs and 'female' jobs is a social construction subject to change over time, women have often wanted to do 'male' jobs, and we can even find cases of men wanting to do so-called 'women's' jobs. 'Non-traditional'[3] jobs often offer higher pay to women and greater job satisfaction to men than jobs considered appropriate for their gender, but the individuals involved have to deal with a number of challenges focused on gender. Examples of women in non-traditional occupations show the persistence of the gender division of labour and the various mechanisms that enforce the division.

Persistence of gender in 'non-traditional' occupations

Academia offers emblematic examples of the still-persistent links between gender, employment, and domestic life. The presence of a small, elite group of women in organizations such as universities, medical practices, and law firms has led to a fairly widespread perception that gender equality has been achieved in many such fields. Yet a closer look at the career patterns of even the most educated and elite reveals ongoing gender inequalities in who is employed where, with what sorts of rewards and returns, and with what possibilities of advancement.

One of the prolonged patterns in elite professions is the persistent impact of child rearing on career advancement for women but not for men. Reaching the top levels of most professions requires uninterrupted, long-term dedication that includes availability for and willingness to work beyond a 40-hour workweek. Women who stop working for pay even briefly and early in their careers to focus on parenting often find that they never reach the top ranks of their profession because of that work interruption. Women still constitute less than 30 per cent of the members of the academy of university teachers in Canada and remain concentrated in the lower ranks of the profession. Whereas the majority of part-time professors in Canada are women, they comprise only 18 per cent of the number of full professors (CAUT 2006, 1–2). Carmen Armenti found that for women professors, 'the very act of having pretenure children was seen as an obstacle to their career progression' (2004, 12). Women professors with young children do have less time for research and writing because of the time demands of child raising, but the same is not true of parenting male professors, who usually have more opportunity to put career priorities ahead of parenting responsibilities (Armenti 2004, 8, 13).

Other barriers to women's full participation and advancement are the internal structures that characterize the profession. Not only do the work schedules of academics (like those of many other professions) assume the professor's availability for workweeks of more than 60 hours (denying 'normal' amounts of time for family life and caregiving), but embracing some aspects of academic life, such as attending conferences, requires the ability to escape household responsibilities for several consecutive days. Gender issues are embedded in the accounting systems of academic accomplishment. The old adage that to get ahead, women must be seen to work twice as hard as men still seems to have some relevance when it comes to dossiers for promotion and tenure (see Cummins 2005).

The methods of research, the ways of knowing, and the topics of study in most academic fields have also been characterized by gendered and racial exclusions. Changes involving the inclusion of women-centred topics and women's ways of knowing were and still are resisted by some members of the academy. The same is true of understandings based on ethnic difference (see especially Patricia Hill Collins and Elizabeth Spellman). Entire departments as well as individual projects focused on women have often been underfunded and discredited simply because their terrain was new and feminine. In a profession that is supposed to value new ideas, insights, and information as contributions, the contributions originating in feminine and ethnic minority perspectives were devalued primarily because they were new. Topics centred on women's lives were accepted as scholarly when Mary Ellen did her master's and doctoral research at Carleton and the University of Alberta in the late 1990s, but even then there were variations from one department and university to the next in the extent of openness to gender-focused analysis. During the same period, women's studies scholars at one Canadian undergraduate university tried to have the creation of a women's studies program approved. But even though the university offered women's studies courses in two divisions and seven departments, the scholars were unable to establish an independently funded women's studies program. Since there was precedent for the creation of programs smaller than this one, many scholars believed that the main obstacle was the fact that some of the people with decision-making power still did not value research and study emphasizing women as much as they valued other themes. A female colleague, now retired, who coordinated development of the women's studies program, had seen comparable episodes before. She recalled watching a doctoral-level classmate during the 1970s being required to assemble significantly more data than other doctoral students simply because her thesis topic focused on the lives of women. This is what a gender hierarchy in what is valued means: work culturally associated with men and masculinity is still sometimes treated as more important and valuable than work associated with women and femininity, although there is no real logic to that process of evaluation.

Barbara Bagilhole (2002) describes experiences such as glass ceilings (or invisible barriers to advancement through the ranks of the profession), pressures to be more qualified than male colleagues in order to get the same or lesser opportunities, and sexual harassment as 'dynamics of exclusion and marginalization' (2002, 6). She classifies university teaching and scholarship as a non-traditional profession for women, and the experiences described above characterize the work lives of many women in non-traditional professions.

Studies of other non-traditional occupations also reveal exclusion, marginalization, and intransigently patriarchal work cultures. A workplace culture is created by the patterns of interaction among people in that workplace, along with the built environment or physical contexts within which the work is performed. Some examples of the classic work culture that made women feel they were entering patriarchal space,

Mary Ellen Connects with the Social Construction of Male Privilege in Non-Traditional Occupations

I wonder as you read this whether your experience as a university student has meant being empowered and whether it has included being degraded or oppressed. I work in an excellent department in which the majority of the sociology professors understand the importance of feminism and seek to improve or restore the self-confidence of the students. That does not mean that our students escape the larger context, which is hostile. A class of 26 students that I am teaching as I write the first draft of this chapter includes a young woman who is coping with the immediate effects of a severe case of sexual harassment and two other female students who suffer from panic attacks for reasons unknown to me. Our campus newspaper in 2006 reported 17 known cases of the use of the 'date rape drug' Rohypnol during the first two and a half months of the year.

While I recognize that this information is frightening, I encourage you not to blame your specific university. Across the country, one in four women experiences a sexual assault while they are university students. This is not a 'chilly climate'; it's a chamber of horrors! With the advent of feminism, most universities offer support services for victims of violence and sometimes even preventive programs. While these are important improvements and allow many strong and determined women to persist and continue their education, it is evident that caring women and men at universities must perpetuate a safer and hospitable climate however they can. At least the number of young women pursuing post-secondary education has been rising, and in our sociology program their number is in proportion to their number in the population. That representative quality breaks down, however, when you look at the number of women from First Nations and visible-minority ethnic populations in Canada.

I can appreciate that the working environment may have been even more toxic and the number of female colleagues in academe even fewer for the generation of women scholars that preceded mine. I am grateful not only for the role models that these women provide but also for the commitment that some of them and a few rare men have shown to building and preserving unions, to developing equity policies, to supporting women's centres, and to fighting for student access to assault services in the community if not right on campus. Many of these struggles are ongoing, so I strive to preserve and perpetuate the place for women alongside men.

Do you know which women are doing this work on your campus? On my current campus, some of the important women's initiatives came from the ideas and energies of undergraduate students. On your campus, as here, there is likely opportunity for you to make your own contribution to educational equity and cultural change.

or space controlled by the men, include pin-up pictures of naked (or near-naked) women, habitual workplace conversations featuring themes of sexual activity, and socializing through highly masculinized sporting events such as football. The consequence of the posters or conversational themes was that some women felt they did not fit in, and some even felt that they were viewed more as objects than as co-workers. Both structural and attitudinal barriers evident historically in accounts of women physicists and foresters, for example, include isolation, exclusion from important networking opportunities, lack of advancement despite demonstrably superior abilities and knowledge (glass ceiling), more direct forms of sex discrimination,[4] sexual harassment, and lack of accommodation for caregiving roles (since professionals are presumed to have a wife, not to be one) (Prentice 1999; Tripp-Knowles 1999). Sometimes female workers are expected to be caregivers in the workplace just because they are female, as Helene Cummins says of her experience as a single childless woman academic (2005, 226–9).

Evidence of positive change must, however, be acknowledged. Livingstone and Luxton (1996) discuss how men's attitudes at the Stelco steelworks in Hamilton started to change after women won the right to be employed there. The association of masculinity and steelworking had a long tradition, and when the first women were employed, reactions were mixed. Yet, as the authors observed, the experience of an integrated workplace often dispelled gendered notions of what were or were not appropriate women's and men's jobs. As one of the male steelworkers said (1996, 126): 'Me, I don't care if it is a man or a woman. Black, white or purple, it don't matter to me, you know. . . . I am not prejudiced about anything.'

Boundary maintenance, or protecting 'our turf'

People's identities can be deeply caught up in a gendered sense of who they are, and who they are as workers is frequently part of this. Sometimes, economic concerns and gender identities seem to congeal into a unified resistance to change.[5] Workers' ability to bargain with employers in an effort to improve working conditions and maintain or increase wages depends on recognition that their labour power and skills are valuable to the employer. Established workers often experience an influx of new workers, whether they be women and/or new immigrants, as a direct threat to their bargaining power. (While many feminists now try to unite oppressed people in opposition to class, gender, and racial threats, an oppositional history among those groupings still must be overcome.) Established workers have used a variety of tactics to maintain the value of their labour by keeping out new workers and maintaining gender boundaries. There were many structural ways of protecting male employment levels, as Janet's research on postal workers and telephonists in the summary below indicates. After human rights legislation forbade outright discrimination in hiring policies, highly masculinized workplace cultures have sometimes perpetuated the exclusion of women at a cultural level.

Established workers have often appealed to public 'common sense'—actually the indoctrination of gendered stereotypes—in order to preserve the gender exclusivity of their workplaces. Men have sometimes forcibly resisted the inclusion of women in workplaces that had been all-male domains and have done so with the support of a

Janet's Research on Gender-Segregated Jobs

I did my PhD research on postal workers and telephonists in London, England. I was interested in these two groups of workers for three main reasons—they held highly gender-segregated jobs, they were organized by the same union, and they had in the past officially negotiated restrictions on where and how women and men could be employed. My field work (144 semi-structured interviews) was conducted shortly after both jobs had been restructured to comply with legislation in the UK against sex discrimination. Prior to that, women could work as postal workers but only as temporary workers—they could not be confirmed as permanent employees, which meant that they never had job security or accumulated seniority. Since everything in the postal job was determined by seniority (what job you got, which holiday times you could have), women were systematically allocated the least desirable routes and vacation weeks. Also, the union and management had agreed to leave a certain proportion of the job complement vacant so that there would always be a pool of jobs for men to apply for. Women on temporary contracts would be fired if the vacancy complement fell below the negotiated level. This has to be one of the few officially negotiated instances of women being used as a 'reserve army of labour'. When the arrangement became illegal, women were granted the right to permanent status, but only from the date that the anti-sex discrimination legislation came into effect. For many women, this meant that many years of service were not recognized. A postwoman took both the union and the management to court and won her case against them—her seniority, and that of other postwomen, was fully recognized. This is an interesting case of a job being identified and protected as a man's job by both the union and management. The gendering of the job had little to do with job skills (since women had always done the exact same job as men) and more to do with protecting men's access to a particular type of work.

The telephonists were similar in that both men and women did exactly the same work but under different conditions. Men could work full-time on nights only. Women could work full-time on days only. Night work was more highly paid, but otherwise the work was identical, and the gender segregation of jobs by shift was a way of reserving the more highly paid work for men.

If you are interested in further details on this study, you can find more information in my book *Locating Gender: Occupational Segregation, Wages, and Domestic Responsibilities*.

Such blatant sex discrimination in the structuring of jobs is seldom seen any more, but there continue to be preferences and practices in the organization of employment that result in gendered jobs and employment conditions. Take, for example, the types of things high-tech employers have introduced into their workplaces to attract employees. Would beer fridges, pool tables, or foosball games appeal equally to young men and women? Can you think of other types of jobs where the way the job is organized, or the entrance criteria required, systemically favours one gender or the other?

broader social community. One example can be found in the film *North Country* about a single mother, Lois Jenson, who worked in a northern Minnesota iron mine in the 1970s. The film depicts Jenson's courageous leadership in circumstances of brutal and degrading sexual harassment at the mine; she stands up to the men and the union in spearheading the first sexual harassment class action suit in American legal history.

At the other end of the spectrum, predominantly male unions have also spearheaded campaigns to introduce female-friendly working conditions. While rare, these campaigns are important instances of cross-gender solidarity. In Canada, the most famous example is the case of the Canadian Union of Postal Workers (CUPW) putting maternity leave at the top of its bargaining list in the early 1980s and going on strike over the issue. It was a magnificent initiative in support of a minority group in the membership and a strong message to other male-based unions about the importance of gender equality (White 1993). As the union announces proudly on its website:

> 1981: CUPW argues that maternity leave is needed to eliminate the injustice suffered by female workers who are forced to take a substantial loss in pay due to pregnancy. It takes the position that women shouldn't have to pay a penalty because they are the ones in society who bear children. The union wins paid maternity leave after a 42-day strike, making CUPW the first national union to win this right for its members.

White documents other gendered victories for the CUPW, including their stand in solidarity with (largely female) cleaners whose work was being outsourced to private cleaning corporations without regard for any hazards involved (1993, 195–6).

Experiences of exclusion also occur at the individual level and include processes of identity formation. Christine Overall's book *A Feminist I* offers reflection on how she encountered a series of class-based and masculine-gendered aspects to the culture of scholarly life (1998). Mary Ellen Donnan notes the prevalence of sexual assault in the lives of students at all phases of their academic careers and lack of services appropriate to the depth and prevalence of that issue (2003). Paula Caplan aptly describes the accumulated effects of numerous small exclusions and barriers in academe as 'lifting a ton of feathers' (1993). The examples cited earlier about university gate-keepers rejecting the importance of women's studies as an academic program or women's lives as important enough for dissertation topics were belated attempts to perpetuate a gender hierarchy in which the skills, lives, and concerns of men are more important than those of women. Despite the resistance, sometimes described as a 'backlash', women do overcome these challenges every day. Those who pursue change to the workplace culture often do so in the hope of fostering a more hospitable environment for future scholars of all genders and identities.

Some of the challenges of transforming the gendered segregation of employment come from the general public's cultural assumptions. Cultural discrimination occurs when members of the public assume, for example, that female engineers and blue-collar workers are weaker or less competent than males with the same qualifications (Williams 1999, 228). Outside perceptions and workplace cultures can reinforce each other, as seems to happen in the persistently male-dominated field of engineering. In a study of engineers working in Alberta's energy industry in the 1980s, Gillian Ranson (2005) found that women engineers who were mothers lived complex negotiations of gendered behaviour because of incompatibilities between mothering and being an engineer. Women engineers who did not have children also had to contend with gender differences within their male-dominated work contexts but expressed willingness to 'act like a man' in order to achieve the career success they wanted.

Governance of gender

We have been taught to think that the state (meaning the legal system and the elaborate infrastructure of regulations and social programs that intersect with our day-to-day lives) is a neutral arbiter and that therefore government institutions would not create advantages or disadvantages for people of particular identities (of gender or race, for example). Scholars who have taken a closer look at this question point to how government programs and policies have traditionally supported the breadwinner/homemaker model over other family forms in ways that affect careers. Family allowance was one such program. It was paid as a 'mother's allowance' to give families some extra spending money, since it was assumed that a mother did not work outside the home (Burt 1993, 219; Porter 2003, 54). Unemployment insurance is an example of a social policy that has supported a traditional social construction of gender. Ann Porter traces the historical patterns of how unemployment benefits were strongly gendered—originally to prevent married women from getting such benefits (so that they would not compete with men for jobs). After married women began working for pay in greater numbers, gendering of the program persisted, with denial of unemployment benefits to pregnant women and mothers. The structure of government unemployment insurance policies has changed significantly over the decades, and those changes are somewhat reflective of the growing belief in gender equality in the culture, as is evidenced in maternity leave provisions being legislated under the same program as employment insurance (Porter 2003). At the same time, the recent shift in access to employment insurance for part-time workers, touted as a positive change for primarily female part-time workers, turned out to be a bit of a con. Part-time workers were eligible to pay premiums, but in important circumstances were unlikely to accumulate sufficient hours to claim benefits. For example, it was found that women's pattern of part-time working between the births of the first and second child was unlikely to result in sufficient hours for a woman to be eligible for employment benefits as her maternity leave provision (McKeen and Porter 2003, 118–19).

For a while, the government of Canada was very much seen as a favourable employer for women. Civil service careers offered women better wages and more job security than many other areas of employment, and the government was actually one of the biggest full-time employers of women in the country. This has changed since the 1980s, as ideological rejection of the welfare state led to downsizing of government programs, privatization of Crown corporations, and many cuts to social services. Neoliberalism has had both direct and indirect impacts on the gendering of careers, as we discuss in greater depth in the next section.

Changing workers, changing jobs, or both?

Changing social institutions can be a slow process. In a qualitative analysis of the work lives of women in four non-traditional professions, Barbara Bagilhole found a strong tendency for women to adapt their behaviour to the pre-existing masculine cultural norms of the profession. Based on the cases of women in academia, engineering, construction, and the priesthood (in the Church of England), she found 'little hope for the masculine culture being challenged and changed' (Bagilhole 2002, 186) by the presence of women within the profession. Nonetheless, some of the female Church of England priests believed strongly that they brought unique gifts to the ministry and consciously conducted their work in ways distinct from those of their male colleagues (Bagilhole 2002, 96–9, 165–79). One area of change, however, is the greater acceptance of women as supervisors and bosses—acceptance by both women and men. Much has been written about reluctance to work for a female boss; however, research shows change on this front, with employees appreciating styles of management more typical of female bosses (or of the management positions women more often find themselves in). Krahn, Lowe, and Hughes (2006, 203) discuss research that shows that some gender differences in attitude and effort at work should actually lead to the promotion of women as preferred employees.

Employment stratification also includes segregation of tasks within professions, such as in lawyers', nurses', and doctors' practices or specializations. In legal professions, courtroom roles are scripted according to traditional ideas of gender. For example, when the courtroom strategy requires the litigant to be aggressive, that role is assigned to males 88 per cent of the time (Pierce 2004, 242). Gendered patterns can also be seen in the branch of law that women are streamed into, with more women doing family law, which is less profitable, than corporate law, where men tend to dominate.

Judith Butler's understanding of gender as performative is helpful in clarifying the possibilities for changing how we choose jobs regardless of whether they are traditionally performed by members of another gender. Just because women have traditionally been excluded from many fields of endeavour means neither that women cannot do the job nor that the job cannot change to reflect a greater diversity of employees. Some choices about how to respond to established social roles are ours to make as individuals and as siblings, friends, or co-workers. When people choose not to conform to limiting gender scripts, they make room for all of us to be more fully human. Parents and caregivers encounter interesting decisions about the boundaries between individual expressions of personality and socialized expectations of gender performance, as Christopher Longtin experienced in his employment at a residence for people with developmental disabilities. Everyone who liberates themselves by performing gender in their own way also creates more space within the culture for others to negotiate their identities anew. Transgendered people (such as Brandon Teena, whom you read about in chapter 1), who so recently have gained a voice in the sociological literature, offer unique inspiration on this terrain. Men too may defy social expectations to work in caregiving or service positions as, for example, elementary school teachers, flight attendants, nurses, child care workers, and cosmetologists.

Intersecting oppressions

In many instances, the social construction of gender is intertwined with other social constructions such as race. The concept of race gains its meaning from people investing value into distinctions of ethnicity, nationality, and/or physical characteristics. It

Gender/ed Care

by Christopher Longtin
Sociology MA Program

I spent the summer of 2007 working and living in a community of adults with developmental disabilities. Gender factored into my job in two ways. First, it influenced how I carried out the job. Second, I became interested in the intersection of residents' gender identities and their disabilities. Within this short piece, I consider how gendered perceptions affect 'care' and how persons with disabilities are gendered.

For the most part, unpaid and paid care work continues to carry feminine connotations. In accepting my paid care position, I surprised a number of family members and friends who thought it an unusual choice for a young man. The idea that care work is 'women's work' affected my relationships with residents in ways that were surprising even to me.

My female co-workers, for example, felt their gender contributed to an instant 'maternal' trust with the residents. They were quickly accepted and established as authority figures. Relationships between male assistants, such as me, and residents took a longer time to develop. There was an initial uneasiness that, consequently, led me to be extra attentive to the needs and character of the residents. At the same time, because I was not immediately recognized as experienced in a caring role, the residents appeared more comfortable directing my behaviour. Female assistants were offered less guidance. Whereas I had the benefit of direction when completing tasks, females were forced to rely on personal initiative and, in many cases, guesswork. This lack of direction sometimes had negative consequences. Preparing a resident's breakfast without first asking, for example, often led to frustration, because the resident's independence, adulthood, and personal space were seen as threatened. This is not to suggest that perceptions of my skills were gender-free. In fact, early on, I became a source of security in thunderstorms or the preferred person for setting an alarm clock. I was also drawn on for 'handyman' tasks—such as hanging blinds or fixing furniture.

While gender was negotiated by us as assistants, the residents also had strong gender identities. Many very much wanted to enter into adult relationships with others and to more fully explore their gender identity. However, the exploration of gender by residents was more socially limited. Assistants, living part of the week in the home and part of the week outside of the home, also seemed to bridge private and public spheres. The residents turned to us not only for what was 'cool' but also for knowledge of gender norms. This placed me in an awkward position, because I felt an unjustified influence over the performances and negotiations of gender among the residents. For example, males in the community sometimes adopted feminine accessories. Although occurring most often in the bedroom, these performances occasionally occurred in other areas of the house. If an assistant accepted the behaviour, often by just overlooking the accessory, the frequency of the performance and item increased. The self-confidence of the individual also increased. However, a negative reaction, such as a suggestion that these accessories were just for women, resulted in substantial withdrawal, physically and emotionally.

Two things can be seen here. First, we see the ability of the assistant or 'the public' to influence what is 'masculine', or 'feminine', and therefore 'acceptable'. Gender identities are influenced by outside forces. Second, the limited ability of the resident to encounter different discourses is evidenced. If I want to explore different aspects of my gender, for example, I could engage multiple supportive spaces outside of my own immediate living space. The community residents do not have this ability because of constrained mobility and limited social contacts.

This experience has left me with a better understanding of how experience and perception can gender the individual, his or her job, and the world he or she lives in.

The above discussion suggests that the acceptance of gender performance can differ in public and private spaces. Can definitions of 'inclusive societies' or 'sexual citizenship' facilitate multiple spaces of gender performance? Must one conception of gender always be dominant?

How might ideas of care have connotations of gender and power? Are careers of 'care' the only careers with such connotations?

is precisely the intertwining of hierarchies that necessitates the discussion of racial hierarchies simultaneously with a discussion of gender. Employment patterns in Canada are not a simple dichotomy, with all men's jobs positioned at an advantage to all women's jobs. Racial discriminations create a particularly powerful set of disadvantages among Canadian workers. This section considers how race and gender combine in the employment structures of nursing in Canada, then returns to a more textured discussion of the role of the state in gendering employment with an analysis of women workers hired as non-citizens in Canada.

Two discriminatory patterns have been evident in the nursing profession. One involves the advancement of men, and the other involves discrimination against African-Canadian women. Although men still occupy a small proportion of the nursing positions in Canada, that number had been on the rise. Data from the Canadian Nurses Association in 2004 show that 5.6 per cent of registered nurses in Canada were male. The number of male registered nurses in Canada was 14,007 in 2004, up by 26.5 per cent from 2000 (Canadian Nurses Association 2005).

Further, the men who choose non-traditional employment benefit from what can be called the glass escalator, or a series of invisible mechanisms accelerating their advancement through the ranks of the profession. Men in non-traditional occupations (especially straight men) are more likely than their female colleagues to advance quickly from hands-on caregiving work to administrative positions, which offer higher pay and job status (Williams 1999).

Agnes Calliste (1996) and Tania Das Gupta (2002) have documented racism within Canada's nursing profession. This racism is evident in immigration policy, hiring and advancement practices, delegation of duties, degree of monitoring, disciplinary measures, isolation, scapegoating, and systemic failure to understand or respond appropriately to the racism of patients and patients' families. In a context of severe cutbacks to the health care system, vague and subjective criteria for evaluating medical staff and word-of-mouth recruitment practices work against fair opportunities for women of colour working in the medical field (Das Gupta 2002, 130; see also Armstrong and Armstrong 2003, 178–86). Many Filipino migrant nurses have entered Canada as domestic workers, but they are prevented from practising their profession by a combination of delayed verification of their nursing credentials and a restructured health care system that has restricted opportunities for highly qualified professionals (Stasiulis and Bakan 2003, 160–3). Indeed, the medical profession is characterized by a combination of gender and racial stratifications, with the most powerful, prestigious role of doctoring performed mainly by white men, the relatively secure but less powerful role of nursing (especially nursing management) performed by white women, and Third World women of colour designated to the least secure positions: nurses' aides, laundry workers, cleaners, and food service providers—despite their qualifications for positions involving more recognized skills. Not only are women from the Philippines and the Caribbean doing the most physically demanding work within the health care profession, but as Pat and Hugh Armstrong have noted, the stealthy privatization of health care in Canada has made these service workers at the lower rungs vulnerable to further decline in the quality of their jobs (2003, 184).

In analyzing careers and work opportunities, it quickly becomes evident that an intersectional analysis is required to fathom the complex relationships between culture, identity, and gender that structure work opportunities and women's responses to these opportunities. We have already discussed how a set of social assumptions designates some tasks as feminine and others as masculine. Often, as we saw in the health care example, the least desirable jobs become 'racialized', meaning that the work is devalued and that usually only people of colour are economically and socially vulnerable enough to be willing to do that work. The valuing that characterizes the gendered and racial divisions of labour not only resonates in terms of prestige but also in the economic rewards for the work. Differences in earnings are structured by race as well as by sex. In 2002, the average annual earnings of women in Canada totalled $25,300, compared to $38,900 for men (Biggs and Downe 2005, 196). For every dollar earned by Canadian women belonging to the racial majority, women of visible minority groups earned 85 cents. For every dollar earned by non-Aboriginal women in 1999, Aboriginal women earned only 69 cents (2005, 196).

Since the 1950s, Canada's immigration legislation has exclusively targeted Third World women, especially from the Caribbean, then the Philippines, to look after children and do housework for Canada's wealthier families. The current version of this legislation is the Live-In Caregiver Program (LICP), which replaced the Foreign Domestic Movement program in 1992 (Daenzer 2002, 218). Under the LICP, women allowed into Canada to work as domestics are required to live in the home of their employer, are restricted from changing employment without the approval of the Department of Employment and Immigration, and are exempted from the normal protections of Canadian labour legislation (Stasiulis and Bakan 2003, 47). The 1992 legislation looks after the interests of those needing assistance in the home but completely fails to protect the migrant women from abuse and exploitation. It, in effect, potentially pits one group of women against another. Restrictions to the program have reduced the number of domestic workers who come through legal channels, so a larger proportion of these workers now have the extra vulnerability of being at the whim of their employers because they are in the country illegally (Stasiulis and Bakan 2003, 51–2). Violations experienced by live-in domestic workers in Canada include sexual assault, overwork, lack of privacy, unfair dismissal, and wilful breaking of the terms of their contracts.

Another category of workers permitted into Canada only on temporary work permits is the strongly gendered job of exotic dancer. Macklin argues that the sexualized entertainment industry began to have difficulty filling such positions after the 1990s when the legalization of lap dancing allowed more contact between patrons and performers. Women recruited overseas for this work are frequently manipulated and lied to about their working conditions prior to their arrival in Canada (Macklin 2003, 472).

Statistics indicate that a smaller proportion of First Nations women than non-Aboriginal women work for pay in Canada. Economic rewards from employment for First Nations women are also less. Statistics Canada data show patterns of education for First Nations women as distinct from those of non-Aboriginal women and Aboriginal men. Young First Nations adults (aged 15 to 24) are less likely to be attending school, but many First Nations women return to school during and after their mid-20s (O'Donnell 2006, 197–8). This fits with their higher fertility level and role as sole parents, which are part of the cultural patterns in their communities. Child care may be an even more salient issue for First Nations mothers than for non-Aboriginal women (Donnan 1996, 136–40, 200–7).

> Clearly we were different. We were 'not white' and it showed. However, the historical persistence of our cultural difference generation after generation (despite the best assimilative efforts of both Church and State) is a sign of our strengths and our resistance. That we have historically, and continually, mothered in a way that is 'different' from the dominant culture is not only empowering for our women but is potentially empowering for all women. (Lavell-Harvard and Lavell 2006, 3)

Child rearing is certainly a factor delaying career start and advancement for these women, but what, if any, are the career ambitions of Aboriginal mothers? This issue needs further research, because although we do know that a First Nations perception is that mothering holds a greater relative importance for them than it does for the majority of non-Aboriginal Canadian women (Oullette 2002, 89), we do not have a full understanding of how the balance between earning and caring is understood by First Nations women. We cannot assume that feminist solutions designed by and for non-Aboriginals will be culturally appropriate. Feminist values are questioned by some First Nations authors (see Oullette 2002, 15–28). The lack of information around these issues points to a need for localized specificity about employment contexts and a richly inclusive framework for analyzing gender and career in Canada.

The ways we understand and measure work are also socially constructed, so it is wise to be alert to factors of both gender and culture within those constructions. For example, the unemployment rate for Aboriginal women is twice as high as it is for other women in all age categories. The difference is particularly steep in the 15 to 24 age group, with 57 per cent of non-Aboriginal but only 35 per cent of Aboriginal women working for pay (O'Donnell 2006, 198). However, Vivian O'Donnell notes that there are limitations to the applicability of the Statistics Canada data used in that calculation:

> Official unemployment rates . . . may not always reflect work that is carried out for which no payment is received. Work of this type is common in many Aboriginal communities where large amounts of time are spent fishing, trapping, hunting, sewing and caring for children of friends and family members. Also there is much seasonal work in many Aboriginal communities. (2006, 199)

As researchers and writers, we must be careful not to impose our ideas and agendas, because unpaid work may be more important to a First Nations woman's well-being and self-concept than paid work would be. The issue of colonialism is more than just a question of the British and French invasions of Canada and the processes of taking land away from First Peoples. Colonialism also occurs with every cultural process that assumes that the mainstream culture (with more access to economic, political, and military power) is superior to the colonized cultures. The structures of colonialism intersect with social constructions of gender to create deeper disadvantages for some women than for others.

GENDER CONSEQUENCES OF GLOBALIZATION

Sociology offers a variety of analytical tools for studying the national and international political context of recent decades and implication of changes in this context for the study of gender. As Pat and Hugh Armstrong say of changes to the public health system, 'All of these developments are profoundly gendered in terms of both the assumptions on which they are based and their consequences' (2003, 181). Cutting the public sector involved the state in privileging some Canadians over others in a gendered and racial way at an even steeper intensity than at any time since the creation of a welfare state in the 1940s and 1950s. This section discusses ways in which neo-liberalism is a deeply gendered process within Canada. There are growing gaps between advantaged and disadvantaged segments of the labour force. These are persistently described as economically prosperous times for the country, and average income has increased, but this situation is deceptive because it entails significant increases in income for upper echelons, while middle- and lower-income recipients have continued to struggle. National Council of Welfare data show an after-tax increase of income of more than 14 per cent for the richest 20 per cent of families between 1980 and 2003 but an increase of less than 5 per cent for the poorest 20 per cent of families (NCW 2006). This is a gendered pattern, with women—especially lone-parent mothers—overrepresented among the poor. We explain how this polarization reinforces gendered divisions in the labour force, with more precarious employment and fewer secure jobs for women, worsening of conditions for garment workers, and more privatization of caregiving labour. We also briefly address neoliberalism as a national-level reflection of, and support for, transnational processes of globalization that have gender implications.

Comprehension of the current employment context requires knowledge of some of the dynamics between corporations, national policy-makers, and international market forces. The context in Canada is characterized sociologically as 'neo-liberal globalization'. 'Neo-liberal' refers to a policy direction (enacted federally and provincially) that minimizes government social welfare supports and maximizes market freedoms for corporations. The inclusion of *globalization* along with neo-liberalism in the descriptor identifies a multinational political and economic process of increasing the volume of trade networks across the world. Canada has participated actively in the globalization process, with some questionable political decisions, such as signing the North American Free Trade Agreement (NAFTA) and the General Agreement on Trade in Services (GATS). Many sociologists object to these agreements because a series of steep monetary penalties in the agreements prevents the Canadian government from protecting Canadian citizens, resources, and environments from international market exploitation (see McQuaig 1991; 1998; Clark and Barlow 1997). That exploitation includes a worsening of the polarity of employment structures, with the many women and immigrants who were already disadvantaged being pushed precariously to the edges of survival (Shalla 2006).

Since the mid-1970s, many government services, including social supports, medical systems, and funding for education, were reduced in a process summarized by the term 'downsizing'. Downsizing and privatization meant fewer government jobs for Canadian workers. Many government jobs were 'standard jobs' characterized by reasonable levels of job security, some opportunity for advancement, medical and dental benefits, and a pension. Because of the public demand for equity in hiring, the Canadian government was one of the employers most likely to give women access to standard jobs. Nursing was one of those public-sector professions:

> Between 1994 and 1996, 12 per cent of the nursing staff lost their jobs (Wagner and Rondeau 2000, iv). Most of those employed by the public sector have part-time, part-year or temporary employment. By the beginning of this century, only 52 per cent of those working in health care had full-time employment. (Armstrong and Armstrong 2003, 181)

Other sectors that mainly hired women, like clerking and service work, already primarily offered non-standard jobs or precarious employment, with low pay, part-time hours, no benefits, and minimal job security, so the gender division for career prospects became even wider.

Cuts to the public sector also have implications for women who work in other sectors. Whether or not women have children, they often face mid-life time shortages because of the social expectations of caregiving. Susan McDaniel, for example, observes a caring crisis that began emerging in the 1990s because women in mid-life have less non-work time than was previously the case. This is partly due to neo-liberal cuts to public health care, which effectively moved care work back into the home (Armstrong and Armstrong 2003, 171) and has translated into women caring for elderly relatives and thus becoming part of the 'sandwich' generation (see chapter 4). Some of this mid-life cohort of women is simultaneously experiencing extended responsibilities because high youth unemployment means that parents must look after young-adult children who cannot find enough work to be self-sustaining for a longer period (McDaniel 1995; 1996).

Deregulation and a rise in non-standard work create patterns of even more significant gender and racial stratification. Deep inequalities generated by colonialist policy and structural racism have become even worse with the advent of neo-liberalism and increased corporate power at the global level. While a tiny portion of women enjoy job security and good, safe, rewarding working conditions, for other women employment patterns have gone from bad to worse. Trends in wage data show an interesting picture. Between 1967 and 1997, the earnings of full-time, full-year female workers increased as a percentage of men's wages—but the increase was only 14 percentage points. That is little more than a four percentage point increase per decade for the group of female workers most comparable to men! In part, the increase was due to the fact that men's wages increased by very little over the same period, making it easier for women to catch up (Jackson and Robinson 2000, 19–20). However, only about half of the women employed in Canada work full-time, full-year. The circumstances of part-time, part-year workers have deteriorated, as little by little employers have been able to remove what minimal protection had been available to these workers.

Deborah Barndt (2002) traces the life of a tomato as it is planted in Mexico, transported through the US, and sold/purchased in Canada as a way of revealing the deteriorating conditions for female workers wrought by the increasing globalization of agricultural production. All along this chain, women work in precarious jobs, for low pay, with no or minimal benefits, little chance of advancement, and often close supervision. Barndt finds that globalized production depends on the gendered division of labour, with management of several sectors expressing clear preference for women workers over men:

> The packing plant is one of the places where entrenched gender ideologies clearly reign. Women are considered both more responsible and more delicate in their handling of the tomatoes; and because the appearance of the product is so critical to tomato exporters, there is at least some recognition of this work as a skill, even if it is considered innate rather than part of female socialization. (Barndt 2002, 186)

Despite the skill required not to bruise the tomatoes, the expectation that gentleness comes 'naturally' to women devalues the skill. Wages are so low since the North American Free Trade Agreement that meeting basic needs requires the wages of five workers in a family. Jobs requiring physical strength, the exercise of authority, and technical knowledge are reserved for men (Barndt 2002, 184).

As highlighted previously, First Nations and immigrant women experience some of the worst employment conditions in Canada. Employment is more precarious than it was before the 1970s (Cranford et al. 2006). Working conditions under new management strategies that pursue ever-greater 'economic efficiency' have deteriorated, with effects including worsening health problems, more restrictions on workers, and increasing racial tensions in restructured workplaces (Fox and Sugiman 2006, 76, 85–6).

Globalization treats gendered and racialized bodies distinctly, sometimes not allowing international travel, other times restricting travel conditions. Stasiulis and Bakan (2003, 2) note that in the current era, Third World women of colour face especially steep barriers to gaining the advantages of citizenship entitlements.

> . . . invidious distinctions made between migrants in migration policies which are based on North–South relations, their class positions, race/ethnicity, gender or other markers of difference including disability and sexual orientation are reproduced through a hierarchy of citizenship statuses. (Stasiulis and Bakan 2003, 12)

At the bottom of the hierarchy of workers in Canada are workers admitted since 1973 under a collection of regulations termed the Non-Immigrant Employment Authorization Program (NIEAP). These workers are admitted to work for a specified employer on a temporary contract without the opportunity to apply for more permanent residency (Bains and Sharma 2006, 211). Under this program umbrella are a series of regulatory processes under which women may be employed as domestic workers, agricultural workers, or exotic dancers. They can be deported at their employer's pleasure, as Melca Salvador's boss tried to do to her in the incident described at the opening of this chapter. The conditions of employment in Canada require payment of taxes but do not offer standard civil, legal, or social protections to the workers.

Women were excluded from the Foreign Agricultural Resource Management Services (FARMS) until 1992, but they now pick and pack produce and work in greenhouses. Only certain women, however, are considered eligible for the work. One of the Mexican workers in the program explains that most participants are widows while some are single mothers or divorcees, but married women are excluded because of the perceived risk that they might try to stay in Canada (Barndt 2002, 160). The women who are mothers are frequently assisted by extended family members back home who look after the farm labourer's children while she is away for months at a time. Although many of the women do similar work in their home country, Canadian jobs are preferred because at $56 per day, they earn about seven times as much (Barndt 2002, 162).

Gender and country of origin combine to shape employment opportunities for many of the immigrant women who arrive in Canada without good language skills in English or French. The hyper-exploitation of many immigrant women who do home work, especially for the clothing industry, is attributable in some measure to the processes by which they were categorized under Canada's immigration system. Many garment manufacturers prefer that their seamstresses work in their own homes, because the employee, not the company, has to supply the sewing machine, and when they are working in isolation, the women have much less opportunity to organize or collectively bargain for minimum wage instead of piecework rates. For the seam-stresses, the result is rates of pay often well below what labour laws allow. Most of them are foreign-born immigrant mothers with a first language other than English or French who arrived in Canada within the 'family class' immigration category. The 'family class' designation relieves the government of any responsibility for language training, but without supports or teaching aids, family members in Canada often do not provide that instruction either, leaving the women with very few employment options (Ng 1998; 1999).

The market 'freedoms' allowed by our government under policies of neo-liber-alism are expanding the gendered divide between good quality careers and work that barely allows people to survive. The film *The Corporation* explains how corporations have gained legal rights greater than many people enjoy. Corporate goods and dollars move freely across borders that many people are prevented from crossing; corpora-tions are protected from 'unfair' competitive practices, but workers are not. While the global processes of market expansion have been frequently depicted as beneficial to all or at worst neutral, they are politically motivated in pursuing the best interests of the wealthiest segments of Canadian and international populations. The rise of transnational corporations has led to production being dispersed into more eco-nomically disadvantaged sectors of the globe and the loss of industrial jobs here. Con-way notes that more than 180,000 jobs were lost within the Greater Toronto Area (constituting about one-tenth of its employment base) between 1989 and 1992 (2004, 108, footnote 14). Ng shows how market competition and corporate opportunity to globalize resulted in ethnic-minority female seamstresses in Toronto's garment indus-try being pushed during the 1990s from unionized factory work to piecework, sewing at home under terribly exploitive conditions that evade Canadian labour codes (2000). The implications of a GWG/Levis garment factory closure in Edmonton (after 93 years of operation) were especially bad for immigrant workers, because it had been a unionized workplace with some sense of community and possibilities for learning English within the work environment (Fenwick 2007).

As discussed in more detail in the upcoming section on how to change gender inequality in careers, many forces intersect in the structuring of employment oppor-tunities, and equity gains made recently in some sectors have been counter-balanced by losses in other sectors.

With globalization, the vulnerability of Third World women has increased. When women were subsisting on the products of their own small plots of land, they were not contributing to the national Gross Domestic Product (GDP) of their country, but they were able to feed and live with their families. International organizations claim to be helping countries by encouraging them to export more goods and raise their GDP, but that whole agenda has a gender subtext in which men, who are more involved in the cash economy, profit more than women, who tend to be direct providers rather than wage workers (Waring 1988). The development of export processing zones and other forms of industrialization that pushed people off their lands leaves women—many of whom are the sole supporters of children—with no choice but to sell their labour under whatever conditions allow them and their families to survive a little longer. Export processing zones are infamously hazardous areas where authorities exempt corporations from taxes, environmental restrictions, and labour codes as an incentive for them to choose the zone as a site for their manufacturing process. Many factors, ranging from the gendered wage scales and hiring preferences of corporations to military roles for men, mean that it is often women who leave home to go to a different region to work at manufacturing product for export or to a different country in search of whatever wages can be secured for their families. Taking work in another country is frequently the best option for women in less economically privileged nations, even though that work takes them away from home and family. There is an interconnected, international web of corporate influence and military might (called neo-colonialism by some) by which the profits of production are filtered away from these women workers and the structural and social advantages of the already wealthiest (white men) are perpetuated (Eisenstein 1998; 2004).

Clearly, the starting points for career opportunities are unequal across identities of gender and ethnicity as well as statuses of citizenship. Beyond that, the rewards from employment and the opportunities for advancement are very uneven. Can recognition of this injustice lead to change in the processes that produce career inequity or redistribution of the gains from paid work?

IMPROVING ON CAREER INEQUALITIES AND IMAGINING INCLUSIVE SOLUTIONS

One of the prevailing myths in Canadian society is that in career terms, you get what you deserve in life because career choice is equitable and advancement is based on merit. Sociology destroys that myth, but not without also offering the hope of a better system to come. In this section, we outline traditional solutions to career inequity from social theory and political practice, including from unionization, from other social movement activity, and from equity legislation. We then analyze the limitations of those traditional solutions and, finally, explore newer strategies of social change.

Traditional solutions

As mentioned in the introduction to this chapter, critical sociology is meant to lead us to the realization of liberal and humanist goals such as equality of opportunity, freedom, justice, and fair distribution of the benefits of belonging to a society. There is a long history of women and men who have challenged the social structures that foster gender discrimination in employment. Historically, it was a struggle for women to gain the educational opportunities to train for jobs that were outside of the narrow gender scripts of women in domestic roles. Many of the changes in women's employment in Canada and elsewhere can be attributed to the work (both ideological and practical) of social movements, including the women's movement, the labour movement, and anti-racist organizations. As you can imagine, since there are many structures and processes complicit in the making of gendered career hierarchies, efforts on many fronts are required to dismantle them. Activists and workers in Canada have fought gender inequalities in the work world by lobbying for the removal of barriers and fighting for equity and against discrimination in the courts, as well as by forming and expanding unions.

The women's movement in Canada has a powerful history of engagement with the state. Jill Vickers writes that an orientation towards political processes (especially in the case of the anglophone women's movement) and a commitment to dialogue are two of the main characteristics of Canadian feminist practice (1992, 40). Women in the political realm have also retained some optimism about being able to exert their influence collectively. Arscott and Trimble document several cases of female Canadian politicians uniting across partisan differences to push for women's interests (1997). One such case saw the right to sexual equality enshrined in the Canadian Constitution. This means that discrimination in hiring on the basis of sex is illegal. Although the process can be slow and costly, the Constitution provides an important avenue for fighting discriminatory practices. It took three years of contention in the courts (ending at the Supreme Court of Canada) for a female firefighter, Tawney Meiorin, to demonstrate that fitness tests for firefighters were discriminatory because they demanded physical abilities not necessary for good job performance (Hamilton 2005, 127).

Academic attention has focused on issues of discrimination for decades now, certainly since the report of the Royal Commission on the Status of Women in 1971. Sixty-two of the 167 recommendations in the commission's report were directed towards employment, not counting child care recommendations. Unlike the situation in our current political context, the federal government of the 1950s through the early 1970s had a serious interest in promoting the social welfare of Canadians. Commissioning the Status of Women report was part of that, and as a follow-up to the report, politicians took suggestions of the National Action Committee on the Status of Women under advisement. One of the reasons for listening to an advisory body was the significant gendering of elected representatives to the House of Commons. At the federal and provincial levels, political representation in Canada is overwhelmingly dominated by males. The more general theory concerning women's political influence is that a critical mass of 30 per cent female representation is required for an effective influence on politics. That 30 per cent mark has only been crossed in the Quebec legislature which, with 38 women elected out of 123 representatives, reached 31 per cent between 2003 and late 2007. With this exception, the percentage of women in federal and provincial parliaments has ranged between 9 and 26 per cent over the past decade (Library of Parliament 2006; Parliament of Canada 2006). Nonetheless, despite the lack of representation, some gains were made in employment equity.

The initial employment equity strategies, based on the principle of equal work for equal pay, did little to amend gender employment inequity because, as you have just read, women and men were working in different sectors and doing distinct jobs more than they were working side-by-side. The momentum then shifted to equal pay for work of equal value, which was legislated under section 11 of the Canadian Human Rights Act in 1977 (Fudge 2000, 324). The intention of the legislation was to create substantive equality by challenging the diminution of the contribution made in traditionally female jobs: 'The legislation required places of employment to develop job evaluation plans that compare, along a variety of dimensions, jobs usually done by men with those usually done by women' (Hamilton 2005, 76). It is a cumbersome mechanism for challenging gender inequity, because the process of getting a settlement takes many years. Fudge (2000) and Hamilton (2005) also see limits to the strategy, since its effectiveness has been weakened by changes to provincial legislations and corporations have developed other strategies for subverting applicability of the legislation since the 1980s (as we discuss below). Overall, a feminist perspective suggests that the implementation of equal pay for work of equal value is highly problematic, and the results have been mixed in recent economic contexts (Armstrong, Cornish, and Miller 2003).

Since World War II, the classic solution to job/career inequalities and concerns has been unionization. Through collective bargaining processes, workers in many places restored a balance of power with employers, which lasted for some time. Women experienced some resistance within many unions (Briskin and McDermott 1993), as did people of colour, but distinct gains were made by women who had more favourable working conditions to begin with. 'Canadian women unionists have successfully pressured unions to take up issues of child care, reproductive rights, sexual harassment, pay equity and employment equity among others' (Briskin 2005, 212). Linda Briskin insists that unions are still effective, providing evidence that women workers in Canada make 31 per cent more if they are unionized. Specifically, part-time women workers who are unionized bring in 40 per cent more than non-union part-time women workers. Further, the gender wage gap between unionized women and men is smaller than that between non-unionized women and men (2005, 210). Grace-Edward Galabuzi sees great potential for improvement of the work lives of racialized people in Canada through collective bargaining, because unions need them as members (they are younger on average than current union members) as much as the racialized workers need the power of unions (2006, 235–46).

The support of free market ideologies and workplace restructuring have limited the effectiveness of both equal pay for work of equal value and collective bargaining as means of creating an overall move towards gender equity in Canadian employment.

> In the neo-liberal climate pay equity legislation is seen as special pleading rather than an attempt to redress systemic inequalities, and provincial governments have moved to take the teeth out of the process or abolish it altogether (Evans and Werkerle 1997, 23; Findlay 1997, 235). More seriously the growing conversion of full-time permanent jobs to part-time, temporary and contracts effects an end run around pay equity legislation. (Hamilton 2005, 79)

Roxana Ng's analysis of the impact of restructuring on the textile industry in Toronto demonstrates that the unionization of immigrant women workers in Toronto sweatshops provided only temporary improvement of conditions for the women, mainly from Asia, whose work lives were also conditioned by caregiving responsibilities and limited understanding of Canada's official languages. Competition from overseas manufacturers led to the closure of most of Toronto's garment factories and substitution of an in-home piecework production process, which devalued the work of the seamstresses to the extent of about \$2.50 per hour for a very efficient worker (Ng 2000). It is much more difficult for the women to unionize again now that workers are scattered among private homes around the city.

Affirmative action is another strategy for combating gendered and racial divisions of labour. Sociological research shows us that people belonging to particular groups (for example, recent immigrants from Africa and Asia or First Nations people) are likely to have experienced a series of social and economic disadvantages in life, including racial prejudice. These disadvantages make it less likely that people from these groups will manage to achieve the same levels of education and experience that people of other groups have, and consequently we see fewer of them holding good jobs. This understanding is the starting point for affirmative action programs. There are often many qualified people for any single job. Affirmative action programs use various strategies, such as quotas, to encourage employers to choose the qualified people belonging to groups currently under-represented among their high-level employees. This process recognizes that achieving the same credentials means overcoming extraordinary obstacles for some segments of the population and seeks to restore a better balance of reward for efforts made. Affirmative action strategies also have inter-generational potential because of the development of role models for other members of the disadvantaged groups.

The size of an organization also has to be considered in an affirmative action strategy if it is to be effective in fully integrating diverse people into large organizations. Full inclusion and embracing the benefits of diversity within our population (as opposed to assimilation) implies that previously marginalized people can contribute at all levels of an organization and have the power to negotiate changes to reflect diverse perspectives.

If they represent a numerical minority within a group, they could be tokenized (Carty 1993; Andersen 2006, 139–41). Tokenism means that the institution has superficially met the need for the appearance of inclusion but members of the previously excluded group are isolated and prevented from exercising effective influence over the organization. Alternatively, as active members of a minority group, they could be required to meet excessive demands for participation and representation. Janet Conway documents a social planning committee in Toronto that experienced this problem when it recognized that every subcommittee would benefit from minority representatives yet only a few such representatives were available (2004).

First Nations organizations offer insights for bringing more gender and racial equity to employment patterns in Canada. The Native Women's Association of Canada has called for affirmative action policies for articling positions in the legal profession and examination of racial and gender bias in the law school acceptance test (NWAC 1992, 3, 5). Inuit women have, with the support of government funding, developed business models for women of their communities. These models emphasize Inuit themes of balancing responsibilities, sharing culture, serving as a role model, and providing work for others in the community over the more mainstream goals of earning profits (Jamieson n.d.). Notice that these strategies require attention to gendered and racialized ways of knowing. In other words, if the agenda of economic development in the North is going to be taken up by First Nations people, what is needed is economic development that does not take the form of invasion or exploitation by outsiders.

Neo-liberal policies have widened and deepened the gendered and racialized gaps between employment sectors. Many service jobs that were once part of the public health care and social welfare systems have been cut or privatized. Pat and Hugh Armstrong help us to understand that the changes to which roles are defined as within the public sphere versus within the private are implicated in the gendering and devaluing of caring work. In the public sphere, wages and status have been more evenly distributed among women, as well as between women and men (Armstrong and Armstrong 2003, 179). Once that work was contracted out, the quality of the work declined, and the gender wage gap (as well as other indicators of work equality) between the subcontracted jobs and public-sector jobs expanded. A corollary of that finding might be that job inequities could be reduced again by expanding the public sphere.

> A profit-based system bases choice, as well as power, on ability to pay. Because most women have fewer financial resources than most men, and distribution of these resources is racialized as well as gendered, inequality between women and men and among women is greater the greater the strength of the for-profit sector. (Armstrong and Armstrong 2003, 174)

Since the private sector is governed by a profit motive, while the public sector has a broader scope of concern, including notions of social well-being, the public sector plays an important role in reducing inequalities of condition.

Solutions such as pay equity, affirmative action, and unionization have proved to be limited in the scope of their effectiveness. Moderately prosperous segments of the labour market benefited greatly from these strategies for sharing the profits of work more equitably with the workers, but none of these three solutions challenge the larger international structures that are the biggest actors in the hyper-exploitation of women of colour and the perpetuation of gender inequality.

Ideological limits of traditional solutions

Over the past 20 years, seemingly insurmountable obstacles have been placed in the path of traditional solutions to social inequity, including employment stratification. Canadian women historically pursued both state-focused and grassroots routes to equality (Adamson et al. 1988), but the efficacy of the former has become increasingly doubtful over the past two decades. Since the mid-1980s, a significant lack of social concern has been evident in the neo-liberal policy trajectory. Writers in the social work tradition have linked countless stories of poverty, social isolation, hunger, homelessness, and suffering to the new policy regime. Sheila Neysmith et al. have documented heart-rending accounts that illustrate how cuts to the public sector within a context of welfare-state restructuring have altered the lives of all but those at the highest income levels in Canada (Neysmith, Bezanson, and O'Connell 2005). Great suffering has resulted, including economic and social insecurity, physical and mental ill-health, and job losses. Canada has an underclass of racialized workers who are familiar with hunger and homelessness (Galabuzi 2006). Publicizing these conditions and making evident the link to political policy has not significantly changed the policy climate.

The persistence of this climate means that change must be pursued in ways beyond appealing to the social conscience of our politicians. Labour unions and employment equity and affirmative action programs challenge problems at the level of the individual workplace, but all of these workplaces are embedded in a broader social context that is influencing the employer–employee relations. In other words, the scale of the problem is bigger than individual workplaces and therefore needs an equivalently scaled response. Politicians and media pundits have tried to shift the blame on vague international forces (globalization and technological advancement), which are touted as inevitable or incontrovertible. There are often disconnections between the scale on which policy-makers think about their economic strategies and the scale on which local and national lobbyists view the situation.

Gender inequalities cannot be eliminated with conservative or narrow policy frameworks limited to the actions of individual employers or corporations. People's lived experiences of gender inequalities are significantly intertwined with a variety of other social and economic structures. All of these intertwining structures need to be addressed if a complete understanding is to be reached and inclusive solutions devised. New Zealand feminist economist Marilyn Waring convincingly argues that the notions of value upon which the global economic system rests are deeply skewed (1988). She notes that neither the value of unwaged caring labour, nor the damages of environmental destruction have been included in accounting processes that define national economic success or difficulty. Her analysis includes concrete and practical solutions for redressing the imbalances in international accounting.

Resolving gender inequalities from within more traditional frameworks that are centred on the role of the federal state, and especially those perspectives that accept corporate globalization and neo-liberalism as necessary or inevitable, simply does not generate the depth of cultural, social, and political change that is needed.

The sociological imagination, via embracing diversity and the politics of alter-globalization while rejecting neo-liberalism and decentring the state, can envision both a social system that is beyond gender discrimination in careers, and processes that can take us from where we are towards that more equitable state. Such a theo-retical perspective draws from post-colonial and post-structural thought alongside feminism and anti-racism.

Another aspect of gender equality that has been getting worse with globalization is the question of political voice. Women remain under-represented in electoral poli-tics at the federal and provincial levels. Additionally, the locus of decision-making has been shifting to non-democratic (meaning not elected by the populace of the coun-try) institutions often working at supra-national levels. Much to the dismay of Maude Barlow, Tony Clarke, and other activists, transnational corporations working through such institutions as the Business Council on National Issues and the World Trade Organization (WTO) are exerting more influence over political and social decisions in Canada than the citizenry is. Not only are the corporate representatives who sit on international decision-making bodies like the WTO almost exclusively male, but their agendas benefit the already rich (namely, white males) much more than other segments of the population, and they do serious harm to those (such as Third World women) who begin from a disadvantaged economic position. Policy critics insist that Canadian government policy-makers could reverse the neo-liberalism that encourages reductions in standard jobs and expansion of precarious employment (Bains and Sharma 2006). While right-wing economic theories claim that the benefits of free-market competition will trickle down to all segments of the populace, the evidence from employment patterns in Canada since neo-liberalism do not support such an assertion. Regulations and tariffs have been used in the past to protect local producers and manufacturers from competition and to encourage market development within the country, so it is not inconceivable that such processes could begin working again. The political voices of the women disadvantaged by neo-liberal policies and men who do not want to see deeper gender polarization of incomes need to be rallied and organized in opposition to the loss of democracy. It is interesting to notice, as Nick Scott does in the research he describes below, that even our forms of political protest have gendered nuances.

Equality in Difference? Gender and Political Protest

by Nick Scott
Sociology PhD Program

The gender division of labour and socialization in Canada and other Western countries has generated various stereotypes and norms about the different political competencies of men versus women. Feminist sociologists have demonstrated how unequal access to power has drawn on and reinforced ideologies of 'masculine' political occupations as demanding rationality and 'hawkishness'. Women, by contrast, have been rewarded for reconciling their civic involvement with expectations that they prioritize familial obligations and take on nurturing and social service roles. These factors have been used to help explain historically higher rates of formal engagement in the political sphere among men.

Is this analysis of political participation outdated? The fact that seats of formal political power throughout the electoral system in Canada remain so badly skewed towards male occupancy suggests not. But what of unconventional forms of involvement that have diffused across post-industrial democracies over the past several decades, such as boycotts, demonstrations, and strikes? Because they straddle work *within* and the fight *against* governing institutions, I would argue that contemporary protest activities may constitute an important bellwether of participatory equality.

On one level, gender clearly remains an important mediator of the protest experience, evident in campaigns that use explicitly gendered criteria for recruitment or to frame movement goals and identities. On the level of individual participation, however, gender may be less relevant. My multivariate analysis of recent national survey data (Scott 2007) suggests that, in line with women in other Western countries, Canadian women are today no more or less likely to employ protest tactics than men. The finding is a partial indicator of gender parity within protest participation. Importantly, it captures the manifold contests over highway construction, school closures, and other local concerns rather than simply the mass movements that are most likely to garner national media attention.

The picture becomes more complex, however, once we move beyond simple additive regression models to consider the intersection of gender with class and ethnicity. Indeed, my research also suggests that women of visible-minority status are significantly less likely to participate in protest activities than males who are not white, regardless of income levels and other factors related to gender, such as parental, marital, and employment status. The negative influence disappears, however, upon controlling for educational attainment. That is, depressed participation among minority women appears to reflect their lower access to a key socio-economic resource—the human capital manifested in higher learning—rather than the direct influence of either their ethnicity or their gender.

Such quantitative analysis of protest participation often emphasizes visible 'public' actions or routinized events over 'private' behaviours and the meanings that participants themselves give to their actions. Identifying protest behaviour with visible public events overlooks, however, the performative, discursive, and cultural forms of resistance that have, for example, played a key role in sustaining the women's movement between peaks of stirring mobilization.[6] It also neglects everyday practices that may bracket political protest. Environmental sociologists have argued that women not only engage in environment-friendly practices more frequently in their daily routines but they are also more likely than men to connect such behaviours to the broader environmental movement.[7]

In short, gender differentiation of protest participation persists and bears a complexity that is usefully addressed by interrogating the 'political' and exploring how civic actors understand their behaviour. Still, crucial puzzles remain. At what point do gender differences of resources, style, and opportunity to protest reflect *inequalities*? What sorts of social patterns of engagement point to meaningful equality?

Perhaps most pressingly, given the current state of our relationship with nature and the planet, how might we diffuse more broadly the kinds of environmental stewardship associated with maternalism and parenthood? Should children or teens, whose politics may diverge from that of their parents, be trained to use non-violent protest tactics, and if so, who should teach them? Would you expect young women and men to be motivated by the same political issues and protest strategies?

Gender relations are fragmented by relations of race, citizenship, economic opportunity, and international power structures. This situation offers many challenges to the way policies are developed and political movements are organized. A variety of theories and approaches to social analysis have been developed that are helpful for understanding differences within and across genders. An early effort was strategic essentialism, which focused on women's shared bodily experiences and commonalities of oppression around which women's political activism could be united. Even though the intention was to emphasize gender-based differences without reproducing them, the strategy ultimately seemed to create a hierarchy of oppressions and place gender as primary. Chantal Mouffe and others found that the process of deconstructing identities rather than essentializing them ultimately offered deeper possibilities for personal liberation and political alliance (Mouffe 1992). Building coalitions for common causes between varied groups that each maintains its own central focus offers another strategy for social change. Beyond multiculturalism and coalition-building, we now have a new series of insights on political and social change that builds on the realization that difference offers a source of strength. We turn our attention to these insights now.

New solutions

Solutions on a different scale are going to be required to get to the roots of the problems of which the gendering of careers is only one part. In the actions of the anti-globalization (or alter-globalization) movement and in the writings of many thinkers who are pushing the boundaries of gendered research, including Chandra Talpade Mohanty, Zilla Eisenstein, Julie Katherine Gibson-Graham, and Jodi Dean, we can find new gender-based strategies for social change. Some of their key insights are that local contexts are effective sites for participation in global struggles, that differences of identity and location do not prevent solidarity across gender, and that ideological change can build political change.

Although the predominant social pattern perpetuates career structures of gender and racial hierarchy, people at many locations within those hierarchies are interested in change, and theories of how to develop solidarity are improving. Just ignoring difference perpetuates the inequalities, because flows of advantage and disadvantage will continue until we (or someone) change them. Solidarity is not genuinely inclusive if it is developed in a position that amounts to the rule of the majority, but deconstructions of identity along multiple lines of difference, and openness to oppositional voices, can allow a *reflexive solidarity* that can inform inclusive politics. As developed by Jodi Dean, reflexive solidarity offers a conscious political perspective informed by a sense of responsibility and a commitment to reciprocity that can allow for development of mutually supportive political positions not only within but across genders (1996).

Earlier in this chapter, the spread of global capitalism was identified as an obstacle for achieving a better balance of power and income across differences of gender and race. Another source of inspiration and insight regarding positive political possibilities is work that shows that capitalism's power is not inescapable and that non-capitalist economic realities already exist in localized examples. Such examples can be found in Ladahk's Ecological Development Group (Norberg-Hodge 1992, 172) and in a series of community economy projects discussed by Julie Katherine Gibson-Graham (2006). Another inspiring example is captured in Naomi Klein and Avi Lewis's film *The Take* in which factory workers of both genders become the masters of their own economic destiny. People are already changing social organization in ways that build communities, and Julie Katherine Gibson-Graham (1996; 2006) argues that this kind of change can begin right now from our current social locations. We can see within the life experiences of Perez Nyamwamge how women can play many roles simultaneously and build success from the skill of balancing numerous goals and commitments within each day.

Reflections on Personal Experiences as a Woman of Colour Playing Multiple Roles

by Perez Nyamwamge
Sociology MA Program

What struggles and challenges do women have to cope with in their personal and professional lives? Reflecting on some of my own personal experiences, I realize that my level of participation in family, school, work, and community activities and, more importantly, the meanings that I bring to bear upon all these engagements have a significant impact on my thoughts about the social and cultural obligations of women's multiple roles.

About six years ago, I participated in a short-term program that was designed to encourage women to enter the field of information technology (IT). Because I had been unemployed for a long time, I saw this as my golden chance to acquire skills that would open up many opportunities for employment in both the public and private sectors. In addition, since I did not have any Canadian experience (except as a gender intern for nine months at the International Development Research Centre), and as mother of two, I felt that it would take a long time before I could ever get on any career path. In short, I was desperate.

Three weeks into the IT program, I discovered that I was expecting my third child. I remember experiencing mixed emotions. Because I was determined not to quit or give up such a golden opportunity, I immediately approached the co-ordinator of the program and made my pledge to attend all the classes and to fulfill all the requirements of the course. I also pleaded with her to schedule my three-month work placement after the baby was born so that I could still benefit from the second component of the program. Once I had completed negotiating my participation in the program, all that was left was to manage myself and meet my family obligations as well as to find strategies for navigating around the daily demands and challenges of the program.

One thing I remember vividly is my classmates asking me constantly how I was able to cope with two young children (both under five years), a husband, a home, and attending the IT course as a full-time student. It was this constant probing that increased my awareness of my multiple roles and the level and quality of participation demanded by each one. One of the things I realized was that I did not want to use any of the roles as an excuse, because that would allow my classmates as well as friends and family members to make excuses for me. In other words, because I was concerned about the common stereotypes associated with women, visible minorities, motherhood, and marriage, I made every effort not to have anyone use these labels on me.

Furthermore, as a woman of colour, I felt the pressure to excel and succeed in order to participate in a field that is largely male-dominated. That is, I had unwittingly internalized the goals of the program, and therefore, I felt obligated not to waste the valuable resources invested in this effort to encourage women to explore careers in IT.

Reflecting back, there were a number of personal issues that I had to address and resolve. First, as a mother, I had to ensure that I was meeting all the emotional, nutritional, social, and spiritual needs of my two toddlers. One thing that helped was teaming up with another mom in my neighbourhood who stayed at home full-time to care for her own children. That way, I was assured that my children were given good-quality care while I was attending classes. Second, I was fortunate to have the valuable support of my spouse, who encouraged me throughout all my endeavours. As someone who had known me for many years as a graduate student, and since I supported him through his program in law school, he always admired my ability and determination to balance all aspects of my life. This marital support was evident when I completed the program and had to participate in the three-month work placement. In terms of my family life, it was a great sacrifice for me to work as a volunteer and incur child care costs as well as additional costs as a full-time worker. In this situation, what helped me greatly was the fact that my spouse and I discussed our family goals and collectively agreed on what we were willing to sacrifice and for how long. Although this is an area we are constantly negotiating and renegotiating, I feel that having someone who is understanding and support-ive provided a conducive environment for me to come to terms with the external and social pressures that I had to cope with as woman of colour, mother, wife, and student.

My reflections on these experiences have made me more aware of social, economic, political, and cultural barriers that sometimes inhibit women from perceiving their lives as an integrated whole in which their many roles affect the achievement of their goals.

The key question for me is: how do the different roles we play at home, at school, within our family, and in the community influence our perceptions, our active participation, and our negotiations as women? In what ways does playing multiple roles put women at a disadvantage (or at advantage)? Can you think of any examples of possible benefits of the multiple roles that women play? And what about men? Do they also play multiple roles? And if so, are there differences between women and men? Are these mainly gender differences, or are these gender differences also shaped by ethnicity, class, and culture?

Mohanty argues that feminist anti-imperialist processes can challenge and undermine the American nexus of economic and military power. Her clear and simple logic is grounded in the gendered struggles of Third World women of colour. The imperialist machine of economic globalization relies on women's bodies: it is a deeply gendered process in which women produce many of the products sold, entertain and sexually satisfy the troops of the armies supporting the economic enterprises, and purchase the goods that are produced.

> The argument I am making here is very simple: imperialism, militarization, and globalization all traffic in women's bodies, women's labor, and the ideologies of masculinity/femininity, heteronormativity, racism and nationalism to consolidate and reproduce power and domination. Thus, it is anti-racist, anti-imperialist, anti-capitalist, multiple gendered feminist praxis that can provide the ground for dismantling empire and re-envisioning just, humane and secure homespaces for marginalized communities globally. (Mohanty 2006, 9)

Those marginalized communities in Mohanty's analysis include women who live in the 'First World' under 'Third World' conditions alongside those who are located geographically in the less industrialized countries usually called the 'Third World'. The efforts to theorize inclusively have required a commitment to listen to the voices of the subaltern populations of the world and reflect deeply on power relations. Although Mohanty was one of the first thinkers to introduce the concept of 'Third World women' to feminist theorists and did so with the intention of enriching inclusivity, she has since come to believe that a slightly different terminology would be more appropriate. The term 'Third World' has come to stand for ways in which these women are disadvantaged at the expense of discussion about the competencies, successes, and other dimensions of their experience. As well, the numbers 'Third' and 'First' very subtly rank them below people of the 'First World'. The numerical significance of those disadvantaged by global capitalism and the power imbalances of neo-colonialism are better captured by identifying the disadvantaged group as the 'Two-Thirds World' (since they constitute at least that proportion of the world's population). In this reframing, those of us wielding more than our fair measure of power and wealth are identified as the 'One-Third World' (Mohanty 2003).

Within a project such as Mohanty's are hopes for career equity built upon a value system that is not skewed by differentials of gender and race. This is the type of solution that does not deepen the exploitation of Two-Thirds World women while equalizing the opportunities of One-Third World women and men. It is a huge project, involving changes to the way we think, the way we organize ourselves as societies, and the balance between economics, environments, and politics, and perhaps most significant for our consideration of careers, we need a change in values that honours characteristics or behaviours labelled 'feminine' in balance with our appreciation for the masculine and in ways that are open to cultural diversity.

CONCLUSION

The careers of Canadian workers continue to reflect traditional gender patterns to a greater extent than one might expect at a time when most members of both sexes spend at least part of their lives in the paid workforce. While the worst stereotypical associations of masculinity with physical strength and femininity with nurturing have faded, gendering of occupations and gender segregation within career structures persist in more subtle forms. Where women and men are both present within job classifications, women are frequently concentrated at the lower levels of the career structure, and where Two-Thirds World women are included at all, they are overrepresented in the least desirable and most poorly rewarded occupations.

Over time and across differences of gender and country of origin, the Canadian state has had a changing and contradictory role in relation to careers. For a time, the civil service offered some of the best jobs for women in the country, but these opportunities have been curtailed over the past 20 years with the shrinking of government roles in health care and social services. Women from non-European countries continue to experience prejudicial treatment in the career windows and citizenship opportunities available to them under government policy. Neo-liberal globalization has significant negative impacts on gender relations and equity. The expansion of the private sector with its exclusive profit motive results in more unpaid and poorly paid work for women while enhancing the careers of wealthier One-Third World men.

Some aspects of gendered career inequalities have been remedied through legislation and unionization. Women and men are entering non-traditional fields of work, and when possible women are working to overcome barriers to their career progress. However, since the value of one kind of skill or contribution over another is a socially constructed measure, pay equity has not always brought results that women workers find fair. Still, equal work is now more likely to return equal pay regardless of the gender identity of the worker, and critical analysis continues to provide opportunities for rethinking what the value of 'feminine' work is.

Solidarity within and across genders is still possible. While there is a tendency to think that capitalism in general and transnational corporations specifically have become irresistible social forces that are polarizing the economy, there is also evidence of other possibilities. When we look at the gendered divisions of resources and opportunities within some local communities, we can see that systemic supports for equity and mutual benefit are also possible. Our active involvement in the rejection of sexist, racist, and imperialist ideologies can push back against imperial power, contributing both locally and globally towards a social world where opportunity is no longer defined by gender in any of its forms.

Research Questions

1. Do you know of anyone—male or female—who works in a non-traditional job? Ask them how it feels to be in a gender minority in their workplace. Is there anything about how their workplace is organized or the way people act that makes them feel included or excluded from the predominant culture of their workplace?

2. Try to find images of jobs in magazines, newspapers, or advertisements. Do the images portray the jobs as gender-neutral, or are there messages in the images to suggest that these jobs are gendered?

3. Form groups of four to six with roughly equal numbers of males and females; discuss your answers to each of the following questions. Take notes about what you learn and write up the results focusing on gender differences and similarities.
   - What are your current career aspirations?
   - Do they fit in traditional or non-traditional employment patterns?
   - How were your career ideas formed, and who or what were your biggest influences in that decision?
   - What would an alternative career choice be for you, and how does it fit in the pattern of gendered careers?
   - What forms of paid work have you done?
   - What was the gender breakdown of the management in those workplaces?

Discussion Questions

1. Why and how have immigrant women been disadvantaged in Canada's job market?
2. How do women's experiences of non-traditional occupations compare to men's experiences of non-traditional occupations?
3. Why doesn't the strategy of equal pay for equal work remedy the inequalities of the Canadian labour force?
4. How has neo-liberalism affected the gendering of employment in Canada?

Further Reading

Galabuzi, Grace-Edward. 2006. *Canada's Economic Apartheid: The Social Exclusion of Racialized Groups in the New Century*. Toronto: Canadian Scholars' Press. An important book for demonstrating that economic and social inequalities in the lives of racialized Canadians are direct consequences of continuing social and economic policies pursued by our governments.

Gibson-Graham, J.K. 2006. *A Postcapitalist Politics*. Minneapolis: University of Minnesota Press. Challenges the assumption that capitalism is everywhere and all-powerful with a series of explications of the presence of post-capitalist subjects, economies, and communities.

Porter, Ann. 2003. *Gendered States: Women, Unemployment Insurance, and the Political Economy of the Welfare State in Canada, 1945–1997*. Toronto: University of Toronto Press. A compelling analysis of how Canadian women workers' historical experiences of high levels of income insecurity are attributable more directly to social and economic policies than to the competencies of the workers themselves.

Shalla, Vivian, ed. 2006. *Working in a Global Era: Canadian Perspectives*. Toronto: Canadian Scholars' Press. A collection of articles that will develop your understanding of what 'globalization' is and how these processes of political/economic change affect diverse workers distinctly in ways that tend to lessen their control over their work environment while creating greater social and economic disparity between workers of varying identities.

Films

North Country. 2005. A fictionalized account of the response of women workers at a mine in Minnesota who were harassed on the job but eventually confronted their co-workers and their community to claim their space alongside the men.

The Take. 2004. <www.thetake.org>. Documenting the inspirational case of autoparts workers in Argentina who resist a globalized attempt to discard them as workers, confront political corruption, and revive their factory on a socialist model.

The Corporation. 2003. Documentation of the pathological mode upon which corporations are constructed and the destructive implications of that fact.

El Contrado (The Contract). 2003. National Film Board of Canada documentary film about the constrained choices of Mexican men working as migrant labourers in southern Ontario and their desire for dignity and respect.

Websites

www.genderwork.ca
Offers a scholarly database on gender and work in Canada analyzing gender and work from a feminist political economy perspective under six modules: Heath Care, Migration, Precarious Employment, Technology, Unions, and Unpaid Work.

www.cleanclothes.org
An activists' website supporting an international campaign to improve working conditions in the garment and sportswear industries.

www.justicia4migrantworkers.org
Maintained by a non-profit group focused on promoting the rights of Caribbean and Mexican workers admitted to Canada under the Seasonal Agricultural Workers Program.

www.canadians.org
Website of the Council of Canadians, a non-profit, non-partisan group focusing on the well-being of Canadians through issues such as fair trade, clean water, energy security, and public health care.

Chapter 6

Analyzing the Complexity of Gender: Intersectionality and Beyond

Chapter Objectives

1. To demonstrate different scholarly positions concerning the usefulness of intersectionality as a way to theorize and research the complexity of gender.
2. To illustrate challenges in analyzing the complexity of gender relations in Canada with the example of gender-based analysis in policy assessment and development.
3. To encourage students to be open to ongoing questions and new developments in the sociological analysis of gender.
4. To consider issues of gender and good research practice in the production and validation of knowledge.

INTRODUCTION

Throughout this book, we have interwoven sociological theory with personal, theoretical, and political narratives. As educators, we are convinced that as students you learn more when you are able to connect sociological material to 'real world' events as they unfold around you—in your family and neighbourhood, in newspapers, on the Internet, and on TV. In this final chapter, we reflect in further detail on a key theme in the second shift in the sociological analysis of gender. We bring together our thoughts, and those of others, on the recent theoretical developments and practical applications of intersectionality as an approach to understanding the complexities of gender. Much of the chapter is organized as a series of questions. This reflects the fact that many of the issues discussed are matters of ongoing debate and development. As more advanced sociological students, it is important for you to begin thinking about sociology as a collection of knowledge that is open-ended, contested, and always changing as new challenges and ways of thinking emerge. The questions posed in this chapter are ones that many of you will confront and engage with in your honours papers and even perhaps in your graduate work, should you decide to pursue your sociological interest in gender at an advanced level of study.

To begin the discussion, we ask you to consider the complexities of gendered experience in one of the most horrific cases of serial murder in Canada. The story, with which you may already have some familiarity, is often referred to as the case of the Missing Women. Spanning over 30 years, the story unfolded in a courtroom and on the east end streets of Vancouver as well as on a farm nearby in Port Coquitlam. At the heart of the story are more than 60 women who one by one went missing, with barely any notice on the part of the police or the wider community. Most of the missing women were economically impoverished and belonged to ethnic minority groups. Many were Aboriginal. Almost all were engaged in sex work. Some, probably a large proportion, were suffering addictions. The first woman went missing in the early 1980s, but the authorities did not begin a systematic investigation until decades later. Many critics have asked how long it would have taken authorities to act if the missing women were middle-class, white, young, female schoolteachers. As it was, the missing women were on the wrong side of class, race, occupation, health, citizenship, housing, age, and gender divides. The coincidence of their multiple disadvantages made them socially invisible and their disappearance of little official consequence. For indigenous women, the Sisters in Spirit Campaign, launched by the Native Women's Association of Canada in 2004, states the problem clearly: 'Although indigenous women represent only 3 per cent of the Canadian population, they are overrepresented as victims of racialized, sexualized violence. . . . Sadly, many indigenous women are seen as less than human, or not as human beings at all.'[1] The brutal, callous treatment of the missing women's bodies is ugly evidence of the truth of this statement.

While the Missing Women story clearly highlights some of the tragic ways that intersections of gender, class, and ethnicity matter for women, it is also a story about men positioned very differently in relation to the events of this case. On a positive note, it is also a story about a group of indigenous men, Brothers in Spirit, who are acting in solidarity to support the Sisters in Spirit campaign. A different positioning is that of Don Morrison, the Vancouver police complaints commissioner, who was forced to resign from his post, largely because of his inattention to complaints about police inaction on the case. Morrison was, however, on the right side of the gender, race, and class divide, and although he left his post in disgrace, he received a handsome sum of severance money. The most notorious male in these events is the pig farmer Robert William Pickton. He confessed to murdering 49 women altogether while claiming regret at not achieving his target of 50. He has been convicted of six murders and is charged with several others. As a white, property-owning male positioned in a relation of power and control over a group of low-income, mainly ethnic minority and Aboriginal women, Pickton represents yet another configuration of the complex intersections of gender, class, and race.

As detailed in the insert by Kristen Gilchrist, a PhD student in sociology at Carleton, the story of the Missing Women shows how crucial it is to understand and identify the consequences of intersecting disadvantages. It also highlights the importance of recognizing that these intersections have an impact not only on individual stories and personal experience but also on institutional, cultural, and broader structural contexts. The Missing Women case tells us about more than the sick and dangerous actions of one man. It reveals to us the institutional and structural conditions that not only allowed the disappearances and murders to happen but also allowed some to attempt to profit from them.

Multiple Disadvantages:
The Missing and Murdered Women of Vancouver

by Kristen Gilchrist
Sociology PhD Program

Given their race, class, sexualized occupation, and criminalized lifestyle, the women who went missing from the Vancouver area dubbed 'Canada's poorest postal code' did so without attracting much attention (Jiwani and Young 2006). Their deaths have become a symbol of the structural violence that can be perpetrated on individuals who become socially invisible, and even disposable, because of multiple, interconnecting disadvantages.

The Missing Women case extends far beyond the appalling actions of the convicted murderer, Robert Pickton. It raises issues of how gender, occupation, ethnicity, health status, and culture affect the valuing of human life and limit the extent to which all citizens are offered the protection or consideration of social institutions such as the police, the law, and the news media.

For several years prior to Pickton's arrest, the families and friends of the missing women accused Vancouver police, the RCMP, and the mayor's office of denying any link between their failure to act on the disappearances and the women's marginal status as sex workers and drug addicts. When police did act by posting a $100,000 reward for the capture of a suspect relating to the Missing Women case, they were further criticized for offering the same reward for the arrest of two separate home-invasion suspects in affluent Vancouver suburbs (Lowman 2000).

This case highlights other issues of sociological and political significance. First, it points to the extreme vulnerability of street sex workers to predatory violence. An American study of serial killers from 1960 to 1995 found that 78 per cent of their victims were sex workers (Egger 1998). Gary Ridgeway, the infamous 'Green River Killer' who pleaded guilty in 2003 to the murders of 48 street sex workers in Seattle, Washington, professed in open court that he targeted street sex workers 'because they were easy to pick up without being noticed'. Ridgeway went on to say, 'I picked prostitutes because I thought I could kill as many of them as I wanted without getting caught.'

Second, a large proportion of the victims in this case were Aboriginal women. This underscores the extreme vulnerability faced by Aboriginal women in Canada. The Native Women's Association of Canada (Jacobs 2002) and Amnesty International (2004) estimate that more than 500 Aboriginal women from all walks of life have gone missing and/or been murdered in Canada in the past two decades. Many are believed to be victims of sexual violence and murder. Their disproportionate

victimization raises serious questions about whether Aboriginal women are being specifically targeted because they are so marginalized in Canadian society (Gilchrist 2007). It is worth noting that Aboriginal women make up 70 per cent of street sex workers in Vancouver's Downtown Eastside and most often they work in the most dangerous and low-paying areas (Culhane 2003).

Finally, even after their deaths, these women of Vancouver's Downtown East-side continue to be marginalized and demonized (Jiwani and Young 2006). The news media, in particular, have been taken to task for exploiting and sensation-alizing the gory details and horrific brutality perpetrated against the women in order to boost ratings and/or sell newspapers. Police and the press continue to use police mug shots to depict the victims. Such representations de-emphasize the victims' humanity by one-dimensionally positioning them as criminal, deviant, and drug-addicted.

Feminist media critics have further questioned the media's widespread depiction of the perpetrators of violent crimes, such as Robert Pickton, as sick or deranged, without examining broader social issues. Instead, critics are shifting the focus onto the ways that the multiple locations of disadvantage faced by Aboriginal women and street sex workers render them vulnerable on many fronts. Marginal women are not only at risk of victimization, they are also at risk of structural violence and of being discarded and neglected by police, news media, and the wider Canadian public. By extension, an important issue that deserves further consideration is how and why it is that sexual and physical violence against women remains such a widespread and systemic social problem—and specifically asking what steps can be taken to challenge and prevent violence.

We have tried to demonstrate in the preceding five chapters that gender relations are highly diverse and that patterns of intersecting identities can intensify gendered experience. The complexities and dynamics of gender are revealed in sharp relief in extreme situations such as the Missing Women case. They are also present in less extreme, more mundane, everyday actions and encounters. The ways in which our gender intersects with a range of other significant social characteristics matters greatly in terms of how we are viewed and treated by our friends, colleagues, family, the media, the police, the courts, the schools, and the communities where we live, play, and work.

For children, adolescents, and younger and more mature adults, gendered experience varies according to a host of social processes and relations. Not only are gender relations often classed and racialized, experiences of gender can also be structured by and vary according to many other dimensions of social life such as age, dis/ability, sexuality, and culture. There is a widespread consensus in the sociological literature on gender that in order to adequately and fully capture the diversity in women's and men's experience, the concept of gender needs to be specified and contextualized. To specify the concept of gender, we need to identify exactly which women and men are being referred to—older? single? poor? university-educated? white? heterosexual?

Aboriginal? new immigrant? But these more specialized identifications are not in themselves meaningful. We must also identify the social context within which these categories of experience are produced as meaningful and have consequences for the individuals concerned. Context is largely a matter of the social processes and relationships shaping the life-world of individuals. It is these processes and relationships that make specific forms of gendered experience meaningful.

Although sociologists generally agree that gendered experience needs to be specified and contextualized, there are different views as to how this should occur. That is, while there is a strong sociological consensus that gender is a complex and multifaceted phenomenon, this still leaves open questions of how to move on from this starting point to create insightful and useful sociological knowledge. In attending to these questions, sociologists and feminist scholars have and continue to put forth different analytical strategies. More specifically, in this final chapter we discuss some of the different ways that feminist scholars and sociologists are approaching the use of intersectionality as a way of analyzing the complexity of gender.

THEORIZING COMPLEXITY: FROM ADDITIVE MODELS TO INTERSECTIONALITY

In chapter 1, we traced the lines of critique and analysis that led to a general endorsement of some version of intersectional analysis as the way to understand and theorize the diversity of gender experiences and the structures that enable and constrain change. Key lines of critique focused on the use of unspecified gender categories. One strand of this critique focused on the exclusion of race and ethnicity. A second strand pointed to the significance of class differences among women and the limitations of remedies for gender inequality that heightened inequalities among women. A third strand argued that theories of gender presumed heterosexual orientations and thus effectively contributed to the marginalization and pathologizing of other sexual identities and practices. A fourth strand argued for the importance of dis/ability differences.

While there is considerable consensus on the need to consider other aspects of oppression and disadvantage when researching the experience and structure of gender inequality, the question of exactly *how* to theorize diversity has been of equal concern and much debate. An early issue that arose, for example, related to whether all of these aspects of experience, and what were often termed 'structures of oppression', should be treated as equally significant or, alternatively, was there a hierarchy of oppressions? This question led, in turn, to the practice of adding up oppressions and instances of inequality and what came to be called, and ultimately dismissed, as the 'additive' approach to understanding gender diversity and inequality.

The initial lens for understanding the diversity of gendered lives was identified as an 'additive' model. In an additive approach, one would add to a gender analysis considerations of race, class, disability, ethnicity, citizenship, age, visible-minority status, and so on. However, it did not take long before feminist sociologists and other scholars were strongly opposing this additive method of analysis. The problem they identified was that it falsely distinguished as separate dimensions aspects of identities and circumstances that are integrated and inseparable. In the United States, Spellman argued: 'One's gender identity is not related to one's racial and class identity as the parts of pop-bead necklaces are related, separable and insertable in other "strands" with different racial and class "parts" ' (1988, 15). At the same time, some described the divisions between women as a consequence of issues such as race, sexuality, nationality, ethnicity, and class experiences as constituting 'contradictions of oppression'. In the UK, Ramazanoglu (1989) argued that such divisions created oppositions that could not easily be overcome either in theory or in political practice.

In Canada, an ardent critic of the additive approach, Himani Bannerji was equally strong in her condemnation of its false 'political arithmetic' (1995, 113). She argued passionately for a form of social analysis that would not only theorize forms of experience in relation to each other but also create an inclusive and integrated social analysis in the service of social change. Her vision was of an analysis that would reveal, and help to challenge, socially organized relations of domination 'encoded as gender, race and class' (1995, 89). These critiques led scholars and activists to begin to think about the ways in which oppressions interlocked, interconnected, and intersected.

By the late 1980s and into the 1990s, scholars were more routinely attending to the diversity within gender categories and were working with a more finely tuned understanding of how complex patterns of identity and circumstances can both heighten privilege and deepen disadvantage. In the United States, Andersen and Collins wrote about an approach based on a 'matrix of domination' model in which there are 'multiple interlocking levels of domination that stem from the societal configuration of race, class, and gender relations [and] affect individual consciousness, group interactions, and group access to institutional power and privileges' (1992, 3). Similar ideas were developing in Canada, where Gillian Creese and Daiva Stasiulis (1996) outlined the importance of a multi-dimensional approach to inequality with no presumption of the relative importance or particular configuration of any dimension. Creese (1999) follows up on these insights with detailed research on how intersections of gender, class, and race become institutionalized through the union and management practices of a large public-sector utility company in BC. Also in Canada, Sherene Razack was writing about a theory of 'interlocking systems of domination', arguing about the existence of interconnected and interdependent systems of inequality and, more generally, systems of women's oppressions. In an edited collection on the pervasive racism experienced by feminist scholars working within Canadian universities, Linda Carty (1991, 31) has noted: 'As Black women, we experience our femaleness and Blackness together, always at the same time, and we challenge whether it is possible for white women to be white or female because we see them as white and female.' As Vijay Agnew (2002, 7) reflects, 'it became the norm to use the term *intersectionality* to refer to the crosscutting nature of oppression in different identities.'[2]

A key feature of an intersectional approach is that it understands the categories of inequality and oppression to be relational. This point is well revealed in Sherene Razack's book (1998), *Looking White People in the Eye*. She ends her book with a discussion of the ways in which some white feminists do not seriously engage with their complicity in the disadvantages faced by other women. She makes the provocative claim that no one is innocent in the story of race. One example is the way that greater financial independence and personal autonomy for middle-class white women in

North America occurs partly because of the work of much lower-paid child care and domestic workers (as the story of Melca Salvador in the previous chapter illustrates). While, as we noted in chapter 4, many feminists have made this critique, it is also important to draw out the ways in which this occurs relationally between women of different classes and ethnicities. Most notably, women of colour or first-generation immigrant women take up these lower-waged jobs, which support other women and, of course, men. As Razack highlights, we need to attend to the relational dimensions of inequality. That is, who is constrained or enabled by particular social arrangements, and further, who is complicit in the constraining or enabling of others? Throughout her book, Razack thus urges feminists to reflect on the theme of complicity and more specifically on the ways in which white, middle-class North American women and men are complicit in continuing relations of inequality for Aboriginal and immigrant women and men. Razack's *Looking White People in the Eye* is thus a call for women of colour to look at white women and for white women to look at themselves.

It is now fairly common for sociologists to regard the categories of intersectional analysis as relational. There is also now a more expansive understanding of how diverse gender categories are. We have travelled very far into the matrix of possible divisions, complexities, and intersections. Ten years ago, Janet Chafetz (1997) noted that intersectionality was a 'hot topic'. It remains a hot topic today, but the enthusiasm with which we embrace it is tempered by questions of how we move on from this point.

DEVELOPING AN INTERSECTIONAL APPROACH: QUESTIONS AND CHALLENGES

There has been a great deal of agreement among feminist scholars, activists, and sociologists about the uses and application of intersectional analyses to understand women's inequalities in relation to men as well as social and experiential differences among women. Although there continue to be questions about the reach of intersectional analysis—for example, how well it can cover the complex nexus of disadvantages and marginalizations experienced by persons with disabilities (Meekosha 2006; 2008)—scholars are interested enough in its possibilities to seriously examine its potential. One area requiring extensive examination is how to apply such analyses to social life and the everyday worlds of women and men. The ongoing debate and discussion over how intersectional analysis may be used to analyze the everyday lives of women and men reflects the fact that this analytical lens is still very much in development. In this section, we outline some of the areas of contention and continuing debate. We ask six questions to help identify key points at issue and to guide our discussion of recent developments.

(i) Is gender assumed to be significant as a starting point of analysis?

The first question is whether intersectional analysis should begin with a specific idea of the content or substance of gender in relation to other dimensions of social inequality. That is, in developing their projects, should researchers start with a position that assumes precisely how gender is significant in people's lives?

Most authors working with an intersectional approach are inclined to investigate rather than assume the significance of gender. Joan Acker (2006), for example, urges us to begin with gender (and class, race, sexuality) as starting points of analysis whose exact shape and meaning emerge through the analytical process. Evelyn Nakano Glenn (2002) is also of this view, arguing that a goal of analysis must be to *discover* the specificity and historical variability of classed, raced, and gendered experience. What this means is that analysts do not want to predetermine what gender relations might mean and look like in their research investigations. However, it also means that analysts are prepared to begin with an assumption that gender will matter in some way—the research question is *how*.

Another issue, still on the general question of 'starting points', involves a more radical departure. The issue here is whether or not *any dimensions of experience* will be presumed to be significant at the outset of the analysis. With this position as a starting point, we would be prepared to discover that in the specific instance under investigation, gender *is not significant* as a structural or experiential focus. For example, in Janet's case studies of occupational segregation in the UK (1994; 2002), she found that what had been identified as a gendered pattern of job segregation was primarily a pattern of segregation by relations to household responsibilities. The gender skew in the jobs she researched was part of a larger pattern of wage segregation that distinguished two types of jobs: component-wage jobs in which people (both men and women) could not earn enough money to support themselves; and full-wage jobs that paid enough to allow people to live as independent adults. Other researchers have elaborated on this idea in their investigations of job structures in the US (Pratt and Hanson 1993) and in the wider occupational structure in the UK (Rubery 1997). Leslie McCall's (2001) recent work on the 'complex inequality' of American labour markets also shows that in some municipalities, gender is not the primary fault line of wage inequality. Marshall summarizes this point succinctly when she argues that we must (2000, 162) be open to 'relinquishing gender's hegemony as a starting point for analysis, looking instead to if and how it emerges as significant in particular circumstances'.

While some people have difficulty accepting that we may need to regard the importance of gender as a question for analysis rather than an assumption of it, we must recognize that such a situation reflects any number of historical and specific conditions—including the successes of feminist political campaigns and the profoundly negative realities of other forms of oppression and discrimination. Perhaps the bottom-line question, however, is: *what can we determine in advance?* Stasiulis (1999) cautions theorists and analysts to guard against bringing new forms of essentialism into intersectional analysis. She argues, using examples of race and culture, that intersectional analysis does not necessarily eliminate essentialist thinking either in terms of what is significant or how it is significant. She concludes: '*Which* social relations in the seemingly dizzying array of differences should be accorded particular salience or significance in any given theoretical framework is impossible to predict a priori' (1999, 378). This more open, heuristic approach echoes the one endorsed by Joy Parr, who counsels us to 'presume less' about the relevance of categories of difference and their relation to configurations of daily life in specific settings (1990, 231). Her detailed historical analysis of the dramatically different configurations of gender, class, age, ethnicity, and religion in the workforce of two Ontario manufacturing

towns demonstrates the interpretive value of keeping an open mind about what theoretical categories may be analytically relevant and useful.

(ii) What assumptions are made about the relative positioning of the many dimensions included in the analysis? Are some more important than others?

As analysts try to work with formulations of intersectionality, they generally reject
any notion of conceptual hierarchy. Creese and Stasiulis set this argument out clearly
in the introduction to their special issue on intersectionality in *Studies in Political
Economy*. What they argue for explicitly in the case of political economy applies just
as readily to sociology: 'When we shift our theoretical lens to the intersections between
and among relations of gender, race, class and sexuality, we extend the boundaries of
political economy by challenging the "categorical hegemony" attempted by many
Marxists with class, many feminists with gender' (Creese and Stasiulis 1996, 8). For
many, this involves rejecting class as the primary structure of social relations, with
race and gender folded in as modifications of an already existing structure of class
inequalities. This position is also adopted by Seccombe and Livingstone in their investigation of group consciousness in the context of work. They aim to 'break with a
"class first" framework that treats gender, generational and race relations as subsidiary
to, or somehow derived from, class relations' (1996, 131). Evans and Wekerle (1997)
also reject conceptual ranking in their analysis of the development of the Canadian
welfare state.

The advantage of regarding the relative positioning of dimensions of inequality
as a variable feature of social relations is illustrated very strikingly in McCall's (2001)
case studies of different configurations of wage inequality in four American cities.
She discovered, for example, that in the industrial city of Detroit, gender inequality
was typically higher than the national average, while racial inequality was lower. This
pattern contrasts with the post-industrial city of Dallas, where racial inequality was
higher than the national average and gender inequality was typically lower. Both these
patterns in turn contrast with the high-tech manufacturing city of St Louis, where
both racial and gender inequality were higher than the national average. In McCall's
study, class inequalities were most extreme in the city of Miami. This is interesting
evidence of how, a priori, sociologists cannot tell which dimensions of inequality will
be the most significant. As McCall says (2001, 192), 'In one configuration, gender
might be present in the starkest divisions, while in another it might be race or class,
or in yet another it might be some combination.'

The significance of intersectionality for policy analysis is also emphasized in
Neysmith et al.'s (2005) analysis of how neo-liberal approaches to social policy in
Canada have been lived by individuals and their households. Complexities of class,
gender, household composition, locality, age, race, ability, and social networks were
all important in helping to decipher and understand how equally complex interconnections of policies and programs shape daily lives. Such an approach, they argue, can
help to explore and reveal differences in and struggles over meaning—an aspect of
policy impacts that is as important as struggles over resources. It helps to answer the
question (2005, 208): what differences and divisions matter?

In Andrea's research on Canadian primary caregiving fathers, she started out questioning the significance of gender in parenting. The title of her book, *Do Men Mother?*, was partly conceived as a way of asking whether or not there were gender differences in the practices and identities associated with parenting. She was also aware of the need to include a diversity of fathering experiences across class, ethnicity, and sexuality in order to investigate diversity of gendered experiences. Thus, her study included interviews with 17 fathers of visible minorities, nine gay fathers, and men from varied levels of income and occupational status. Her strategy was not to assume difference but to include diversity of experience and social location in order to explore where and how differences mattered. As detailed in the excerpt from her book in the insert below (2006, 202–4), the way in which intersectionality played out varied across social settings. What was noteworthy was how a key resource of masculinity—'earning'—and class mattered in how fathers were viewed, and accepted, by others as primary caregivers.

Resources of Masculinity, Class, and Earning:
'It Might Be Different If I Was a Plumber'

For many men, being primary caregivers without having achieved success as breadwinners signals something out of sync with what many communities consider as a socially acceptable identity for a male and for a father. Fathers without jobs or those in low-income jobs, particularly single fathers in such scenarios, can also be viewed with particular suspicion within communities. Stay-at-home fathers fare slightly better, although not working could still ring community alarm bells if it seemed that the father may have lost his job and was not in his caring situation due to a family 'choice'. A key resource of hegemonic masculinity—that of social status acquired through being a family provider, especially in a high-income or high-status profession—helps to increase fathers' ability to cross into the socially gendered identity of caregiver, cushioning them from being viewed with suspicion.

Henry, for example, highlighted how his lower social class, combined with the fact that he was out of work, was one of the reasons why his house was not viewed as an acceptable option for his daughter's sleepovers:

'My daughter sleeps over at a friend's place right across the street, and her friend never comes back. I push it in the sense that it isn't fair. I actually try to mention it to the parents and stuff, but it's no big deal. They live in a nice big detached house. The girl mentioned has two full sets of parents that both live in nice big detached houses with multiple cars, or that kind of thing. And I live in this town-house co-op place.'

On the other hand, Jacob, a physician in training, pointed out that sleepovers were not a problem at his house, either for his two sons or for his 11-year-old daughter. He reflected on how this and his acceptance as a frequent helper in his children's schools could be rendered unproblematic, partly because his occupation was one of high status:

> 'I am involved in the school. I help out on field trips. I go in and help to read whatever I can. I am also the head lice co-ordinator. Once or twice a month I go and look at heads! I know the teachers and the principal and a lot of the kids. I also know them from ringette and hockey. I feel very accepted. . . . Being a doctor may be part of it. It might be different if I was a plumber.'

What is playing out here are the links between hegemonic masculinity and earning. In effect, the economically unsuccessful male caring for children represents a form of double jeopardy because he is judged as being a *failed* male (i.e., not a breadwinner) and as a *deviant* man (i.e., a primary caregiver). On the other hand, a male who is visibly providing economically for his family, or has temporarily left a career that allows him to do this, often feels more comfortable in himself and more accepted in his community as a caregiver. Meanwhile, gay fathers often face what theorists have termed 'multiple jeopardy', because both gender and sexuality and, in some cases, social class are working against their acceptance within communities. One example is Jean-Marc, a French-Canadian 43-year-old gay and divorced father of seven-year-old twin boys. Living in a small town, he has remained wary of the community's perceptions of him as a gay father:

> 'I have not met any of their teachers yet (long sigh). . . . I am perhaps somewhat timid. I don't know. I just didn't know what to expect. It's a situation where their teacher is married to a police officer in the town. Everybody knows me. I will go. . . . I want them to know that "hey, I am a good father. I am involved. And you may have heard that I am gay and that is absolutely correct. But I am not some riff raff off the street."'

(iii) What dimensions of experience need to be included in the analysis?

As intersectional analysis became an accepted way of understanding gendered lives, it became clear that other, more analytical tools were needed in order to understand inequalities. While there has been a growing general agreement that we need to move beyond the conceptual 'trinity' of class, gender, and race in intersectional analysis, there is still the question of how we know what else needs to be included. Various writers have introduced dis/ability, religion, sexuality, citizenship status, language, nationality, migration experience, and health status as relevant dimensions for an intersectional approach to the analysis of gender.

There is some disagreement in the literature about how long the set of diversity dimensions should be. Indeed, some have drawn a contrast between modern and post-modern approaches to intersectional analyses on just this point. For example, DiPalma and Ferguson (2006) suggest that modernist sociological approaches to gender and diversity attempt to move towards creating coherent and stable locations for subjects with intersecting characteristics. In contrast, they suggest that post-modern approaches to gender and diversity celebrate multiplicity for its potentially destabilizing and disrupting possibilities. In this sense, theorists influenced by post-modernism might be inclined to open up their analyses to unlimited sets of dimensions intertwined with gender, while more modernist approaches might be inclined to draw tighter analytical boundaries around possible diversities in gendered experience.

Post-modern sensibilities underlie recent attempts to widen understandings of race and ethnicity to make them more differentiated and contextual. For example, in Canada, feminist scholars have reflected on how 'race' can be configured differently for different groups of racialized women. As Jiwani puts it:

> The designation of Black has different meanings in the United States and Canada. In speaking about racialised women of colour, I am cognizant that Aboriginal and White women are also racialized. However, Aboriginal women have a different history, as indigenous people of this land. My position as an immigrant and an Other makes me painfully aware of how immigration itself was structured in the interests of forging the Canadian nation and grounded in the displacement and genocide of Aboriginal peoples. (2006, xviii)

In addition to recognizing differences within and between racialized groups, the concept of 'immigrant woman' also came under scrutiny. For example, Roxana Ng's (1986) investigation of a community-based employment counselling and placement agency in Toronto reveals the minute acts and assumptions that come together to create 'immigrant women' as a distinct category of labour.

(iv) Are dimensions mutually constituted?

When we have a sense of which dimensions of experience are interacting with gender, there is the very important question of *how* we conceptualize the relationships between these diverse experiences. There is a great deal of ambiguity and little agreement in this area of intersectional analysis. Glenn (2002, 12) argues that social constructionism can be used to forge an integrated analysis of how race and gender are 'mutually constituted systems of relationships organized around perceived differences'. Within this integrated framework, race, class, and gender share at least three characteristics: they are relational concepts; they each involve issues of representation and material relations; and each involves relations of power. The advantage of examining race, class, and gender as mutually constituted is that this approach will facilitate the analysis of specific and historically variable social situations. In considering how disability needs to be integrated into intersectional analysis, Meekosha (2006; 2008) also sees little value in analyzing dimensions of inequality and oppression as if they were separate dynamics. She presents a strong argument for an intercategorical examination of disability, class, gender, ethnicity, and race that recognizes their mutual constitution.

While Acker (2006) agrees with Glenn that analyses characterized by specificity and historical variability are desirable, she disagrees on how the relationship between gender, race, and class should be conceptualized. Acker's preferred idea of how to push forward an analysis of the complexity of gender draws heavily on the sociological approach of Dorothy Smith. Her preference is to use gender, class, and race as starting points or entry points in analysis—as heuristic devices for uncovering what is not seen, identified, or heard by mainstream investigations. Her view is that gender is always classed and raced; class is always gendered and raced; and race is always gendered and classed. How these general interconnections emerge and operate within specific social contexts is a matter for research. She further objects to the idea of mutually constituted relations, saying that: 'Although the concept of gendered and racialized class relations depicts class, gender and race as inherently interconnected, these concepts also represent difference that may be lost to view in the effort to approach them as mutually constituted' (2006, 51–2).

There is no clear consensus on this issue, and there continues to be much debate and disagreement over the ways in which multiple differences and inequalities intersect and indeed matter. Beginning in the late 1990s, feminist researchers, in the process of conducting empirical research on women's lives, began to recognize that sometimes one structure or experiential dimension of inequality—such as race or sexuality—might be the dominant one in a particular context—and relatively innocuous in other contexts. For example, Jane Ward (2004) has argued that 'not all differences are created equally' and that at times 'counting and ranking' inequalities may be a sound political strategy. That is, intersectionality appears in varied ways, with diverse and unique intersections being mapped out between gender, class, ethnicity, and sexuality at different points in the life course and in different sites (family, work, communities, schools). Canadian political scientist Radha Jhappan also discusses this approach by referring to a strategy called strategic essentialism. According to Jhappan (1996, 52): 'Strategic essentialism . . . sees identity as a function of context and allows us to stress one or several aspects of our identities according to the axis of oppression at issue in particular situations, without necessarily tying individuals to a specific identity for all time and purposes.'

Different authors use distinct terms to identify the nature of the relationship between gender and other dimensions of difference. Some talk of 'simultaneity' (Stasiulis 1999; West and Fenstermaker 1995), while others prefer the term 'mediation' (Dei 2005). McCall (2001) insists that while intersections of class, race, and gender occur, the underlying processes of inequality are distinct—at least in terms of wage inequality by class, race, and gender in four American cities. To the extent that any consensus is developing on this matter, it is to the effect that grand generalizations about the nature of relationships between categories of experience are of little use. While this does not necessarily resolve the question of what processes create intersections of gender and other dimensions of experience, it does encourage us to seek answers in the specifics of people's everyday lives. As Neysmith et al. (2005) have shown, the complexity of these lives requires attention to fine and highly significant details.

(v) Intersections as structure or experience?

There is common ground in the promotion of intersectionality as requiring a focus on process and social relations. However, authors have different ideas of where the emphasis has been either too strong or insufficient. According to American sociologist Patricia Hill Collins, intersectionality 'refers to particular forms of intersecting oppressions, for example, intersections of race and gender, or of sexuality and nation. Intersectional paradigms remind us that oppression cannot be reduced to one fundamental type, and that oppressions work together in producing injustice' (2000, 18). Collins also draws a distinction between intersectionality as operating at the level of experience and identity and 'the matrix of domination', which refers to 'how these intersecting oppressions are actually organized'. Here, Collins is explicitly pointing to how intersectional analysis works at the level of both structure and agency.

While the analytical terms 'structure' and 'agency' are constantly being conceptually redefined, the important issue to highlight here is that issues of difference and disadvantage can work at multiple levels of analysis. On the one hand, this analysis can operate at the level of identity or agency (e.g., 'I feel discriminated against as a Black woman, not just as a woman and not just as a Black person, but as a Black woman'). On the other hand, discrimination is also rooted in the ways in which social institutions are set up, that is, the ways in which families, workplaces, state policies, and laws are set up. This point is also well made in the work of Canadian sociologist Himani Bannerji, who draws on Dorothy Smith's presentation of the significance of experience as an analytical starting point. Bannerji urges us to move forward with intersectional analysis by beginning investigations with many experiences and descriptions of differences 'as the widest point of entry into a social analysis of mediation of those social relations—encoded as gender, race and class' (1995, 89). Meanwhile, Acker agrees that the experiential has been overwhelmed by attention to ideas of intersecting systems and structures. McCall (2005), by contrast, sees her role as rectifying a lack of attention to how intersections are structured.

(vi) What kind of data and analysis are required?

Intersectional analysis developed initially as a theoretical argument. Its real proof of viability and use, however, has to be its capacity to inform a research practice for both academic and policy purposes. As McCall states, 'despite the emergence of intersectionality as a major paradigm of research in women's studies and elsewhere, there has been little discussion of *how* to study intersectionality, that is, of its methodology' (2005, 1771).

McCall discusses how researchers have responded to the complexities involved in intersectional analysis—and here we speak in more detail about two of them: *intra-categorical* analysis and *inter-categorical* analysis. While both forms of analysis adopt a critical stance towards categories of analysis, they differ in the focus of their analytical approach.

The main focus of the intra-categorical methodology is to reveal the experiential realities of individuals and groups positioned at specific intersections of oppression. As McCall notes, this type of exploration of intra-categorical complexity is typically qualitative and draws on the rich developments within feminist research practice designed to reveal and express the depth and complexity of lived experience. Rose (2001) has discussed the advantages of qualitative analysis in the 'contextualization of experience', allowing a closer look at the multiple dimensions of inequality within women's lives.

As McCall notes, however, this type of intra-categorical analysis provides a rich but limited view of intersectionality. She makes the point that in this form of analysis, 'complexity derives from the analysis of a social location at the intersection of single dimensions of multiple categories, rather than at the intersection of the full range of dimensions of a full range of categories' (2005, 1781). For the latter analysis, she recommends an inter-categorical approach.

In order to appreciate the systemic and structured nature of intersecting multiple dimensions of inequality, it is important to examine complexity as a feature of relationships between as well as within all categories of the dimensions of interest. If gender is operating in a particular context as a structuring mechanism of inequality, we need a comparison between men and women to establish this. If we are then interested in the intersection of gender and visible minority status, we need to contrast and compare the experiences of men and women within each category of visible minority status, as well as contrast and compare the experience of all visible minority groups within each gender category. Such an inter-categorical analysis would be able to tell us which dimensions are having a structuring effect and whether any existing effects are modified or contextualized by their intersection with other dimensions. This type of approach can only be conducted in practice with quantitative forms of analysis, which can handle inter-categorical complexity.[3]

There is talk in discussions of feminist methodology in Canada of revisiting quantitative methodologies to find ways of claiming them for feminist purposes (for an example, see Rose 2001), and in this light, McCall's argument is very interesting. She presents a strong case for the value of certain forms of quantitative research in advancing the analysis of intersectionality. The report of her own quantitative inter-categorical analysis of the relative weight of gender, class, and race on wage inequalities in four American cities piques one's interest in the possibilities of this approach, because it supports the need for place-specific and contextualized policy development that much recent feminist research in Canada is calling for.

While intersectional analysis has become a widely accepted form of analysis within sociology and feminist scholarship, we have tried to outline how its uses and applications have been hardly straightforward. It is, as we noted earlier, an analytical lens that is still in the process of development. We have explored six key lines of inquiry, which have been particularly salient in Canadian discussions of intersectional analysis over the past decade. These lines of inquiry have included questions about gender as a starting point of analysis, its relative weight and relationship to other dimensions of analysis, its status as both experiential and structural dimensions, and how intersectional analysis can inform research practice. We now turn to how intersectional analysis has been taken up in policy issues in Canada.

INTERSECTIONAL APPROACHES AND GENDER-BASED ANALYSIS IN CANADA

In this discussion, we turn our attention to a specific example of a policy-focused research practice that speaks to diverse gender experiences. There has been a lot of developmental work in Canada, in academic circles, among activists, and in government policy departments addressing questions of gender and diversity. We begin this discussion with a consideration of how far policy-based research has progressed in this area. Canada has been a leader in pioneering 'gender-based analysis' as a research tool to help in the production of gender-sensitive policy and programs. From the start, gender-based analysis was described as a method that acknowledged differences *within* gender categories. However, finding a methodology to put the consideration of the diversity of gendered experiences into practice has proved challenging. Our discussion addresses a key analytical challenge facing those interested in the analysis of gender today: that is, how to find a way to address the specificity of experiences of gender while at the same time attending to broader commonalities and configurations that have social and political significance.

Gender and diversity in gender-based analysis
Canadian commitments to the implementation of gender-based analysis in policy development, implementation, and assessment have from the beginning included the awareness that gender categories are not homogeneous. Differences among women and among men in terms of, for example, class, racialization, language, disability, and so on have been recognized from the start as significant aspects in the structure and experience of inequality in Canada. By the time the federal government was preparing its commitments to be presented at the Fourth UN World Conference on Women in Beijing in 1995, there was significant recognition that gender-based analysis needed to be conducted with the importance of diversity acknowledged and integrated. For example, paragraph 23 in the federal plan (*Setting the Stage for the Next Century: The Federal Plan for Gender Equality, 1995–2000*) states:

> A gender-based approach ... acknowledges that some women may be disadvantaged even further because of their race, colour, sexual orientation, socio-economic position, region, ability level or age. A gender-based analysis respects and appreciates diversity.

While the *idea* of the significance of diversity for a full analysis of gender inequality was present, the *practice* of gender-based analysis was more often than not limited to an analysis of inequalities between men and women as distinct and undifferentiated groups. While one might argue that in the context of government policy, any form of gender analysis is better than none, a simple analysis of male versus female differences is a crude implementation of gender-based analysis. The inadequacy of this approach has become a matter of concern—within government practice and among inequality activists and academics.

Within federal government practice, there have been important efforts to move beyond a crude implementation of gender-based analysis in order to take into account variations in experience and inequality within gender categories. Four recent forms of action in this respect are worthy of note. First, in 1997, Status of Women Canada (an agency within the federal government) launched an initiative entitled the Integration of Diversity into Policy Research, Development and Analysis.[4] The call for proposals asked researchers to reflect on the policy implications of diversity among women. Several papers were published from this initiative, and two in particular (Bakan and Kobayashi 2000; Rankin and Vickers 2001) report on comparative research that shows the need for specificity in addressing gender and diversity in policy analysis and development.[5]

Second, also in the late 1990s, the Federal–Provincial–Territorial Working Group on Diversity, Equality and Justice was created and produced an analysis tool referred to by its acronym IDEAS—the Integrated Diversity and Equality Analysis Screen.[6] The screen is proposed as a tool to assess the possible effects of a proposed course of action on various groups identified as having been vulnerable to disadvantage within the justice system. It is cross-referenced with background information on and profiles of all identified groups (women, youth and children, seniors, Aboriginal peoples, racial and ethno-cultural minorities, refugees, recent immigrants, persons with disabilities, persons with literacy problems, social assistance recipients and the poor, religious groups, and GLBTs). The screening instrument asks analysts to consider potential impacts on all of these groups as well as potential impacts on 'individuals who belong to more than one of these groups'.

The third noteworthy action on integrating gender and diversity involves Citizenship and Immigration Canada (CIC). This department is in a unique position within the federal government because since 2002, it has had a statutory obligation to include in its annual report to Parliament a gender-based analysis (GBA) of a specific political initiative—the Immigration and Refugee Protection Act. The statutory requirement to report to Parliament on gender impacts is unprecedented, and the department is, in this sense, very much in the lead in terms of developing and legitimating the efficacy of gender-based analysis. In this role, Citizenship and Immigration gives weight to the need to examine inequalities within as well as between gender categories. In their first gender-based analysis of the Immigration and Refugee Protection Act, CIC states that GBA is 'an analytical framework that assesses the differential impacts of policy, programme and legislation for men and women and for different groups of men and women'.[7]

Fourth, significant steps have been taken in the area of health. A notable example has been the establishment of regionally based Centres of Excellence across Canada to promote research and education on women's health. Each centre has been actively involved in pursuing gender-based analyses of health, and because of their regional specificity, these analyses contextualize women's health needs by variations in regional characteristics. In addition to this degree of diversity, the centres have been active in advocating for a form of gender-based analysis that focuses on differences within women's health experiences in even more specific locales (such as cities and neighbourhoods) and situations.

These are all important achievements showing a measure of commitment within the federal government to use a form of gender-based analysis that is sensitive to diversity. However, as the review of the five-year Federal Plan for Gender Equality by Status of Women Canada (2001) noted, there is a long way to go in realizing the goal of gender and diversity-sensitive policies and programs. In particular, the Status of Women report highlights the need for further progress in the development of analytical resources capable of reflecting diversity and its complex relations to gender. They also note the need to respond to and keep pace with an ever-changing political environment, in particular the increasing shift of policy involvement and responsibility from federal levels of government to provinces and municipalities. The assessment highlights the need for new forms of inequality and policy analyses that can handle both greater specificity and complexity. As in academic research, analysts in the policy field are turning to the possibilities of intersectional analysis.

Beyond gender and diversity: Putting intersectional theory into practice

In many ways, the Status of Women review of federal action on gender equality in the latter half of the 1990s is a milder version of what was being said by many activists and academics. As different groups and individuals in Canada prepared for Beijing +10 and generally assessed the achievements of gender mainstreaming, there was growing disenchantment with the value of gender-based analysis (CRIAW [Canadian Research Institute for the Advancement of Women] 2005; Hankivsky 2005). One problem identified was the gap between the theoretical understanding of gender and methodological practices of gender-based analysis. The prominent understanding of gender in current academic circles—described in this book as more fluid, contested, relational, and contingent—clashed with the more rigid, fixed presentation of gender in gender-based analysis. Using our terminology from chapter 1, we could say that academia had made the second shift in the conceptualization of gender but policy thinking had not. Another issue identified was that the intention to integrate diversity issues into gender-based analysis gave a priori primacy to gender inequality. The primary significance of gender may or may not be the case in specific instances of inequality—even for women—and, as we identified in our previous discussion, a number of analysts and activists have called for a form of intersectional analysis that does not presume the primacy of any particular dimension of inequality. Some have gone as far as to suggest (Hankivsky 2005) that we should drop the idea of gender mainstreaming altogether and focus instead on diversity mainstreaming. These criticisms of the 'gender and diversity approach' in the context of gender-based analysis resonate with directions in academic research towards a focus on intersectionality (Dua 1999; Biggs and Downe 2005; McMullin 2004). Intersectional analyses can provide the detailed specifications of complex inequality configurations required to determine the equality policy implementation strategies likely to be most effective for specific policy jurisdictions and locales. As in the academic literature and research, however, progress requires the development of a suitable research practice.

We can see forms of McCall's intra-categorical analysis in Canadian policy research. For example, one of the research reports in the Status of Women *Integration of Diversity* initiative (Côté et al. 2001) looked at the experiences of French-speaking, family-sponsored immigrant women living in Ontario—an intersection of disadvantages along dimensions of gender, language, immigration class, and visible-minority status. Another (Kenny et al. 2002) examined experiences of culture, education, and work among Aboriginal women—not considered as an undifferentiated group but distinguished by diversity in their Aboriginal ancestry (Inuit, First Nations, Métis) and regional circumstances. Good examples of inter-categorical analysis are Nick Scott's MA research described in chapter 5, as well as other recent research on civic engagement in Canada (Tossutti et al. forthcoming).

The observation that policy must be more specific and contextualized features prominently in the Status of Women papers produced for the *Integration of Diversity* initiative. Papers by Rankin and Vickers (2001), Bakan and Kobayashi (2000), and Kenny et al. (2002) are particularly strong on this point. These papers argue against a 'one size fits all' approach to policy-making. Not only do they make this argument in terms of recognizing diversity within gender categories, but they also call for policy-delivery mechanisms that are as contextualized and situation-specific as possible. Bakan and Kobayashi's analysis of employment equity policy in Canada's 10 provinces is perhaps the most forceful on this point, and it represents an argument that is coming to the fore in Canadian policy debate. Their first recommendation is that employment equity policy needs to be tailored to the specifics of the 'legislative and public service cultures' in *each* province (2000, 57). Their second recommendation is that employment equity policies should be tailored to the specific characteristics and needs of *local* communities. While all designated groups need to be included in any employment equity initiative, it may be necessary, given the specifics of the configuration of employment inequality in any particular place, to identify specific groups for special priority attention.[8] The point made here by Bakan and Kobayashi is similar to the one made by McCall (2005)—no single form of policy implementation is going to be suitable for all contexts—and the applicability of the logic of Bakan and Kobayashi's argument is equally relevant for policies other than employment equity.

The Canadian Research Institute for the Advancement of Women has led the way in steering widespread consultation and workshop activities to create a framework for approaching intersectional analysis. Identified as an Intersectional Feminist Framework, this approach has been developed for the specific purpose of putting intersectional analysis at the service of policy development and activist campaigns.

GENDER RELATIONS AND ISSUES IN THE PRODUCTION OF NEW SOCIOLOGICAL KNOWLEDGE

The analysis of diverse forms of gender relations presents multiple challenges to academics and policy-makers. Theorists, researchers, and policy-makers all face dilemmas about how to move their work forward. It is important to recognize that the significance of diversity also applies to the resolution of these dilemmas—that is, there may be a multiple number of viable analytical paths forward. Nevertheless, there are some common problems to be resolved that are rooted in current practices of knowledge production. These common analytical problems stem from the fact that the methodologies of knowledge production typically used in sociological research have come under attack for being themselves imbued with a gender politics. In the final section of this chapter, we trace recent historical developments in the intersections between gender, power, and knowledge production. Our aim is to introduce you to the ways in which relations of gender and power have been implicated in the production of reliable and valid knowledge. We also hope to give some indication of how, as a student of sociology and gender relations, you might think about doing your own research. As a start, you need to do what all of us involved in this book are also doing—trying to think about the types of research approaches that would help to

Intersectional Feminist Frameworks:
A New Direction for the Canadian Research Institute
for the Advancement of Women (CRIAW)

Intersectional Feminist Frameworks (IFFs) aim to foster understanding of the many circumstances that combine with discriminatory social practices to produce and sustain inequality and exclusion. IFFs look at how systems of discrimination, such as colonialism and globalization, can impact the combination of a person's:

- Social or economic status;
- Race;
- Class;
- Gender;
- Sexuality;

- Ability;
- Geographic location;
- Citizenship and nationalities; and
- Refugee and immigrant status.

While IFFs are not new, many social activists face an ongoing challenge of developing, understanding, and applying these frameworks. However, CRIAW has identified emerging approaches and principles of IFFs. . . . Some common underlying themes of IFFs include:

- Using tools for analysis that consider the complexities of women's lives;
- Making sure policy analysis is centred on the lives of those most marginalized;
- Attempting to think about women's lives in holistic ways when making policies;
- Valuing self-reflection in our social justice beliefs so that we are aware of how we are all caught up in systems of power and privilege;
- Integrating world views and knowledge that have historically been marginalized;
- Understanding that women's varying histories have created many social identities, which place them in different positions of hierarchical power;
- Making efforts to challenge binary thinking that sustains inequalities, such as able/disabled, gay/straight, white/black, man/woman, West/East, North/South; and
- Revealing that this binary thinking is a result of unequal power relations.

From these themes it's clear that Intersectional Feminist Frameworks (IFFs) are:

- Fluid, changing, and continuously negotiated;
- Specific to the interaction of a person or group's history, politics, geography, ecology, and culture;
- Based upon women's specific locations and situations rather than upon generalizations;
- Diverse ways to confront social injustices, which focus on many types of discrimination rather than on just one; and
- Locally and globally interconnected.

Source: CRIAW-ICREF. 2006. *Intersectional Feminist Frameworks: A Primer*, 6, 7 (slightly abridged), at <www.criaw-icref.ca/indexFrame_e.htm>.

push further the analysis of gender when approached as highly diverse and complex sets of structured relationships.

What method best suits research on the diversity of gender relations in Canada?

Just over a quarter of a century ago, Lorraine Code, a Canadian feminist philosopher, posed what she called an 'outrageous question'. She asked, 'Is the sex of the knower epistemologically significant?' (Code 1981). In other words, she was asking whether being a male researcher or a female researcher had any impact on the process and outcome of research. Code was one of many feminists in many disciplines who undertook to grapple with gender issues embedded in relations of knowledge creation.

Early on, feminist researchers began exposing masculine bias in research practice, including the valuing of characteristics traditionally associated with 'masculine' approaches to knowledge (e.g., reason, rationality, autonomy, emotional disconnection) and other forms of gender bias in the collection, interpretation, and organization of research data. In sociology, early manifestations of this methodological critique focused on the inadequacy of research in the sociology of work and in social stratification. In both of these areas, women were often excluded as research subjects because their life experiences were seen as either not significant or as too complicated for the research questions investigated (Siltanen 2008). Whether or not women had a class position independent of their husbands was both a theoretical debate and a debate about research practice that went on in sociology for many years (Clement and Myles 1994).

Dorothy Smith has been a key voice in these debates about women's place within research practice and within sociology more widely. She argued (1974, 7) that 'sociology . . . has been based on and built up within the male social universe' while further lamenting in her seminal work, *The Everyday World as Problematic* (1987), that the lives of women were largely left to novelists or poets. Thus, female-dominated domains, such as domestic work and the care of children and the elderly, were rendered largely invisible within the knowledge academies. Subsequently, and not surprisingly, when women's lives *were* studied and theorized, it occurred with malestream lenses; that is, women's lives were viewed and analyzed according to how they fit into frameworks that had been derived from studying men. As we noted in chapter 1, British sociologist Hilary Graham (1983) eloquently asked, 'Do her answers fit his questions?' when she observed that women's experiences were being investigated with surveys designed on the basis of men's lives. Researchers in sociology also noted that the much-celebrated 'scientific' virtues of quantitative survey analysis were less useful in addressing the intricate and sensitive details of personal experience that were of central importance in investigating gender relations. Writing at about the same time in Canada, Ann Duffy, Nancy Mandell, and Norene Pupo addressed the issue of the inclusion of women's voices within sociological scholarship by drawing together quantitative data and in-depth qualitative interviews on women's lives as workers and as carers. Two decades ago, they wrote:

> Although there is now considerable quantitative data in North America documenting the double day, there are few in-depth studies presenting rich detail on women's

day-to-day struggles. Nor are there many intensive examinations of the lives of full-time mothers and housewives. Too often this group is demeaned and rendered sociological invisible . . . [W]e hope to reclaim and re-envision women's lives by giving women a forum in which to voice their perspectives. (1989, 14–15)

What was required, then, to overcome the historic male bias in sociological research practice? In thinking about how to do research to further the significance and dynamics of gendered intersections, it was clear that an obvious place to start was to consider the possibility of a feminist methodology. But, did, or does, such an approach exist? Several feminist sociologists tackled this question.

A noteworthy piece in thinking about this issue of feminism and methodology was written by Ann Oakley (1981) and still stands as one of the most cited articles within this discussion. Writing nearly a quarter of a century ago, Oakley argued that some methods were better suited to feminist aims and that they could be viewed as feminist methods. Oakley suggested that, contrary to an objective, standardized, and detached approach to interviewing, the goal of finding out about people through interviewing was 'best achieved when the relationship of interviewer and interviewee is non-hierarchical and when the interviewer is prepared to invest his or her own personal identity in the relationship' (1981, 41). Drawing on her interviews with mothers, she maintained that her own identity as a mother came to act as a leveller against a power hierarchy in the interviewee–interviewer relationship.

A second landmark contribution to the discussion about the possibility of a feminist method or methodology also came from the UK in the work of Caroline Ramazanoglu. Drawing inspiration from the work of Dorothy Smith, she identified five practices as forming an early consensus about the contours of a feminist methodology. These practices were: allowing women to express their own experience; acknowledging the importance of theory in selecting and interpreting experience; taking account of power; validating subjective knowledge; and avoiding the objectification of research subjects (1989, 52–5).

While many feminist scholars were initially positively inclined to the possibility of a feminist methodology and worked hard to set out specifically feminist research practices, it has been difficult to distinguish a feminist methodology from simply a good methodology. Moreover, features that have been identified as hallmarks of a feminist approach to research have since been criticized. For example, notions of mutuality and equality in interviews have been criticized, highlighting how differing, as well as shared, structural characteristics can impede mutuality and reciprocity. Attention to this issue became especially acute as awareness of the significance of differences among women increased. Rosalind Edwards (1993, 184) cautioned that 'if . . . we accept that there are structurally based divisions between women on the basis of race and/or class that may lead them to have some different interests and priorities, then what has been said about woman-to-woman interviewing may not apply in all situations.' Similar observations have been made about power and privilege differences within the research process more generally. In the preface to her edited collection *Feminist Dilemmas in Field Work*, Diane Wolf discusses how her research inadvertently exacerbated the inequalities between herself and her research subjects in Java, Indonesia:

I would go on to finish my dissertation, get a PhD, get a job based on a talk about this research, make enough money in one month to sustain an entire village for several months. . . . Despite my good intentions, I was making a situation for myself based on structures of poverty and gender inequality. (1996, x)

While the search for a feminist methodology had good intentions, scholars are discovering that methodological changes intended to achieve feminist ends— increased collaboration, greater interaction, and more open communication with research participants—may have inadvertently reintroduced some of the ethical dilemmas feminist researchers had hoped to eliminate: participants' sense of disappointment, alienation, and potential exploitation. As Nancy Naples observes (2003), feminist research continues to be charged with practices of 'othering', exclusivity, and domination by post-colonialist, queer, and other social researchers.

Most sociological researchers have taken these charges on board and are endeavouring to find ways to respond to the critique. Some, like Naples, for example, continue to see possibility and promise in uniquely feminist methods as strategies for research that are informed by key feminist theoretical debates, including recent developments in intersectional analysis. At the same time, many feminist sociologists are not convinced by the idea of a distinctive feminist methodology. Instead, they have suggested that feminist research is simply good research that is related to the general aims of empowerment and reducing or alleviating gender inequalities. It is also research that is intricately linked to theoretical concerns emanating out of intersectional analysis and, specifically, the need to be attentive to structural and experiential differences between and within gender categories. Certainly today, with developments in post-positivist methodology and a diverse interest in progressive research practices, there are strong sympathies in the research methods identified as aligned with the possibilities of progressive social change. While there is no distinctive methodology associated with research on the diversity of gender experiences, sociologists interested in the investigation of contemporary gender configurations have embraced particular characteristics in their research work. We explore these characteristics below.

Characteristics of good practice in gender relations research

Good gender research practice is anchored in the wish to produce useful sociological knowledge that will have a positive impact on society. In this sense, it shares many characteristics with what is developing as a post-positivist research practice in sociology generally (Flyvbjerg 2002; Denzin and Lincoln 2005; Bryman 2006). While there are many characteristics of such research, we will highlight seven here.[9] Not all research on gender relations has all these characteristics, and depending on the research questions asked, some aspects of the list may be more or less appropriate. Nevertheless, most discussions of feminist-inspired, post-positivist research practices highlight these seven characteristics.

First, research should not be just *on* people but *for* people. This means that gender research is concerned with issues of broader social change and social justice. A commitment to transformative social change is an anchor in most gender relations research. This includes the eradication of diverse forms of gender inequality and the celebration of positive ways of being female and male. It is important that research on gender relations pay attention to dynamics of change so that we may all learn how the negative aspects of gendered structures and experiences can be overcome.

Second, we must recognize that good research is also conducted *with* people. This idea draws our attention to two related dimensions in the process of research. In the first place, it means that we must recognize the constructed and relational character of sociological data. We do not go 'into the field' to gather data that is waiting for us to simply 'collect'. We actively construct our research data—through observation, conversation, and other forms of social interaction. Our research subjects are also active in the construction of our research data, and post-positivist researchers are finding ways to acknowledge this co-construction of sociological data. In the second place, many researchers argue that to be good, research needs to address and engage with community interests and needs. This can involve varying levels of engagement. At one end of the spectrum—for example, for those committed to a participatory action research approach—community engagement takes a front seat, steering the purpose as well as the practice of the research. For others, community involvement is an important foundation of research and a way to recognize and respect the highly significant contribution research subjects make to the production of academic knowledge. It is also a process to help ensure that the results of social science are 'for people'. As Flyvbjerg sets out (2002), for social science to 'matter', it must engage with issues that are of concern to individuals as they live their daily lives. Deborah Barndt (1999) and Nancy Naples (2003) are two feminist researchers who frame their own research around the importance of community-connected, inclusive forms of research design and research practice.

Third, good research embraces a multi-method approach. Researchers have actively engaged with methodological innovation through challenging conventional or mainstream ways of collecting, analyzing, and presenting data. Initially, this involved challenging positivist frameworks and the dominance of quantitative methods and experimenting with novel ways of documenting and representing women's experiences or everyday worlds. Much research on gender relations continues to be qualitative, with a focus on intensive research designs and thick descriptions of experience. More recently, however, quantitative methods have been recognized as adding important knowledge, and discussions are underway about how to mould quantitative analysis in ways that complement a progressive research agenda (McCall 2005; Oakley 1998; McDaniel 2002).

Fourth, gender-related research should recognize the links between theory, method, methodology, and epistemology. As Sandra Harding (1987) laid out convincingly, feminist-inspired research should closely intertwine methods (techniques for gathering evidence), methodology (a theory and analysis of how research should proceed), and epistemological issues (issues about an adequate theory of knowledge or justificatory strategy). In this vein, research on gender relations must be flexible and able to move and change with the data that emerges as research proceeds. This issue is picked up by Aimee Campeau, who writes about how her MA research changed mid-stream because the information she encountered about the positioning of girls

Encounters with Gender 'in the Field'

by Aimee Campeau
Sociology PhD Program

The journey that was my master's thesis took many unexpected turns that resulted in changing my research focus and my theoretical framework. In turn, this caused me to reconfigure my methodological frameworks. My initial project, based in feminist political economy, sought to examine the invisibility of the informal labour undertaken by girls in developing countries. Yet the project I *ended up* producing was based in post-development theory and examined a history of the constitution of the 'girl-child' in international development discourse (Campeau 2006). Below, I discuss my experience with the master's thesis as a process of being open to the emergence of new problematics when researching gender 'in the field'.

Although I attempted to prepare myself by establishing a solid theoretical understanding of my methodological approach before entering 'the field', it was not until I began my interviews and began to read internal documents that I experienced the divide between research methods in theory and in practice. I began reading documents that presented data on girls in the developing world and discovered a marked shift in how children, and girls particularly, were constructed as subjects of the development process. What became interesting to me was a shift within development discourse from a historical focus on the 'needs' of children to one centred around their 'rights'. This new discourse, which framed girls as *agents* and *participants* within the development process, led me to wonder: why is there a shift to a rights-based discourse? Why now? How does this emerging discourse attempt to make girls responsible for their own development? These new questions sparked the beginning of new theoretical and methodological directions in my research.

In particular, I began to feel that my methodological framework did not support the way that I wanted to theorize my research topic. Themes of power in institutional ethnography, which was my initial methodological approach, were too confining and lacked the complexity that I felt was operationalized within development discourse and intervention strategies. I felt that my new problem was best conceptualized through the lens of post-development and post-colonial theories. I also immersed myself in post-structuralist accounts of discourse analysis, a method I felt could help unpack the complex dynamics of productive forms of power and knowledge generation within mainstream development discourse.

Through the framework of discourse analysis, I was able to trace how girls became a perceptible category of analysis (a problem that required a strategic response). I was also able to account for the subsequent knowledges produced about girls as newly defined development subjects. Additionally, I was able to critically examine how child-centred and gender-based policies had historically neglected to account for the complexities of the lives of girls and women. This was exemplified by the problem that under neo-liberal objectives of economic empowerment, gender relations were conceptualized in isolation from issues of age, family culture, and ethnicity. Thus, discourse analysis provided a foundation upon which I could orient a historically informed discussion of what was highlighted and what was 'left out' in the constitution of girls as development subjects.

Although this decision to 'begin again' required that I dramatically alter my MA thesis, I was satisfied with my decision to do so. Quite simply, this new project presented me with a more challenging intellectual puzzle—one that only came about from being open to alternative research paths.

Engaging with and being aware of the different directions that your research can present to you allows you to be open to changing your mind and your position in relation to your research topic. The emphasis needs to be on 'process' and on being reflexive so that your research can move beyond safe theoretical spaces when contradictions or alternative research opportunities present themselves. I think I am now open to these moments and will continue to welcome them as they emerge.

Have your ideas about gender relations ever been challenged, and possibly changed, as a result of encounters with people or documents or events in the 'real world'?

Can you think of examples of Canadian research on gender relations in which researchers could have gained more insight if they had used a more diverse and complex conceptualization of gender?

in international development forced her to rethink her theoretical framework and, consequently, her methodological approach.

Fifth, research on gender relations includes the recognition that power is inherent in sociological research practices. The focus of much current feminist sociological scholarship has moved on from the question of *whether* there are power inequalities between researchers and respondents to consider *how* power influences knowledge production and construction processes. Questions about who produces knowledge—who can be a knower? whose knowledge? who speaks for whom?—have become critical in contemporary feminist, post-modern, and post-colonial climates.

Sixth, since research practices involve representing the narratives, experiences, and lives of others, there is a need to question how 'voices of participants are to be heard, with what authority, and in what form' (Olesen 1998, 315). The dangers of presuming to speak or advocate for others have been noted. Lorraine Code echoes the views of many feminist researchers grappling with dilemmas around knowing, representing, and advocating for others. She writes:

> Only rarely can we presume to understand exactly how it is for someone else even of our own class, race, sexual orientation and social group. These issues become exacerbated when feminists claim to speak for others across the complexities of difference, with the consequences that the politics of speaking for, about, and on behalf of other women is one of the most contested areas in present day feminist activism and research. (1995, 30)

Racialized women working within Western contexts and feminists working in Two-Thirds World settings have highlighted 'otherness', exclusion, racism, and ethnocentrism. Key issues have included the question of whether feminist researchers in dominant cultures can ever *know* gender relations or women's and men's experience in subaltern cultures (Mohanty 1988; Bannerji 2000) and the challenges of knowing transnational lesbian and gay identities (Gopinath 2005). Issues of power are also present in our attempts to come to know the intimate details of others who live in close proximity to us. Even when researchers and respondents share structural and cultural similarities of, for example, gender, ethnicity, class, and age, this does not guarantee knowing—or 'better' knowing.

Seventh, good research on gender relations displays a commitment to reflexivity. (Mauthner and Doucet 2003; Doucet 2008; Siltanen et al. 2008). In part, this derives from the concern with power and its presence within the practices of research. Feminist sociological research emphasizes accountable and responsible knowing, including the critical importance of being reflexive and transparent about our knowledge construction processes. This means taking time within the research process to reflect on the position and role of the researcher and all research relationships in the production of knowledge.

CONCLUSION: MOVING UNDERSTANDINGS OF DIVERSE GENDER RELATIONS FORWARD

We have emphasized throughout this book the importance of recognizing variation and diversity in gender relations in Canada. Over the years, scholars have made great efforts both to recognize the social and political significance of gender and to problematize its use as a homogeneous category. We are now at the point where we need to move the analysis of diverse gender relations forward—both theoretically and methodologically.

As set out in chapter 1, there is a long and rich history of gender relations scholarship in Canada and elsewhere. We attempted to introduce some of that history and to underline how the sociology of gender relations is grounded in everyday-life problems and issues. We also demonstrated the intersections between the personal and the political and tried to encourage you to think about how these connections play out in your own lives. Specifically, we laid out two key conceptual and theoretical shifts within thinking on gender relations. The first shift in the sociological treatment of gender was to recognize its significance; the second was to realize that a better understanding of gender requires a more nuanced and complex conceptualization. This book sits squarely in the problematics of the second shift in sociological thinking about gender.

Chapter 2 used children's experience to make the point that the conceptual foundation of gender has shifted dramatically. Whereas it was once thought to be important to separate 'natural' sex characteristics from 'social' gender configurations and identities, we are now aware that the natural and the social cannot so easily be separated—and neither can the role of nature and nurture in shaping our human selves. There are multiple forms of gender identity, and these forms have a rather contingent relationship to configurations of body parts and properties. Although post-modern society continues to draw our attention to conventional forms of being male and female, it also has ways of celebrating multiple and shifting gender identities.

As we turned our attention to the intensification of gendered experience in the lives of adolescents in chapter 3, we also confronted the idea that although gender comes in multiple forms, there continue to be dominant and subordinate forms. Gender as a power relation hits adolescents and young adults hard as they try to discover just what sort of men and women they are/will become. The many cultural, economic, and other contexts in which this exploration occurs helps us to understand the value of examining how different dimensions of experience intersect to create both a gendered structural context and a social environment in which conflicting, sometimes contradictory, gender messages are played out.

Chapter 4 focused on the adult years of gender relations when earning and caring, paid and unpaid work, occur as central identities and practices for many Canadians. We highlighted conceptual, theoretical, and empirical issues of gender differences and disadvantage, issues of intersectionality in the sites of home and work life, and the connections between home and work and between paid and unpaid work. We also addressed a central puzzle within the study of gender relations: why does a gendered division of labour continue to characterize the lives of Canadian women and men? We examined how and where gender differences persist and their intersections with other structures and experiential dimensions of differences and disadvantages.

In chapter 5, it became clear that issues encountered in other aspects of adulthood, such as career paths, housing and health, citizenship status, and political action, have diverse gendered forms. We were able to make links in this chapter between local, personal experience and global, systemic patterns. The construction of gender, and its contestation, has a global dimension. We pointed out that this further complicates the analysis of gender by requiring us to continually trace the global in our local experiences and vice versa. The spatial and systemic complexities of postmodern production and consumption intensifies and creates new forms of gender inequality. In most cases, these patterns of discrimination, oppression, and exploitation are etched upon those who suffer multiple disadvantages. Possibilities for a politics geared to addressing these multiple disadvantages are emerging as people realize that solidarity does not require sameness. All women do not have to share an exact condition or experience to undertake collective actions, and active support across gender divides is occurring.

In this final chapter, we have attempted to demonstrate different scholarly positions concerning the usefulness of intersectionality as a way to theorize and research the complexity of gender. We have used the example of gender-based analysis in policy assessment and development to illustrate some of the research dilemmas involved in approaching gender as a diverse phenomenon. Both policy analysts and sociological researchers are working towards new ways of bringing the complexity of gender fully into research designs and methodological practices.

We all need to be open to ongoing questions and new developments in the sociological analysis of gender. As we frame our research questions, develop our research designs, and make decisions about how to produce new sociological knowledge, we also need to be aware that gender relations have played a major role in past ideas of what counts as valid knowledge and appropriate research practice. We have set out some of the development in the thinking about the impact of gendered experience on how sociological knowledge is produced and valued. It is generally recognized in social sciences that power relations feature within the practices of research—as well as being an interesting topic for research. Power relations around gender have shaped and continue to operate in what research gets done, how it gets done, and how it is judged. However, there is a growing convergence within sociology between post-positivist and feminist-inspired research practices that suggests a way forward for the analysis of gender as a complex, fluid, and diverse phenomenon. We have set out seven characteristics of good research that capture this convergence, and we indicate future directions for gender research.

Finally, we have shared our own experiences of living and researching gender in order to provide real-life examples of how gender matters both personally and professionally to us as sociologists. We have also been fortunate to be able to share with you the encounters with gender experienced by students in the sociology graduate programs at Carleton University. We hope that by using examples from our own lives and research, we have helped you to connect the material in this book with your own experience. As sociologists-in-the-making, we also hope that we have stimulated your interest in helping to move the understanding of gender relations in Canada forward.

Research Questions

1. Choose a policy initiative at the federal, provincial, or municipal level (for example, student loans, job training programs, income assistance, old age security, employment insurance, homelessness initiatives) and assess how well the policy design and/or program delivery takes into account the diversity of gendered experience.
2. Design a sociological honours project highlighting gender relations that you would like to carry out. Consider the seven points of good research practice, and elaborate on those you decide are relevant for the research question you are asking.

Discussion Questions

1. What are some of the advantages and limitations of using intersectionality as a way of understanding the diversity of gender relations in Canada today?
2. Should we move beyond a one-size-fits-all approach to gender equality policies? Why? Why not?
3. Is it important to keep gender as a separate dimension of analysis, or should we instead incorporate gender into the concept of diversity?
4. If gender experiences are diverse, is it still possible to engage in gender politics?
5. Does research on gender require a unique approach to research?

Further Reading

Jiwani, Yasmin. 2006. *Discourses of Denial: Mediations of Race, Gender, and Violence.* Vancouver: University of British Columbia Press. Explores intersections of race, gender, and violence in Canadian society and includes a powerful critique of media representation.

McCall, Leslie. 2001. *Complex Inequality: Gender, Class, and Race in the New Economy*. New York: Routledge. Examines intersections of gender, race, and class in employment inequalities in four American cities and makes a strong argument for the significance of intersectional analysis for policy development.

Meekosha, Helen. 2008. *Body Battles: Disability, Representation, and Participation*. Sydney: Sage. Includes an assessment of the usefulness of intersectionality for analyzing experiences of disability.

Naples, Nancy A. 2003. *Feminism and Method: Ethnography, Discourse Analysis, and Activist Research*. New York: Routledge. Spirited defence of the viability of a feminist methodology, with interesting case studies and a focus on bridging the complexity of gender analysis and the possibilities of activism.

Neysmith, Sheila, Kate Bezanson, and Anne O'Connell. 2005. *Telling Tales: Living the Effects of Public Policy*. Halifax: Fernwood. Examines detailed intersections in the daily lives of East Coast households to analyze the impact of neo-liberal policy on the well-being of individuals and their households.

Notes

Chapter 1

1. Janet was involved in some of these very early attempts to 'fit women into' existing approaches to stratification. The research reported in Guppy and Siltanen (1977) tried to find out where people would rank 'housewife' in prestige rankings of occupations and also whether knowing the gender of an occupational incumbent would affect how occupations were ranked. Although such approaches to stratification are less prominent today, Goyder et al. (2003) repeated this study to find out whether the impact of gender on occupational prestige has changed. See Siltanen (2004; 2008) for a discussion of early 'fitting in' efforts in the context of Marxist class analysis.

2. This issue of language is still contested in Canada—some prefer the term 'sex' for analytical and political reasons. For example, a lively exchange in the early 1980s debated the relations between class consciousness and sex consciousness (see Armstrong and Armstrong versus Connelly in Hamilton and Barrett 1986). As Hamilton notes (2005), some activists see a focus on gender as a de-politicization of women's movement politics.

3. These publications include Jennifer Baumgardner and Amy Richards' *Manifesta: Young Women, Feminism and the Future* (2000); Mitchell, Rundle, and Karaian's *Turbo Chicks: Talking Young Feminisms* (2001); and Moraga, Hernandez, and Rehman's *Colonize This: Young Women of Color on Today's Feminism* (2002).

4. R.W. Connell, an Australian sociologist who has made many significant contributions to the study of gender, was male in the 1980s and 1990s. He is now a woman. We discuss this further in chapter 3.

Chapter 2

1. Further information on the diversity of biological sex characteristics can be found on the website of the Intersex Society of North America, <www.isna.org>. Intersex refers to an individual who has both male-identified and female-identified biological characteristics.

2. Kathryn Jackson. 1952. *Nurse Nancy*. New York: Simon and Schuster; Toronto: Musson Book Company. This book was published as a companion to *Doctor Dan the Bandage Man* (1950). Both books were re-issued as a 50th anniversary publication by Simon and Schuster. The Nurse Nancy book came with two Band-Aid spots, two Band-Aid strips, and a Band-Aid plastic patch. It was an early effort to use children's play as a vehicle for product advertising.

3. *Dale Evans and the Coyote*. 1956. New York: Simon and Schuster; Toronto: Musson Book Company.

CHAPTER 3

1. <www.phac-aspc.gc.ca/publicat/whsr-rssf/chap_23_e.html>.
2. Information on the transformation of Canadian adolescent/young adult experience is summarized in Beaujot 2004. Further details, and original sources, are available in this report. Similar patterns have been noted in other Western post-industrial countries. See, for example, similar descriptions of change in Irwin (2005) for adolescents in Britain and in Furstenberg et al. (2005) for adolescents in the United States.
3. Susan Bordo. 1995. *Unbearable Weight: Feminism, Western Culture, and the Body*. Berkeley: University of California Press.
4. Pansevski, Bojan. 2007. 'Unhappy as a boy, Kim became the youngest ever transsexual at 12'. *The Daily Telegraph*. 28 January, at <www.telegraph.co.uk>.
5. Encarta® World English Dictionary © 1999 Microsoft Corporation. All rights reserved.

CHAPTER 4

1. This story is based on a newspaper article on Ann Oakley in the British newspaper *The Guardian*, which Andrea read in 1990. The article is no longer available.
2. Statistics Canada. 2001. *Report on the Demographic Situation in Canada*, at <www.statcan.ca/english/freepub/91-209-XIE/91-209-XIE2001000.pdf>.

CHAPTER 5

1. Arundhati Roy, at the World Social Forum, 2003, cited in Mohanty 2006, 7.
2. Buchanan describes the call centre cubical environment in a New Brunswick example as 'public isolation' (2006, 183). This description is consistent with the call centre workplaces discussed in class by several of Mary Ellen's students and another she has seen in Quebec. In comparison, since software companies often expect their employees to contribute long hours of work, they are frequently provided with additional comforts, including work-out rooms and ergonomically designed work spaces.
3. A non-traditional occupation refers to a profession that historically has been numerically dominated by people of the other gender.
4. Before the First World War, Cambridge denied degrees to women even if all qualifications for that degree had been met (Prentice 1999, 129). In Canada, one woman in forestry was initially denied access to graduate school because she was married to a graduate student, and another was told during the 1970s that field positions were not open to women (Tripp-Knowles 1999, 195, 199).
5. There is interesting evidence of this in the analysis by Fine et al. about the self-esteem challenges of blue-collar men facing job shortages and in Espiritu's work on immigrant men who work in food service and cleaning jobs (both in Michael S. Kimmel and Michael A. Messner, eds, *Men's Lives*, 7th edn. Boston: Allyn and Bacon).
6. Staggenborg, Suzanne, and Verta Taylor. 2005. 'Whatever Happened to the Women's Movement?' *Mobilization: An International Journal* 10, 1.
7. Tindall, D.B., Scott Davies, and Celine Mauboules. 2003. 'Activism and Conservation Behavior in an Environmental Movement: The Contradictory Effects of Gender.' *Society and Natural Resources* 16, 10.

Chapter 6

1. <www.nwac-hq.org/en/SISBrochure.html>.
2. For clarity, we have used the term 'intersectionality' rather than interlocking or interconnecting, although we view these as largely synonymous terms. As stated by Canadian political scientist Olena Hankivsky (2005, 993): 'Intersectionality . . . seeks to illuminate the synergistic effect of interlocking forms of oppression.'
3. For further elaboration of this point, see McCall 2005, 1789ff.
4. Hereafter, this will be referred to as the *Integration of Diversity* initiative.
5. These and other publications from the *Integration of Diversity* initiative are available on the Status of Women website, at <www.swc-cfc.gc.ca/pubs/pubspr/index_e.html>.
6. See <www.justice.gc.ca/en/dept/pub/ideas/index.html> for a full copy of IDEAS.
7. The gender-based analysis chart developed by Citizenship and Immigration is available at <www.cic.ga.ca/english/irpa/gender%2Damend.html>.
8. The four designated groups in employment equity legislation are women, persons with disabilities, visible minorities, and Aboriginal peoples.
9. For further discussion, see, for example, Fonow and Cook 2005; Ramazanoglu and Holland 2002; Naples 2003; Smith 2005; 2006; Doucet and Mauthner 2006; 2008; Mauthner and Doucet 2003; Siltanen et al. 2008.

Glossary

Aboriginal. Also known as Founding Peoples, the indigenous people of Canada of First Nations, Inuit, or Métis ancestry, who are politically organized and represented by the Assembly of First Nations, the Legislative Assembly of Nunavut, and the Métis National Council, respectively.

Affirmative action. Policies and guidelines designed to promote access to education or employment for marginalized groups.

Colonialism. The often violent takeover of a territory and its natural resources, as well as the displacement or domination of existing populations, including their culture, customs, and economic systems, by another nation, group, or government.

Community responsibility. The extra-domestic, inter-household, community-based aspects of being responsible for households, children, and their care.

Difference. A prominent concept in discussions about gender inequality and social justice, refers to the recognition of diversity within gender categories.

Doing gender. The idea that gender is not innate or biological but rather must be 'worked at' or 'achieved' through everyday activities.

Dualism. The belief that masculinity/men and femininity/women are fundamentally opposite, often linked to other dualisms such as nature/culture and rational/emotional.

Dynamics of exclusion and marginalization. Social processes that operate to both systemically and overtly divide, rank, and silence particular groups based on gender, ethnicity, or class, for example.

Emphasized femininities. Forms of femininity that comply with hegemonic masculinity (Connell 1987).

Employment equity. A Canadian program designed to eliminate discrimination in employment faced by four specific marginalized groups: women, Aboriginal peoples, persons with disabilities, and visible minorities.

Essentialism. Belief in 'essential', universal, natural, innate, or inevitable characteristics based on gender, race, or some other social phenomena.

Export processing zone (EPZ). A geographical region, often located in Third World countries, in which trade and commerce laws (including for companies that employ women) are relaxed or eliminated in order to attract foreign investment.

Gender-based analysis (GBA). Research methodology used in policy deliberations in Canada and internationally, which recognizes and takes into account the impacts on differences between women and men as well as among women (see **gender mainstreaming**, below).

Gender divisions of labour. The study of how labour is divided by gender in paid and unpaid work.

Gender identity. An individual's own sense of association with maleness, femaleness, multi-genders, or transgender.

Gender ideologies. Loosely defined as a set of social beliefs about men and women's roles and relationships in varied social institutions.

Gender mainstreaming. Efforts, which may or may not include gender-based analyses, by national and international governing bodies to bring gender considerations into the full range of political departments and issues (also used, by Marshall [2000], to refer to the acknowledged centrality of gender to sociological analysis).

Glass ceilings. Systemic barriers that prevent women from attaining professional success in male-dominated professions and positions.

Glass escalators. The gendered nature of paid labour, which allows men to progress quickly to promotion and professional success in female-dominated professions.

Globalization. Controversial phenomenon that has led to the worldwide interconnection of people, places, and economic and political systems; often refers to the ascendancy of free market logic and practices in international trade and government, led by transnational corporations, and argued to have particularly detrimental impacts on Third World women.

Hegemonic masculinity. A form of masculinity that has central prominence and emphasizes physical and social domination over women and over other forms of masculinity.

Heterosexism. The belief that heterosexuality is dominant, inevitable, and more correct than other sexual orientations; associated with the phenomenon of heteronormativity.

Ideology. A collection of ideas or a world view that includes specific visions for society.

Intersectional analysis. A way of understanding inequality that takes into account multiple, connecting dimensions. McCall (2005) distinguishes intra-categorical and inter-categorical forms of intersectional analysis.

Intersex. Individual born with both female and male biological characteristics.

Malestream. A term introduced in the 1980s to characterize the dominance of men, and men's experience within sociology as well as academia more generally.

Multiple genders. The idea that there are more than two genders.

Neo-liberalism. System of governance in which control rests in the private sector more fully than the public one, which limits the social role of the state and emphasizes the individual over society.

Non-standard employment relationship. Also referred to as precarious or contingent employment, includes several types of employment that are very different from a full-time, full-year, permanent paid job, such as part-time employment, temporary employment, self-employment, or multiple job-holding (typically associated more with women's employment but now increasing for everyone).

Non-traditional profession. Refers to a woman or man taking up a profession that has typically been dominated by the opposite gender (e.g., male nurse, female firefighter).

Post-modern (or postmodern). An approach to understanding the social world that highlights connections between knowledge and power, the reflexive and partial positioning of all social and natural scientists, and the collapse of universal propositions or grand 'meta-narratives' of knowledge. This can be a difficult term to grasp and has different meanings and significance in different academic disciplines. Of relevance to this book is the view that a post-modern society is one generally characterized by fragmentations, multiple realities, competing viewpoints, and perspectives that fill the vacuum left by the absence of 'truth'.

Post-positivism. Approach to research that recognizes the socially constructed, and theoretically embedded, nature of data.

Post-structuralism (or poststructuralism). An approach to understanding the social world by studying the relationship between language, being, and interpretation. According to poststructuralist thinkers, concepts (*signifieds*) and the words (*signifiers*) employed to represent them are constantly shifting in meaning, and therefore interpretations of the world are in a continual process of movement and change.

Racialized women. A political and academic term that highlights the idea that race is a politicized social construction with systemic foundations.

Reflexivity. A research practice whereby researchers acknowledge their role in the research process and in the construction of their data.

Relations of ruling. 'Internally coordinated complex of administrative, managerial, professional, and discursive organization that regulates, organizes, governs, and otherwise controls our societies' (Smith 1989).

Sandwich generation. Individuals who are sandwiched between two generations of caring work and are caring for children and for seniors.

Social reproduction. 'The activities required to ensure day-to-day and generational survival' (Luxton 1998).

Social structure. Includes the systems in a society, such as institutions, governments, media, and discourse and the relations between them.

Standard job. Full-time, year-round employment with one employer, benefits and entitlements, and reasonable expectation of continued, long-term employment (more typically associated with men's employment but declining overall for everyone).

Standpoint epistemology. A theory of knowledge that recognizes the importance of social location in people's understandings of the social world.

Systemic barriers. A combination of policies, procedures, and systems that marginalizes and excludes a particular group, though sometimes unintentionally.

Third wave feminism. Encompasses diverse feminist perspectives, associated with the generations of women who came of age in the 1980s and 1990s, that account for differences among women by rejecting the idea of a universal female perspective or experience.

Transgender. A process that takes many forms whereby an individual exhibits or wants to exhibit characteristics that do not correspond to the gender that individual was identified with at birth.

Undoing gender. Subverting and neutralizing gender norms and expectations through everyday practices.

Universal child care. A government-funded, accessible, safe, and affordable child care program, which many feminists in Canada advocate as a way of eliminating systemic barriers to women's full participation in paid labour.

Unpaid labour. Largely invisible work, not included in calculations of Gross Domestic Product, often performed by women in informal settings such as the family and the community.

Voluntary childlessness. A sometimes stigmatized choice not to have children on the part of a man, woman, or couple.

Bibliography

Abdel-Shehid, G. 2005. *Who da' Man? Black Masculinities and Sporting Cultures*. Toronto: Canadian Scholars' Press.

Absolon, Kathleen, and Elaine Herbert. 2005. 'Community action as a practice of freedom: A First Nations perspective', in Brian Warf and Michael Clague, eds, *Community Organizing: Canadian Experiences*, 205–27. Don Mills, ON: Oxford University Press.

Acker, Joan. 1997. 'My life as a feminist sociologist; or, Getting the man out of my head', in Barbara Laslett and Barrie Thorne, eds, *Feminist Sociology: Life Histories of a Movement*, 28–47. New Brunswick, NJ: Rutgers University Press.

———. 2006. *Class Questions, Feminist Answers*. Oxford: Rowman and Littlefield.

Adams, M.L. 1997. *The Trouble with Normal: Postwar Youth and the Making of Heterosexuality*. Toronto: University of Toronto Press.

———. 1998. 'So what's the problem with wussy sports?', *Borderlines* 46 (April): 12–15.

Adamson, Nancy, Linda Briskin, and Margaret McPhail. 1988. *Feminist Organizing for Change: The Contemporary Women's Movement in Canada*. Toronto: Oxford University Press.

Agnew, Vijay. 2002. *Gender and Diversity: A Discussion Paper*. Ottawa: Status of Women Canada.

Albanese, Patrizia. 2006. 'Small town, big benefits: The ripple effect of $7/day child care', *Canadian Review of Sociology and Anthropology* 43, 2: 125–41.

Allen, Sarah M., and Kerry Daly. 2002. *The Effects of Father Involvement: A Summary of the Research Evidence*. Carleton Place, ON: Father Involvement Initiative—Ontario Network.

Amnesty International Canada. 2004. 'Stolen sisters: A human rights response to discrimination and violence against indigenous women in Canada', at <www.amnesty.ca/stolensisters/amr2000304.pdf>.

Andersen, Margaret L. 2006. *Thinking about Women*. Montreal: Allyn and Bacon.

———, and Patricia Hill Collins. 1992. *Race, Class and Gender: An Anthology*. Belmont, CA: Wadsworth.

Anderson, Karen. 1991. *Chain Her by One Foot: The Subjugation of Native Women in Seventeenth-Century New France*. New York: Routledge.

Anderson, Kristin. 2007. 'Who gets out? Gender as structure and the dissolution of violent heterosexual relationships', *Gender and Society* 21, 2: 173–201.

Anderson, Michael, et al. 2006. 'Timespans and plans among young adults', *Sociology* 39, 1: 139–55.

Anisef, P., and P. Axelrod. 2001. 'Baby boomers in transition: Life-course experiences of the class of '73', in V.W. Marshall et al., eds, *Restructuring Work and the Life Course*, 473–88. Toronto: University of Toronto Press.

Arat-Koc, S. 1989. 'In the privacy of our own home: Foreign domestic workers as solution to the crisis of the domestic sphere in Canada', *Studies in Political Economy* 28 (Spring): 33–58.

————. 1999. 'Neo-liberalism, state restructuring and immigration: Changes in Canadian policies in the 1990s', *Journal of Canadian Studies* 34, 2: 31–56.

Arber, Sara, and Jay Ginn. 2004. 'Ageing and gender: Diversity and change', in C. Summerfield and P. Babb, eds, *Social Trends*, 34: 1–14. London: The Stationery Office.

Armenti, Carmen. 2004. 'Gender as a barrier for women with children in academe', *Canadian Journal of Higher Education* 34, 1: 1–26.

Armstrong, Pat, and Hugh Armstrong. 1984. *The Double Ghetto: Canadian Women and Their Segregated Work*. Toronto: McClelland & Stewart.

————. 2003. *Wasting Away: The Undermining of Canadian Health Care*. Don Mills, ON: Oxford University Press.

————, Mary Cornish, and Elizabeth Miller. 2003. 'Pay equity: Complexity and contradiction in legal rights and social processes', in Wallace Clement and Leah F. Vosko, eds, *Changing Canada: Political Economy as Transformation*, 161–82. Montreal and Kingston: McGill-Queen's University Press.

Arscott, Jane, and Linda Trimble. 1997. *In the Presence of Women: Representation in Canadian Governments*. Toronto: Harcourt Brace.

Bader, Ed, and Andrea Doucet. 2005. *Canadian Community Organizations and New Fathers: A Report of the New Fathers Cluster of the Father Involvement Research Alliance* (October). Guelph: University of Guelph.

Bagilhole, Barbara. 2002. *Women in Non-traditional Occupations: Challenging Men*. New York: Palgrave Macmillan.

Bains, Donna, and Nandita Sharma. 2006. 'Migrant workers as non-citizens: The case against citizenship as a social policy concept', in Vivian Shalla, ed., *Working in a Global Era*, 203–25. Toronto: Canadian Scholars' Press.

Bakan, Abigail B., and A. Kobayashi. 2000. 'Employment equity policy in Canada: An inter-provincial comparison', *The Integration of Diversity into Policy Research, Development and Analysis*, at <www.swc-cfc.gc.ca/pubs/pubspr/index_e.html>.

————, and Daiva K. Stasiulis. 1995. 'Making the match: Domestic placement agencies and the racialization of women's household work', *Signs: Journal of Women in Culture and Society* 20, 21: 303–35.

————, eds. 1997. *Not One of the Family: Foreign Domestic Workers in Canada*. Toronto: University of Toronto Press.

Balbo, Laura. 1987. 'Crazy quilts: Rethinking the welfare state debate from a woman's point of view', in A.S. Sassoon, ed., *Women and the State*, 45–71. London: Unwin Hyman.

Bannerji, Himani. 1991. *Unsettling Relations: The University as a Site of Feminist Struggle*. Toronto: Women's Press.

————. 1993. *Returning the Gaze: Essays on Racism, Feminism, and Politics*. Toronto: Sister Vision Press.

————. 1995. *Thinking Through: Essays on Feminism, Marxism and Anti-Racism*. London and Toronto: Women's Press.

————. 2000. *The Dark Side of the Nation: Essays on Multiculturalism, Nationalism and Gender*. Toronto: Canadian Scholars' Press.

Barndt, Deborah, ed. 1999. *Women Working the NAFTA Food Chain: Women, Food and Globalization*. Toronto: Second Story Press.

————. 2002. *Tangled Routes: Women, Work and Globalization on the Tomato Trail*. Aurora, ON: Garamond.

Barnett, Rosalind C., and Grace K. Baruch. 1987. 'Determinants of fathers' participation in family work', *Journal of Marriage and the Family* 49, 1: 29–40.

Barron, C., and D. Lacombe. 2005. 'Moral panic and the nasty girl', *Canadian Review of Sociology and Anthropology* 42, 1: 51–69.

Bastien, Betty. 2004. *Blackfoot Ways of Knowing: The Worldview of the Siksikaitsitapi*. Calgary: University of Calgary Press.

Baumgardner, Jennifer, and Amy Richards. 2000. *Manifesta: Young Women, Feminism and the Future*. New York: Farrar, Straus, and Giroux.

Beaujot, R. 2004. *Delayed Life Transitions: Trends and Implications*. Ottawa: Vanier Institute of the Family.

Belkin, Lisa. 2003. 'The opt out revolution', *New York Times Magazine*, 26 October.

Bem, Sandra Lipsitz. 1993. *The Lenses of Gender: Transforming the Debate on Sexual Inequality*. New Haven, CT: Yale University Press.

Berk, Sara Fenstermaker. 1985. *The Gender Factory: The Apportionment of Work in American Households*. New York: Plenum.

Bianchi, Suzanne M., et al. 2000. 'Is anyone doing the housework? Trends in the gender division of household labor', *Social Forces* 79, 1: 191–228.

Biggs, L., and P. Downe, eds. 2005. *Gendered Intersections*. Halifax: Fernwood.

Blain, Jenny. 1994. 'Discourses of agency and domestic labor: Family discourse and gendered practice in dual earner families', *Journal of Family Issues* 15, 4: 515–49.

Blum, E., et al. 2006. 'Opening the floodgates: The aftermath of an immigrant women's action against violence project and its evaluation', *Canadian Woman Studies* 25, 1, 2: 27–32.

Bock, Gisela, and Susan James. 1992. *Beyond Equality and Difference: Citizenship, Feminist Politics and Female Subjectivity*. London and New York: Routledge.

Bono, Paola, and Sandra Kemp. 1991. *Italian Feminist Thought: A Reader*. Oxford: Blackwell.

Bordo, S. 1995. *Unbearable Weight: Feminism, Western Culture, and the Body*. Berkeley: University of California Press.

Bornstein, K. 1995. *Gender Outlaw: Of Men, Women, and the Rest of Us*. New York: Vintage Books.

————. 1998. *My Gender Workbook: How to Become a Real Man, a Real Woman, the Real You, or Something Entirely Different*. New York: Routledge.

Boushey, Heather. 2005. *Are Women Opting Out? Debunking the Myth*. Washington: Center for Economic and Policy Research.

Bowlby, John. 1953. *Child Care and the Growth of Love*. Baltimore: Pelican.

Boyd, Monica. 1982. 'Sex differences in the Canadian occupational attainment process', *Canadian Review of Sociology and Anthropology* 19, 1: 1–28.

————. 1985. 'Educational and occupational attainments of native-born Canadian men and women', in Monica Boyd et al., eds, *Ascription and Achievement: Studies in Mobility and Status Attainment in Canada*, 229–95. Ottawa: Carleton University Press.

————, et al. 1985. *Ascription and Achievement: Studies in Mobility and Status Attainment in Canada*. Ottawa: Carleton University Press.

Bradbury, Bettina. 1984. 'Pigs, cows and boarders: Non-wage forms of survival among Montreal families, 1861–1881', *Labour/Le travail* 14 (Fall): 9–46.

————. 1993. *Working Families: Age, Gender and Daily Survival in Industrializing Montreal.* Toronto: McClelland & Stewart.

Brannen, Julia, and Peter Moss. 1991. *Managing Mothers: Dual Earner Households after Maternity Leave.* London: Unwin Hyman.

————, and A. Nilsen. 2002. 'Young people's time perspectives: From youth to adulthood', *Sociology* 36, 3: 513–37.

————. 2007. 'Young people, time horizons and planning: A response to Anderson et al.', *Sociology* 41, 1: 153–60.

Bright, R. 2005. 'It's just a grade 8 girl thing: Aggression in teenage girls', *Gender and Education* 17, 1: 93–101.

Briskin, Linda. 2005. 'Sites of struggle/vehicles of resistance: Unions and women workers', in Lesley Biggs and Pamela Downe, eds, *Gendered Intersections: An Introduction to Women's and Gender Studies*, 210–15. Halifax: Fernwood.

————, and Patricia McDermott. 1993. *Women Challenging Unions: Feminism, Democracy and Militancy.* Toronto: University of Toronto Press.

Brown, Lyn Mikel. 2003. *Girlfighting: Betrayal and Rejection among Girls.* New York: New York University Press.

————, and Carol Gilligan. 1992. *Meeting at the Crossroads: Women's Psychology and Girls' Development.* Cambridge, MA: Harvard University Press.

Bruckert, C. 2002. *Taking It Off, Putting It On: Women in the Strip Trade.* Toronto: Women's Press.

Bryman, A. 2006. 'Paradigm peace and the implications for quality', *International Journal of Social Research Methodology* 9, 2: 111–26.

Buchanan, Ruth. 2006. '1-800 New Brunswick: Economic development strategies, firm restructuring, and the local production of "global" services', in Vivian Shalla, ed., *Working in a Global Era: Canadian Perspectives*, 177–97. Toronto: Canadian Scholars' Press.

Bukowski, W., et al. 1999. 'Same and other: Interdependency between participation in same and other-sex relationships', *Journal of Youth and Adolescence* 28, 4: 439–59.

Bumpus, Matthew F., Ann C. Crouter, and Susan M. McHale. 1999. 'Work demands of dual-earner couples: Implications for parents' knowledge about children's daily lives in middle childhood', *Journal of Marriage and Family* 61 (May): 465–76.

Burstyn, V. 1999. *The Rites of Men: Manhood, Politics, and the Culture of Sport.* Toronto: University of Toronto Press.

Burt, Sandra. 1993. 'The changing patterns of public policy', in Sandra Burt, Lorraine Code, and Lindsay Dorney, eds, *Changing Patterns: Women in Canada*, 2nd edn, 212–42. Toronto: McClelland & Stewart.

Butler, Judith. 1990. *Gender Trouble.* London: Routledge.

————. 2004. *Undoing Gender.* New York: Routledge.

Cairns, Alan. 2000. *Citizens Plus: Aboriginal Peoples and the Canadian State.* Vancouver: University of British Columbia Press.

Calliste, Agnes. 1996. 'Anti-racism organizing and resistance in Canadian nursing: African Canadian women', *Canadian Review of Sociology and Anthropology* 33, 3: 361–90.

Campbell, Marie. 1979. *Halfbreed.* Toronto: McClelland & Stewart–Bantam.

Campeau, A. 2006. 'Cultivated gendered "underdeveloped" subjectivities: Tracing the constitution of girlhoods and mainstream development discourse', MA thesis, Department of Sociology and Anthropology, Carleton University, Ottawa.

Canada. House of Commons Standing Committee on the Status of Women. 2005. *Gender-Based Analysis: Building Blocks for Success*. Ottawa: Standing Committee on the Status of Women.

Canadian Nurses Association. 2005. '2005 workforce profile of registered nurses in Canada', at <www.cna-nurses.ca/CNA/documents/pdf/publications/workforce-profile-2005-e.pdf>.

Canadian Women's Health Network. 2007. 'How would you spend $300 million to best improve women's and girls' health in Canada? The HPV vaccination debate rages on', editorial, at <www.cwhn.ca/network-reseau/10-1/10-1pg1.html>.

Caplan, Paula. 1993. *Lifting a Ton of Feathers: A Woman's Guide to Surviving in the Academic World*. Toronto: University of Toronto Press.

Caputo, V. 2001. 'Telling stories from the field: Children and the politics of ethnographic representation', *Anthropologica* 43, 2: 179–89.

Carrel, André. 2001. *Citizen's Hall: Making Local Democracy Work*. Toronto: Between the Lines.

Carroll, W.K., et al., eds. 1992. *Fragile Truths: 25 Years of Sociology and Anthropology in Canada*. Ottawa: Carleton University Press.

Carty, Linda. 1991. 'Black women in academia: A statement from the periphery', in H. Bannerji et al., eds, *Unsettling Relations: The University as a Site of Feminist Struggles*, 13–44. Toronto: The Women's Press Collective.

———. 1993. *And Still We Rise: Feminist Political Mobilizing in Contemporary Canada*. Toronto: Women's Press.

CAUT (Canadian Association of University Teachers). 2006. 'Women in the academic workforce', *CAUT Education Review* 8, 1.

Cavarero, Adriana. 1993. 'Towards a theory of sexual differences', in S. Kemp and P. Bono, eds, *The Lonely Mirror: Italian Perspectives in Feminist Theory*, 189–221. London and New York: Routledge.

CBC (Canadian Broadcasting Corporation). 2004. 'In depth: Daycare in Canada', on-line article, 24 October, at <www.cbc.ca>.

Chafetz, J.S. 1997. 'Feminist theory and sociology: Underutilized contributions for mainstream theory', *Annual Review of Sociology* 23: 97–120.

Chandler, J. 2002. 'Chick clicks and politics: An exploration of third wave feminist ezines on the Internet', MA thesis, School of Journalism and Communication, Carleton University, Ottawa.

Cheal, David. 1991. *Family and the State of Theory*. Toronto: University of Toronto Press.

———. 1999. *New Poverty: Families in Postmodern Society*. Westport, CT: Greenwood.

Chodorow, Nancy. 1978. *The Reproduction of Mothering*. Berkeley and Los Angeles: University of California Press.

Clarke, Tony, and Maude Barlow. 1997. *MIA: The Multilateral Agreement on Investment*. Toronto: Stoddart.

Clement, Wallace, and John Myles. 1994. *Relations of Ruling: Class and Gender in Post-industrial Societies*. Montreal and Kingston: McGill-Queen's University Press.

———, and Clarence Lochhead. 1994. 'Bringing in gender: Postindustrialism and patriarchy', in Wallace Clement and John Myles, eds, *Relations of Ruling*, 142–73. Montreal and Kingston: McGill-Queen's University Press.

Code, Lorraine. 1981. 'Is the sex of the knower epistemologically significant?', *Metaphilosophy* 12 (July/October): 267–76.

————. 1995. 'How do we know? Questions of method in feminist practice', in S.D. Burt and L. Code, eds, *Changing Methods: Feminists Transforming Practice*, 13–44. Peterborough: Broadview Press.

Cohen, Philip N. 2004. 'The gender division of labor: "Keeping house" and occupational segregation in the United States', *Gender and Society* 18, 2: 239–52.

Colapinto, J. 2001. *As Nature Made Him: The Boy Who Was Raised as a Girl*. New York: Harper Perennial.

Collins, Patricia Hill. 1994. 'Shifting the center: Race, class and feminist theorizing about motherhood', in E.N. Glenn, G. Chang, and L.R. Forcey, eds, *Mothering: Ideology, Experience and Agency*, 45–65. London and New York: Routledge.

————. 2000. *Black Feminist Thought: Knowledge, Consciousness, and the Politics of Empowerment*. London and New York: Routledge.

————. 2004. *Black Sexual Politics: African Americans, Gender, and the New Racism*. New York: Routledge.

Collins, W.A., et al. 2000. 'Contemporary research on parenting: The case for nature and nurture', *American Psychologist* 55, 2: 218–32.

Coloroso, B. 1995. *Kids Are Worth It!* Toronto: Somerville House.

————. 2002. *The Bully, the Bullied and the Bystander*. Toronto: HarperCollins.

Coltrane, Scott. 2000. 'Research on household labor: Modeling and measuring the social embeddedness of routine family work', *Journal of Marriage and the Family* 62: 1208–33.

————. 2003. 'Fathering: Paradoxes, contradictions, and dilemmas', in M. Coleman and L.H.T. Ganong, eds, *Handbook of Contemporary Families: Considering the Past, Contemplating the Future*, 224–43. Thousand Oaks, CA: Sage.

————, and Michele Adams. 2001. 'Men's family work: Child-centered fathering and the sharing of domestic labor', in R. Hertz and N.L. Marshall, eds, *Working Families: The Transformation of the American Home*, 72–99. Berkeley: University of California Press.

Connell, R.W. 1987. *Gender and Power*. Cambridge: Polity.

————. 1995. *Masculinities*. London: Polity.

————. 2000. *The Men and the Boys*. Cambridge: Polity.

Connelly, M. Patricia, and Martha MacDonald. 1983. 'Women's work: Domestic and wage labour in a Nova Scotia community', *Studies in Political Economy* 10 (Winter): 45–72.

Connolly, J. 1999. 'Conceptions of cross-sex friendships and romantic relationships in early adolescence', *Journal of Youth and Adolescence* 28, 4: 481–94.

Conway, Janet M. 2004. *Identity, Place, Knowledge: Social Movements Contesting Globalization*. Halifax: Fernwood.

Coontz, Stephanie. 2006. 'Myth of the opt out mom', *Christian Science Monitor*, 30 March.

Coote, Anne, Harriet Harman, and Patricia Hewitt. 1990. *The Family Way: A New Approach to Policy-Making*. London: Institute for Public Policy Research.

Cornell, Drucilla. 2003. *Between Women and Generations: Legacies of Dignity*. New York: Palgrave.

Corsaro, W.A. 2003. *'We're Friends, Right?' Inside Kids' Cultures*. Washington: Joseph Henry Press.

————, and D. Eder. 1990. 'Children's peer cultures', *Annual Review of Sociology* 16: 197–220.

Côté, A., et al. 2001. 'Sponsorship for better or worse: The impact of sponsorship on the equality rights of immigrant women', in *The Integration of Diversity into Policy Research, Development and Analysis*, at <www.swc-cfc.gc.ca/pubs/pubspr/index_e.html>.

Coulter, R. 1993. *Gender Socialization: New Ways, New World*. St John's: Newfoundland and Labrador Women's Policy Office.

Cowan, Ruth Schwartz. 1983. *More Work for Mother: The Ironies of Household Technology from the Open Hearth to the Microwave*. New York: Basic Books.

Craig, Wendy M., et al. 1998. *Bullying and Victimization among Canadian School Children*. Hull, QC: Human Resources and Social Development Canada.

———. 2002. 'The role of the peer group in pre-adolescent behaviour', in J.D. Willms, ed., *Vulnerable Children*, 317–27. Edmonton: University of Alberta Press.

Cranford, Cynthia, et al. 2006. 'The gender of precarious employment in Canada', in Vivian Shalla, ed., *Working in a Global Era: Canadian Perspectives*, 99–119. Toronto: Canadian Scholars' Press.

Cranny-Francis, Anne, et al. 2003. *Gender Studies: Terms and Debates*. London: Palgrave.

Creese, G. 1999. *Contracting Masculinity: Gender, Class and Race in a White Collar Union, 1944–94*. Toronto: Oxford University Press.

———, and D. Stasiulis. 1996. 'Introduction: Intersections of gender, race, class and sexuality', *Studies in Political Economy* 51: 5–14.

CRIAW (Canadian Research Institute for the Advancement of Women). 2005. 'Transforming our social justice work: Towards intersectional feminist frameworks (IFFs)', at <www.criaw-icref.ca/indexFrame_e.htm>.

———. 2006. 'Intersectional feminist frameworks: An emerging vision', at <www.criaw-icref.ca/indexFrame_e.htm>.

Crittenden, Ann. 2001. *The Price of Motherhood: Why the Most Important Job in the World Is Still the Least Valued*. New York: Henry Holt.

Culhane, D. 2003. 'Their spirits live within us: Aboriginal women in Downtown Eastside Vancouver emerging into visibility', *American Indian Quarterly* 27, 3: 593–606.

Cummins, Helene A. 2005. 'Mommy tracking single women in academia when they are not mommies', *Women's Studies International Forum* 28: 222–31.

Daenzer, Patricia. 2002. 'Benevolent patriarchy: The foreign domestic movement, 1980–1990', in Merle Jacobs, ed., *Is Anyone Listening? Women, Work and Society*, 210–26. Toronto: Women's Press.

Dale, S. 2005. *Candy from Strangers: Kids and Consumer Culture*. Vancouver: New Star Books.

Darling, N., et al. 1999. 'Mixed-sex settings and the perception of competence', *Journal of Youth and Adolescence* 28, 5: 461–80.

Das Gupta, Tania. 2002. 'Racism in nursing', in Merle Jacobs, ed., *Is Anyone Listening? Women, Work and Society*, 117–38. Toronto: Women's Press.

Davies, S., and N. Guppy. 2006. *The Schooled Society*. Don Mills, ON: Oxford University Press.

Davis, K., et al., eds. 1991. *The Gender of Power*. London: Sage.

Dean, Jodi. 1996. *Solidarity of Strangers: Feminism after Identity Politics*. Berkeley: University of California Press.

Dei, G.S. 1996. 'The intersections of race, class and gender in the anti-racism discourse', in G.S. Dei, *Anti-Racism Education: Theory and Practice*, 55–74. Halifax: Fernwood.

———. 2005. 'The intersections of race, class, and gender in the anti-racism discourse', in Valerie Zawilski and Cynthia Levine-Rasky, eds, *Inequality in Canada: A Reader on the Intersections of Gender, Race, and Class*, 17–25. Don Mills, ON: Oxford University Press.

Dellasega, Cheryl. 2002. *Surviving Ophelia: Mothers Share Their Wisdom in Navigating the Tumultuous Teenage Years.* Cambridge, MA: Perseus.

Delphy, C. 2002. 'Rethinking sex and gender', in S. Jackson and S. Scott, eds, *Gender: A Sociological Reader*, 51–9. London: Routledge.

Denzin, Norman K., and Yvonna S. Lincoln. 2005. *The Sage Handbook of Qualitative Research*, 3rd edn. London: Sage.

Deutsch, F.M. 2007. 'Undoing gender', *Gender and Society* 21, 1: 106–27.

DeVault, Marjorie L. 1996. 'Talking back to sociology: Distinctive contributions of feminist methodology', *Annual Review of Sociology*, 22: 29–50.

di Leonardo, Micaela. 1987. 'The female world of cards and holidays: Women, families and the world of kinship', *Signs: Journal of Women in Culture and Society* 12, 3: 440–53.

Dinnerstein, Dorothy. 1977. *The Mermaid and the Minotaur: Sexual Arrangements and Human Malaise.* New York: Harper Colophon Books.

DiPalma, Carolyn, and Kathy Ferguson. 2006. 'Clearing ground and making connections: Modernism, postmodernism, feminism', in K. Davis, M. Evans, and J. Lorber, eds, *Handbook of Gender and Women's Studies*, 127–45. Thousand Oaks, CA: Sage.

Doherty, Gillian, Martha Friendly, and Jane Beach. 2003. OECD *Thematic Review of Early Childhood Education and Care: Canadian Background Report.* Paris: OECD.

Dollahite, David C., Alan J. Hawkins, and S.E. Brotherson. 1997. 'Fatherwork: A conceptual ethic of fathering as generative work', in A.J. Hawkins and D.C. Dollahite, eds, *Generative Fathering: Beyond Deficit Perspectives*, 17–35. Thousand Oaks, CA: Sage.

Donnan, Mary Ellen. 1996. 'State feminism and representation of non-geographic difference: A case study of the Canadian Advisory Council on the Status of Women (child services recommendations)', MA thesis, Department of Sociology and Anthropology, Carleton University, Ottawa.

———. 2003. 'Slow advances: The academy's response to sexual assault', in Deborah Keahey and Deborah Schnitzer, eds, *The Madwoman in the Academy: 43 Women Boldly Take on the Ivory Tower*, 123–9. Calgary: University of Calgary Press.

———. 2004. 'The meanings of citizenship: Homelessness in relation to extra-local civic republicanism and local community spirit in Ottawa', PhD dissertation, Department of Sociology and Anthropology, Carleton University, Ottawa.

———. 2005. 'Affordable housing and social sustainability in Canadian cities', *The International Journal of Environmental, Cultural, Economic & Social Sustainability*, at <www.sustainability-journal.com>.

Doucet, Andrea. 2004. 'Fathers and the responsibility for children: A puzzle and a tension', *Atlantis: A Women's Studies Journal* 28, 2: 103–14.

———. 2006. *Do Men Mother? Fathering, Care, and Domestic Responsibility.* Toronto: University of Toronto Press.

———. 2008. ' "From her side of the gossamer wall(s")": Reflexivity and relational knowing', *Qualitative Sociology* 31 (January): 519–33.

———, and Natasha S. Mauthner. 2006. 'Feminist methodologies and epistemologies', in C.D. Bryant and D. Pleck, eds, *Handbook of 21st Century Sociology*, 36–42. Thousand Oaks, CA: Sage.

———. 2008. 'Feminist approaches to qualitative interviews', in Pertti Alasuutari, Julia Brannen, and Leonard Bickman, eds, *Handbook of Social Research Methods.* London: Sage.

Drolet, D. 2007. 'Minding the gender gap: Why do boys seem to underachieve academically relative to girls?', *University Affairs/Affaires universitaires* 48: 9–12.

Dua, E. 1999. 'Beyond diversity: Exploring the ways in which the discourse of race has shaped the institution of the nuclear family', in E. Dua and A. Robertson, eds, *Scratching the Surface: Canadian Anti-racist, Feminist Thought*, 237–60. Toronto: Women's Press.

Dubois, J. 2002. *What Influences Young Canadians to Pursue Post-secondary Studies?* Ottawa: Applied Research Branch, Human Resources and Development Canada.

Duffy, Ann, Nancy Mandell, and Norene Pupo. 1989. *Few Choices: Women, Work and Family.* Toronto: Garamond.

Duncan, N. 1999. *Sexual Bullying: Gender Conflict and Pupil Culture in Secondary Schools.* London: Routledge.

Dusseault, C. 2007. 'UBC confronts gender-related differences in faculty of science', *University Affairs/Affaires universitaires* 48: 34–5.

Duxbury, Linda, Chris Higgins, and Karen L. Johnson. 2004. *The 2001 National Work-Life Conflict Study: Report Three: Exploring the Link between Work-Life Conflict and Demands on Canada's Health Care System.* Ottawa: Public Health Agency of Canada.

Eder, D. 1995. *School Talk: Gender and Adolescent Culture.* New Brunswick, NJ: Rutgers University Press.

Edwards, Rosalind. 1990. 'Connecting method and epistemology: A white woman interviewing black women', *Women's Studies International Forum* 13: 477–90.

———. 1993. 'An education in interviewing: Placing the researcher and the researched', in C.M. Renzetti and R.M. Lee, eds, *Researching Sensitive Topics*, 181–96. Newbury Park, CA: Sage.

Egger, S.A. 1998. *The Killers among Us: An Examination of Serial Murder and Its Investigation.* Upper Saddle River, NJ: Prentice Hall.

Eichler, M. 1980. *The Double Standard: A Feminist Critique of Feminist Social Science.* New York: St Martin's Press.

———. 1988. *Non-sexist Research Methods.* Wellington: Unwin Hyman.

———. 1992. 'The unfinished transformation: Women and feminist approaches in sociology and anthropology', in W. Carroll, et al., eds, *Fragile Truths: 25 Years of Sociology and Anthropology in Canada*, 71–101. Ottawa: Carleton University Press.

Eisenstein, Zillah. 1998. *Global Obscenities: Patriarchy, Capitalism and the Lure of Cyber-fantasy.* New York: New York University Press.

———. 2004. *Against Empire: Feminisms, Racism, and the West.* London: Zed Books.

Elliotte, Michael. 2001. 'Death in Genoa', *Time*, 22 July: 1, at <www.time.com/time/magazine/article/0,9171,168470,00.html>.

Engels, F. 1942. *The Origin of the Family, Private Property and the State.* New York: International Publishers.

Espiritu, Yen Le. 2007. 'All men are *not* created equal: Asian men in US history', in Michael A. Kimmel and Michael A. Messner, eds, *Men's Lives*, 7th edn, 21–9. Boston: Allyn and Bacon.

Evans, J., and B. Frank. 2003. 'Contradictions and tensions: Exploring relations of masculinities in the numerically female-dominated nursing profession', *Journal of Men's Studies* 11, 3: 277–92.

Evans, P.M., and G.R. Wekerle, eds. 1997. *Women and the Canadian Welfare State: Challenges and Change.* Toronto: University of Toronto Press.

Eyler, A., et al. 1997. 'The nine point gender continuum: Results from the University of Michigan Medical Centre Comprehensive Services Program Longitudinal Transgender Health Project', *International Journal of Transgenderism* (XV Henry Benjamin International Gender Dysphoria Association Symposium, at <www.symposion.com/ijt/hbigda/vancouver/eyler2.htm>).

Fast, Janet E., and Norah C. Keating. 2001. *Informal Caregivers in Canada: A Snapshot.* Report to the Health Services Division Health Policy and Communications Branch, Health Canada, Ottawa.

Feiring, C. 1999. 'Other-sex friendship networks and the development of romantic relationships in adolescence', *Journal of Youth and Adolescence* 28, 4: 495–512.

Feldberg, Roslyn L., and Evelyn Nakano Glenn. 1984. 'Male and female: Job versus gender models in the sociology of work', in Janet Siltanen and Michelle Stanworth, eds, *Women and the Public Sphere*, 23–36. London: Hutchinson.

Fenwick, Tara. 2007. 'Learning on the line: Voices of garment workers at Great Western Garment', *Labour/Le travail* 59 (Spring): 215–30.

Ferree, M.M., et al., eds. 1999. *Revisioning Gender.* Thousand Oaks, CA: Sage.

Findlay, Sue. 1997. 'Institutionalizing feminist politics: Learning from the struggles for equal pay in Ontario', in Patricia M. Evans and Gerda R. Wekerle, eds, *Women and the Canadian Welfare State: Challenges and Change*, 310–29. Toronto: University of Toronto Press.

Fine, Michelle, et al. 2006. '[In] secure times: Constructing white working-class masculinities in the late 20th century', in Michael S. Kimmel and Michael A. Messner, eds, *Men's Lives*, 7th edn, 54–65. Boston: Allyn and Bacon.

Fisher, William F., and Thomas Ponniah. 2003. *Another World Is Possible: Popular Alternatives to Globalization at the World Social Forum.* Black Point, NS: Fernwood.

Flyvbjerg, B. 2002. *Making Social Science Matter.* Cambridge: Cambridge University Press.

Folbre, Nancy. 1994. *Who Pays for the Kids? Gender and the Structures of Constraint.* London: Routledge, Chapman and Hall.

———. 2001. *The Invisible Heart: Economics and Family Values.* New York: New Press.

Fonow, M.M., and J.A. Cook. 2005. 'Feminist methodology: New applications in the academy and public policy', *Signs: Journal of Women in Culture and Society* 30, 2: 2211–36.

Fox, Bonnie. 1998. 'Motherhood, changing relationships and the reproduction of gender inequality', in S. Abbey and A. O'Reilly, eds, *Redefining Motherhood*, 159–74. Toronto: Second Story Press.

———. 2001. 'The formative years: How parenthood creates gender', *Canadian Review of Sociology and Anthropology* 38, 4: 373–90.

———, and Meg Luxton. 2001. 'Conceptualizing family', in Bonnie Fox, ed., *Family Patterns, Gender Relations*, 22–33. Don Mills, ON: Oxford University Press.

———, and Pamela Sugiman. 2006. 'Flexible work, flexible workers: The restructuring of clerical work in a large telecommunications company', in Vivian Shalla, ed., *Working in a Global Era: Canadian Perspectives*, 74–92. Toronto: Canadian Scholars' Press.

Francis, A.C., et al. 2003. *Gender Studies: Terms and Debates.* New York: Palgrave.

Frank, B.W. 1997. 'Masculinities and schooling: The making of men', in J.R. Epp and A.M. Watkinson, eds, *Systemic Violence: How Schools Hurt Children*, 113–30. Albany: State University of New York Press.

————, and K.G. Davison, eds. 2007. *Masculinities and Schooling: International Practices and Perspectives*. London, ON: Althouse.

Frenette, Marc, and René Morissette. 2003. 'Will they ever converge? Earnings of immigrants and Canadian-born workers over the last two decades', in Analytical Studies Branch Research Paper Series no. 215. Ottawa: Statistics Canada.

Fudge, Judy. 2000. 'The paradoxes of pay equity: Reflections on the law and the market in *Bell Canada* and the *Public Service Alliance of Canada*', *Canadian Journal of Women and the Law* 12, 2: 313–44.

————, and Leah Vosko. 2001. 'Gender, segmentation and the standard employment relationship in Canadian labour law, legislation, and policy', *Economic and Industrial Democracy* 22, 2: 288–310.

Furman, W., and L. Shaffer. 1999. 'A story of adolescence: The emergence of other-sex relationships', *Journal of Youth and Adolescence* 28, 4: 513–22.

Furstenburg, F., et al., eds. 2005. *On the Frontier of Adulthood: Theory, Research and Public Policy*. Chicago: University of Chicago Press.

Galabuzi, Grace-Edward. 2006. *Canada's Economic Apartheid: The Social Exclusion of Racialized Groups in the New Century*. Toronto: Canadian Scholars' Press.

Galarneau, Diane. 2005. 'Earnings of temporary versus permanent employees', *Perspectives on Labour and Income* (Statistics Canada) 17, 1: 5–18.

————, and René Morissette. 2004. 'Immigrants: Settling for less?', *Perspectives on Labour and Income* (Statistics Canada) 16, 3: 5–16.

Gannagé, Charlene. 1987. 'A world of difference: The case of women workers in a Canadian garment factory', in H.J. Maroney and M. Luxton, *Feminism and Political Economy: Women's Work, Women's Struggles*, 139–65. Toronto: Methuen.

Gaskell, Jane. 1986. 'Conceptions of skill and the work of women: Some historical and political issues', in Roberta Hamilton and Michele Barrett, eds, *The Politics of Diversity*, 361–84. London: Verso.

Gershuny, Jonathon I., and Ray E. Pahl. 1979. 'Work outside employment: Some preliminary speculations', *New Universities Quarterly* 34, 1: 120–35.

Gibson-Graham, J.K. 2006. *A Postcapitalist Politics*. Minneapolis: University of Minnesota Press.

Giddens, A. 1992. *The Transformation of Intimacy: Sexuality, Love, and Eroticism in Modern Societies*. Stanford, CA: Stanford University Press.

Gilchrist, K. 2007. 'Invisible victims: Disparity in print-media coverage of missing and murdered Aboriginal and white women', MA thesis, University of Ottawa.

Gilligan, Carol. 1982. *In a Different Voice: Psychological Theory and Women's Development*. Cambridge, MA: Harvard University Press.

Giulianotti, R. 2005. *Sport: A Critical Sociology*. Cambridge: Polity.

Glenn, E.N. 2002. *Unequal Freedom: How Race and Gender Shaped American Citizenship and Labor*. Cambridge, MA, and London: Harvard University Press.

Godfrey, R. 2005. *Under the Bridge*. Toronto: HarperCollins.

Goetz, Anne Marie. 1995. 'Institutionalizing women's interests and accountability to women in development', *IDS Bulletin* 26, 3: 1–10.

————. 1997. 'Introduction: Getting institutions right for women in development', in A.M. Goetz, ed., *Getting Institutions Right for Women in Development*. London: Zed Books.

Gonick, Marnina. 1997. 'Reading selves, re-fashioning identity: Teen magazines and their readers', *Curriculum Studies* 5, 1: 69–86.

———. 2003. *Between Femininities: Ambivalence, Identity, and the Education of Girls*. Albany: State University of New York Press.

———. 2004. 'Old plots and new identities: Ambivalent femininities in late modernity', *Discourse: Studies in the Cultural Politics of Education* 25, 2: 189–209.

Gopinath, Gayatri. 2005. *Impossible Desires: Queer Diasporas and South Asian Public Cultures*. Durham, NC: Duke University Press.

Government of British Columbia. 1998. *Facts about Bullying*. Victoria: Ministry of Education.

———. 2000. *Helping Our Kids Live Violence Free: A Parent's Guide for Children in Grades K to 7*. Victoria: Ministry of Education.

Goyder, J., et al. 2003. 'The allocation of male and female occupational prestige in an Ontario urban area: A quarter-century replication', *Canadian Review of Sociology and Anthropology* 40, 4: 417–39.

Graham, Hilary. 1983. 'Do her answers fit his questions? Women and the survey method', in E. Gamarnikow, ed., *The Public and the Private*, 132–47. London: Tavistock.

Gruneau, R., and D. Whitson. 1993. *Hockey Night in Canada: Sport, Identity and Cultural Politics*. Toronto: Garamond.

Guppy, N., and J. Siltanen. 1977. 'A comparison of the allocation of male and female occupational prestige', *Canadian Review of Sociology and Anthropology* 14, 3: 320–30.

Haavind, H. 2003. 'Masculinity by rule-breaking: Cultural contestations in the transitional move from being a child to being a young male', *Nora: Nordic Journal of Women's Studies* 11, 2: 89–100.

Hakim, Catherine. 1996. *Key Issues in Women's Work: Female Heterogeneity and the Polarisation of Women's Employment*. London and Atlantic Highlands, NJ: Athlone.

Halbertam, Judith. 2005. *In a Queer Time and Place: Transgender Bodies, Subcultural Lives*. New York: New York University Press.

Hale, Geoffrey E. 2000. 'Managing the fiscal dividend: The politics of selective activism', in L. Pal, ed., *How Ottawa Spends, 2000–2001*, 59–94. Don Mills, ON: Oxford University Press.

Hamilton, R. 1978. *The Liberation of Women: A Study of Patriarchy and Capitalism*. London: Allen and Unwin.

———. 1996. *Gendering the Vertical Mosaic: Feminist Perspectives on Canadian Society*. Toronto: Copp Clark.

———. 2005. *Gendering the Vertical Mosaic: Feminist Perspectives on Canadian Society*, 2nd edn. Toronto: Pearson.

———, and M. Barrett, eds. 1986. *The Politics of Diversity: Feminism, Marxism and Nationalism*. London: Verso.

Handa, A. 2003. *Of Silk Saris and Miniskirts: South Asian Girls Walk the Tightrope of Culture*. Toronto: Women's Press.

Hankivsky, O. 2005. 'Gender mainstreaming vs. diversity mainstreaming: A preliminary examination of the role and transformative potential of feminist theory', *Canadian Journal of Political Science* 38, 4: 977–1001.

Harding, Sandra. 1987. 'Introduction: Is there a feminist method?', in Sandra Harding, ed., *Feminism and Methodology*, 1–14. Bloomington: Indiana University Press; Milton Keynes, UK: Open University Press.

Harper, A.O. 2006. 'Is Canada peaceful and safe for Aboriginal women?', *Canadian Women Studies* 25, 1, 2: 33–8.

Harris, A. 2004. *All about the Girl: Power, Culture, and Identity*. New York: Routledge.

———, et al. 2000. 'Doing it differently: Young women managing heterosexuality in Australia, Finland and Canada', *Journal of Youth Studies* 3, 4: 373–88.

Harris, Olivia. 1981. 'Households as natural units', in K. Young, C. Wolkowitz, and R. McCullagh, eds, *Of Marriage and the Market: Women's Subordination Internationally and Its Lessons*, 136–56. London: CSE Books.

Hawkins, Alan J., et al. 1993. 'Rethinking fathers' involvement in child care: A developmental perspective', *Journal of Family Issues* 14, 4: 531–49.

———, and David C. Dollahite. 1996. 'Beyond the role-inadequacy perspective of fathering', in A.J. Hawkins and David C. Dollahite, eds, *Generative Fathering: Beyond Deficit Perspectives*, 3–16. Thousand Oaks, CA: Sage.

Hearn, Jeff. 1998. *The Violences of Men*. London: Sage.

———, et al., eds. 1989. *The Sexuality of Organization*. London and Beverly Hill, CA: Sage.

———, and M.S. Kimmel. 2006. 'Changing studies on men and masculinities', in K. Davis, M. Evans, and J. Lorber, eds, *Handbook of Gender and Women's Studies*, 53–70. London: Sage.

Held, David, et al. 1999. *Global Transformations: Politics, Economics and Culture*. Cambridge: Polity.

Henry, Frances, et al. 2000. *The Colour of Democracy: Racism in Canadian Society*, 2nd edn. Toronto: Harcourt Brace.

Hepburn, Alexa. 1997. 'Teachers and secondary school bullying: A postmodern discourse analysis', *Discourse and Society* 8, 1: 27–48.

Hermer, Joe, and Janet Mosher. 2002. *Disorderly People: Law and the Politics of Exclusion in Ontario*. Halifax: Fernwood.

Hochschild, Arlie R. 1989. *The Second Shift*. New York: Avon.

Holt, J. 1964. *How Children Fail*. New York: Pitman.

Honoré, C. 2004. *In Praise of Slow: How a Worldwide Movement is Challenging the Cult of Speed*. Toronto: Vintage Canada.

Hughes, Karen. 2006. *Female Enterprise in the New Economy*. Toronto: University of Toronto Press.

Hwang, Pauline. 2003. 'Racism, sexism and Canadian immigration', from the Colours of Resistance website, <www.colours.mahost.org/articles/hwang.html>.

Inness, S.A. 2004. *Action Chicks: New Images of Tough Women in Popular Culture*. New York: Palgrave Macmillan.

Irwin, Sarah. 2005. *Reshaping Social Life*. London: Routledge.

Jackson, A., and D. Robinson. 2000. *Falling Behind: The State of Working Canada, 2000*. Ottawa: Canadian Centre for Policy Alternatives.

Jackson, K. 1952. *Nurse Nancy*. New York: Simon and Schuster; Toronto: Musson Book Company.

Jackson, S., and S. Scott, eds. 2002. *Gender: A Sociological Reader*. London: Routledge.

Jacobs, Beverly. 2002. *Native Women's Association of Canada Submission to the Special Rapporteur Investigating the Violations of Indigenous Human Rights*. Native Women's Association of Canada, Sisters in Spirit Campaign, at <www.nwac-hq.org>.

Jacobs, Merle. 2002. *Is Anyone Listening? Women, Work, and Society*. Toronto: Women's Press.

Jaggar, Alison. 1990. 'Sexual difference and sexual equality', in Deborah L. Rhode, ed., *Theoretical Perspectives on Sexual Difference*, 239–56. New Haven and London: Yale University Press.

James, A. 2004. *Constructing Childhood: Theory, Policy, and Social Practice*. New York: Palgrave Macmillan.

James, Estelle, Alexandrja Edwards, and Rebecca Wong. 2003. *The Gender Impact of Pension Reform: A Cross Country Analysis*. Washington: World Bank.

Jamieson, Mary. n.d. 'Journey to success: Aboriginal women's business planning guide', at <www.ainc-inac.gc.ca/ps/ecd/js/journ_e.pdf>.

Janovicek, N., and J. Parr, eds. 2003. *Histories of Canadian Children and Youth*. Don Mills, ON: Oxford University Press.

Jenkins, H., ed. 1998. *The Children's Culture Reader*. New York: New York University Press.

Jenson, Jane. 2002. 'Against the current: Child care and family policy in Quebec', in R. Mahon and S. Michel, eds, *Child Care Policy at the Crossroads*, 309–32. New York: Routledge.

Jhappan, Radha. 1996. 'Post-modern race and gender essentialism or a post-mortem of scholarship', *Studies in Political Economy* 51 (Fall): 15–63.

———, ed. 2002. *Women's Legal Strategies in Canada*. Toronto: University of Toronto Press.

———, and D. Stasiulis. 2005. 'Anglophilia and the discreet charm of the English voice in Disney's *Pocahontas* films', in M. Budd and M.H. Kirsch, eds, *Rethinking Disney: Private Control, Public Dimensions*, 151–80. Middletown, CT: Wesleyan University Press.

Jiwani, Yasmin. 1997. *Reena Virk: The Erasure of Race*. Vancouver: The FREDA Centre for Research on Violence against Women and Children.

———. 1998. *Rural Women and Violence: A Study of Two Communities in British Columbia*, unedited technical report. Ottawa: Department of Justice.

———. 2000. *The Denial of Race in the Murder of Reena Virk*. Vancouver: The FREDA Centre for Research on Violence against Women and Children.

———. 2006. *Discourses of Denial: Mediations of Race, Gender, and Violence*. Vancouver: University of British Columbia Press.

———, and Mary Lynn Young. 2006. 'Missing and murdered women: Reproducing marginality in news discourse', *Canadian Journal of Communication* 31, 4: 895–917.

Kane, E.W. 2006. ' "No way my boys are going to be like that!" Parents' responses to children's gender nonconformity', *Gender and Society* 20, 2: 149–76.

Kaplan, G., and L.J. Rogers. 2003. *Gene Worship: Moving beyond the Nature/Nurture Debates over Genes, Brain and Gender*. New York: Other Press.

Kaplinsky, Raphael. 2005. *Globalization, Poverty and Inequality*. Cambridge: Polity.

Karaian, L., Allyson Mitchell, and Lisa Rundle. 2001. *Turbo Chicks: Talking Young Feminisms*. Toronto: Sumach Press.

Kaufman, Michael. 2001. 'The White Ribbon Campaign: Involving men and boys in ending global violence against women', in Bob Pease and Keith Pringle, eds, *A Man's World? Changing Men's Practices in a Globalized World*, 38–52. London: Zed Books.

Kenny, C., et al. 2002. 'North American Indian, Métis and Inuit women speak about culture, education and work', in *The Integration of Diversity into Policy Research, Development, and Analysis*, at <www.swc-cfc.gc.ca/pubs/pubspr/index_e.html>.

Kimmel, Michael S. 1994. 'Masculinity as homophobia: Fear, shame, and silence in the construction of gender identity', in Harry Brod and Michael Kaufman, eds, *Theorizing Masculinities*, 119–41. Thousand Oaks, CA: Sage.

———. 2000. *The Gendered Society*. Oxford: Oxford University Press.

Kincheloe, J.L. 1998. 'The new childhood: Home alone as a way of life', in H. Jenkins, ed., *The Children's Culture Reader*, 157–77. New York: New York University Press.

Kline, Stephen. 1993. *Out of the Garden: Toys and Children's Culture in the Age of TV Marketing*. Toronto: Garamond.

Klodawsky, F., et al. 2006. 'Care and the lives of homeless youth in neo-liberal times in Canada', *Gender, Place and Culture* 13, 4: 419–36.

Kostash, M. 2000. *The Next Canada: In Search of Our Future Nation*. Toronto: McClelland & Stewart.

Krahn, Harvey. 1991. 'Non-standard work arrangements', *Perspectives on Labour and Income* (Statistics Canada) 3, 4: 35–45.

———. 1995. 'Non-standard work on the rise', *Perspectives on Labour and Income* (Statistics Canada) 7, 4: 35–42.

———, Graham S. Lowe, and Karen D. Hughes. 2006. *Work, Industry, and Canadian Society*, 5th edn. Scarborough, ON: Nelson.

Lamb, M. 1999. *Parenting and Child Development in 'Nontraditional' Families*. Mahwah, NJ: L. Erlbaum Associates.

Lamphere, Louise. 1989. *From Working Daughters to Working Mothers: Immigrant Women in a New England Community*. London: Cornell University Press.

Lavell-Harvard Dawn Memee, and Jeanette Corbière Lavell, eds. 2006. *"Until Our Hearts Are on the Ground": Aboriginal Mothering, Oppression, Resistance and Rebirth*. Toronto: Demeter.

Lee, J. 1994. 'Menarche and the (hetero) sexualization of the female body', *Gender and Society* 8, 3: 343–62.

Lewis, Jane. 2003. *Should We Worry about Family Change?* Toronto: University of Toronto Press.

Library of Parliament. 2006. 'Women in Parliament', at <www.parl.gc.ca/information/library/PRBpubs/prb0562-e.htm>.

Lindsay, Colin, and Marcia Almey. 2006. 'Chapter 5: Paid and unpaid work', in Statistics Canada, *Women in Canada: A Gender-Based Statistical Report*, 5th edn. Ottawa: Statistics Canada (cat. no. 89-503-XIE).

Littig, Beate. 2001. *Feminist Perspectives on Environment and Society*. Edinburgh Gate, Harlow, UK: Pearson Education.

Livingstone, David, and Meg Luxton. 1996. 'Gender consciousness at work: Modification of the male breadwinner norm among steelworkers and their spouses', in W. Seccombe and D. Livingstone, *Recast Dreams: Class and Gender Consciousness in Steeltown*, 100–29. Peterborough, ON: Garamond.

Lowe, Graham S. 2001. 'Youth, transitions, and the new world of work', in V. Marshall et al., eds, 29–44. Toronto: University of Toronto Press.

———, and Harvey Krahn. 2000. 'Work aspirations and attitudes in an era of labour market restructuring: A comparison of two Canadian cohorts', *Work, Employment, and Society* 14, 1: 1–22.

Lowman, J. 2000. 'Violence and the outlaw status of (street) prostitution in Canada', *Violence against Women* 6, 9: 987–1011.

Lux, Maureen K. 2001. *Medicine That Walks*. Toronto: University of Toronto Press.

Luxton, Meg. 1980. *More Than a Labour of Love: Three Generations of Women's Work in the Home*. Toronto: Women's Press.

———. 1998. *Families and the Labour Market: Coping Strategies from a Sociological Perspective*. Ottawa: Canadian Policy Research Networks.

———, and June Corman. 2001. *Getting by in Hard Times: Gendered Labour at Home and on the Job*. Toronto: University of Toronto Press.

———, and Leah F. Vosko. 1998. 'The census and women's work', *Studies in Political Economy* 56 (Summer): 49–82.

MacAlpine (Foster), K. 2005. 'Ask and you shall receive: An exploration of salary expectations and the gendered earnings gap in Canada', MA thesis, Department of Sociology, University of Waterloo, Waterloo, ON.

McCall, L. 2001. *Complex Inequality: Gender, Class, and Race in the New Economy*. New York: Routledge.

———. 2005. 'The complexity of intersectionality', *Signs: Journal of Women in Culture and Society* 30, 3: 1771–1800.

Maccoby, E. 2000. 'Parenting and its effects on children: On reading and misreading behaviour genetics', *Annual Review of Psychology* 51: 1–27.

———, and C.N. Jacklin. 1974. *The Psychology of Sex Differences*. Stanford, CA: Stanford University Press.

McDaniel, Susan A. 1995. 'The family lives of the middle-aged and elderly in Canada', in Maureen Baker, ed., *Families: Changing Trends in Canada*, 3rd edn, 194–210. Toronto: McGraw-Hill Ryerson.

———. 1996. 'Family/work challenges among mid-life Canadians', in Marion Lynn, ed., *Voices: Essays on Canadian Families*, 195–216. Scarborough, ON: Nelson Canada.

———. 2002a. 'Women's changing relations to the state and citizenship: Caring and intergenerational relations in globalizing Western democracies', *Canadian Review of Sociology and Anthropology* 39, 2: 125–50.

———. 2002b. 'Born at the right time? Gendered generations and webs of entitlement and responsibility', *Canadian Journal of Sociology* 26, 2: 193–214.

McKeen, Wendy, and Ann Porter. 2003. 'Politics and transformation: Welfare state restructuring in Canada', in Wallace Clement and Leah F. Vosko, eds, *Changing Canada: Political Economy as Transformation*, 109–34. Montreal and Kingston: McGill-Queen's University Press.

Mackie, M. 1987. *Constructing Women and Men: Gender Socialization*. Toronto: Holt, Rinehart and Winston of Canada.

———. 1991. *Gender Relations in Canada: Further Explorations*. Toronto: Butterworths.

Macklem, G.L. 2003. *Bullying and Teasing: Social Power in Children's Groups*. New York: Kluwer Academic/Plenum Publishers.

Macklin, Audrey. 2003. 'Dancing across borders: "Exotic dancers," trafficking, and Canadian immigration', *International Migration Review* 37, 2: 464–500.

McMullin, J. 2004. *Understanding Social Inequality: Intersections of Class, Age, Gender, Ethnicity, and Race in Canada*. Don Mills, ON: Oxford University Press.

McPherson, K., et al. 1999. *Gendered Pasts: Historical Essays in Femininity and Masculinity in Canada*. Don Mills, ON: Oxford University Press.

McQuaig, Linda. 1991. *The Quick and the Dead: Brian Mulroney, Big Business, and the Seduction of Canada*. Toronto: Penguin.

———. 1998. *The Cult of Impotence: Selling the Myth of Powerlessness in the Global Economy.* Toronto: Penguin.

McQuillan, Kevin, and Zenaida R. Ravenera. 2006. *Canada's Changing Families: Implications for Individuals and Society.* Toronto: University of Toronto Press.

Maglin, N.B., and D. Perry. 1996. *'Bad Girls'/'Good Girls': Women, Sex, and Power in the Nineties.* New Brunswick, NJ: Rutgers University Press.

Magnusson, Warren. 1998, 'Globalization, movements, and the decentred state', in W.K. Carroll, ed., *Organizing Dissent: Contemporary Social Movements in Theory and Practice,* 2nd edn, 94–113. Toronto: Garamond.

Mallan, K., and S. Pearce. 2003. *Youth Cultures: Texts, Images, and Identities.* London: Praeger.

Mandell, N. 2005. *Feminist Issues.* Toronto: Pearson Education Canada.

Maroney, Heather Jon, and Meg Luxton, eds. 1987. *Feminism and Political Economy: Women's work, Women's Struggle.* Toronto: Methuen.

Marquardt, R. 1998. *Enter at Your Own Risk: Canadian Youth and the Labour Market.* Toronto: Between the Lines.

Marr, N., and T. Field. 2001. *Bullycide: Death at Playtime.* London: Success Unlimited.

Marshall, B.L. 2000. *Configuring Gender: Explorations in Theory and Politics.* Peterborough, ON: Broadview Press.

Marshall, Katherine. 1993. 'Employed parents and the division of housework', *Perspectives on Labour and Income* (Statistics Canada) 5, 3: 23–30.

———. 2003. 'Benefiting from extended parental leave', *Perspectives on Labour and Income* (Statistics Canada) 15, 2: 5–11.

Marshall, V.W., et al., eds. 2001. *Restructuring Work and the Life Course.* Toronto: University of Toronto Press.

Marsiglio, William. 1993. 'Contemporary scholarship on fatherhood: Culture, identity and conflict', *Journal of Family Issues* 14, 4: 484–509.

Martin, E. 1987. *The Woman in the Body: A Cultural Analysis of Reproduction.* Boston: Beacon.

Martin, K.A. 2005. 'William wants a doll. Can he have one? Feminists, child care advisors, and gender-neutral child rearing', *Gender and Society* 19, 4: 456–79.

Mathews, F. 2002. 'The Invisible Boy', paper presented at the Conference on the Status of Male Children in Canada, Toronto, at <www.open.uguelph.ca/cdnboys/cb_highlights.pdf>.

Mauthner, Natasha S., and Andrea Doucet. 2003. 'Reflexive accounts and accounts of reflexivity in qualitative data analysis', *Sociology* 37, 3: 413–31.

Mazzarella, S.R., and N.O. Pecora. 1999. *Growing up Girls: Popular Culture and the Construction of Identity.* New York: P. Lang.

Meehan, Elizabeth M., and Selma Sevenhuijsen, eds. 1991. *Equality Politics and Gender.* London: Sage.

Meekosha, H. 2006. 'What the hell are you? An intercategorical analysis of race, ethnicity, gender, and disability in the Australian body politic', *Scandinavian Journal of Disability Research* 8, 2, 3: 161–76.

———. 2008. *Body Battles: Disability, Representation, and Participation.* Sydney: Sage.

Meissner, Martin, et al. 1975. 'No exit for wives: Sexual division of labour and the culmination of household demands', *Canadian Review of Sociology and Anthropology* 12, 4: 424–39.

Messner, M.A. 1997. *Politics of Masculinities: Men in Movements.* Thousand Oaks, CA: Sage.

Milkie, Melissa A., and Pia Peltola. 1999. 'Playing all the roles: Gender and the work balancing act', *Journal of Marriage and the Family* 61, 2: 476–90.

Miller, Nancy K. 1997. 'Public statements, private lives: Academic memoirs for the nineties', *Signs: Journal of Women in Culture and Society* 22, 4: 981–1015.

Mingione, Enzo. 1988. 'Work and informal activities in urban southern Italy', in R.E. Pahl, ed., *On Work: Historical, Comparative and Theoretical Approaches*, 548–78. Oxford: Basil Blackwell.

Mitchell, Allyson, Lisa Bryn Rundle, and Lara Karaian. 2001. *Turbo Chicks: Talking Young Feminisms*. Toronto: Sumach Press.

Mitchell, Juliet. 1974. *Psychoanalysis and Feminism*. New York: Pantheon Books.

———. 1980. 'On the difference between men and women', *New Society*, 12 June: 234–5.

Mohanty, Chandra Talpade. 1988. 'Under Western eyes: Feminist scholarship and colonial discourses', *Feminist Review* 30 (Fall): 61–88.

———. 2003. ' "Under Western eyes" revisited: Feminist solidarity through anticapitalist struggles', *Signs: Journal of Women in Culture and Society* 28, 2: 499–535.

———. 2006. 'US empire and the project of women's studies: Stories of citizenship, complicity, and dissent', *Gender, Place and Culture* 13, 1: 7–13.

Monture-Angus, Patricia. 1999. *Journeying Forward: Dreaming First Nations' Independence*. Black Point, NS: Fernwood.

Moraga, Cherrie, Daisy Hernandez, and Bushra Rehman. 2002. *Colonize This! Young Women of Color on Today's Feminism*. Berkeley, CA: Seal Press.

Morgan, David H.J. 1992. *Discovering Men*. London: Routledge.

———. 2001. 'Family, gender and masculinities', in S.M. Whitehead and F.J. Barrett, eds, *The Masculinities Reader*, 223–32. Cambridge: Polity.

———. 2006. 'The crisis in masculinity', in K. Davis, M. Evans, and J. Lorber, eds, *Handbook of Gender and Women's Studies*, 109–24. London: Sage.

Moser, Caroline. 1993. *Gender Planning and Development: Theory, Practice and Training*. London: Routledge.

Mouffe, Chantal. 1992. 'Feminism, citizenship, and radical democratic politics', in Judith Butler and Joan W. Scott, eds, *Feminists Theorize the Political*, 369–84. New York: Routledge.

Mouttapa, M., et al. 2004. 'Social network predictors of bullying and victimization', *Adolescence* 39, 154: 315–35.

Murphy, Brian K. 1999. *Transforming Ourselves Transforming the World*. Halifax: Fernwood.

Musgrave, S., ed. 2001. *Nerves out Loud: Critical Moments in the Lives of Seven Teen Girls*. Toronto: Annick.

Naples, N.A. 2003. *Feminism and Method: Ethnography, Discourse Analysis, and Activist Research*. New York: Routledge.

NCW (National Council of Welfare). 2006. 'Poverty facts 2003' (July), at <www.ncwcnbes.net>.

Nelson, A. 2000. 'The pink dragon is female: Halloween costumes and gender markers', *Psychology of Women Quarterly* 24, 2: 137–44.

———. 2006. *Gender in Canada*. Toronto: Pearson Prentice Hall.

Neu, Dean, and Richard Therrien. 2003. *Accounting for Genocide: Canada's Bureaucratic Assault on Aboriginal People*. Halifax: Fernwood.

Newson, Jon, and Elizabeth Newson. 1968. *Four Years Old in an Urban Community*. London: Allen and Unwin.

Neysmith, Sheila, Kate Bezanson, and Anne O'Connell. 2005. *Telling Tales: Living the Effects of Public Policy*. Halifax: Fernwood.

Ng, Roxana. 1986. 'The social construction of immigrant women in Canada', in Michele Barrett and Roberta Hamilton, eds, *The Politics of Diversity: Feminism, Marxism and Nationalism*, 269–86. London: Verso.

———. 1998. 'Work restructuring and recolonizing Third World women: An example from the garment industry in Toronto', *Canadian Women Studies* 18, 1: 21–5.

———. 1999. *Home-Working: Home Office or Home Sweatshop? Report on Current Conditions of Home-Workers in Toronto's Garment Industry*. Toronto: New Approaches to Lifelong Learning, Ontario Institute for Studies in Education.

———. 2000. 'Restructuring gender, race, and class relations: The case of garment workers and labour adjustment', in Sheila Neysmith, ed., *Restructuring Caring Labour*, 226–51. Toronto: Oxford University Press.

Nicholson, Linda. 1994. 'Interpreting gender', *Signs: Journal of Women in Culture and Society* 20, 11: 79–105.

Noble, Jean. 2004. *Masculinities without Men? Female Masculinity in Twentieth Century Fiction*. Vancouver: University of British Columbia Press.

Norberg-Hodge, Helena. 2002. *Bringing the Food Economy Home*. Halifax: Fernwood.

NWAC (Native Women's Association of Canada). 1992. 'Aboriginal women and gender bias in the legal profession', paper prepared for the Canadian Bar Association Task Force on Gender Bias in the Legal Profession, Toronto, 22 January.

———. 1999. 'Equality for all in the 21st century', Second National Conference on Bill C-31, Edmonton, 14–16 May.

Oakley, Ann. 1972. *Sex, Gender and Society*. New York: Harper and Row.

———. 1974a. *The Sociology of Housework*. London: Martin Robertson.

———. 1974b. *Housewife*. London: Allen Lane.

———. 1981. 'Interviewing women: A contradiction in terms', in H. Roberts, ed., *Doing Feminist Research*, 30–61. London: Routledge and Kegan Paul.

———. 1998. 'Gender, methodology and people's ways of knowing: Some problems with feminism and the paradigm debate in social science', *Sociology* 32, 4: 707–31.

O'Brien, C.A., and L. Weir. 1995. 'Lesbians and gay men inside and outside families', in N. Mandell and A. Duffy, eds, *Canadian Families, Diversity, Conflict, and Change*, 111–39. Toronto: Harcourt Brace Canada.

O'Brien, Margaret. 2005. *Shared Caring: Bringing Fathers in the Frame*. Manchester, UK: Equal Opportunities Commission.

O'Brien, Mary. 1981. *The Politics of Reproduction*. Boston: Routledge and Kegan Paul.

O'Connell, P., et al. 1999. 'Peer involvement in bullying: Insights and challenges for intervention', *Journal of Adolescence* 22: 437–52.

O'Connor, P. 2006. 'Young people's construction of the self: Late modern elements and gender differences', *Sociology* 40, 1: 107–24.

O'Donnell, Vivian. 2006. 'Chapter 8: Aboriginal women in Canada', in Statistics Canada, *Women in Canada: A Gender-Based Statistical Report*, 5th edn. Ottawa: Statistics Canada (cat. no. 89-503-XIE).

OECD (Organisation for Economic Co-operation and Development). 2004. 'Early childhood education and care policy: Canada Country Note', Paris: OECD.

Olesen, Virginia. 1998. 'Feminism and models of qualitative research', in Norman Denzin and Yvonna S. Lincoln, eds, *The Landscape of Qualitative Research: Theories and Issues*, 300–32. Thousand Oaks, CA: Sage.

Oulette, Grace. 2002. *The Fourth World: An Indigenous Perspective on Feminism and Aboriginal Women's Activism*. Halifax: Fernwood.

Outhwaite, W. 2006. *The Future of Society*. Oxford: Blackwell.

Overall, Christine. 1998. *A Feminist I: Reflections from Academia*. Toronto: Broadview Press.

Pahl, Ray E. 1984. *Divisions of Labour*. Oxford: Basil Blackwell.

Palameta, Boris. 2003. 'Who pays for domestic help', *Perspectives on Labour and Income* (Statistics Canada) 15, 3: 12–15.

Parliament of Canada. 2006. 'Women. Current provincial and territorial standings', at <www2.parl.gc.ca/Parlinfo/lists/PartyStandings.aspx?Language=E&Section=03d93c58-F843-49b3-9653-84275c23f3fb&Gender=E>.

Parr, Joy. 1990. *The Gender of Breadwinners: Women, Men, and Change in Two Industrial Towns, 1880–1950*. Toronto: University of Toronto Press.

Parsons, Talcott. 1967. *Sociological Theory and Modern Society*. New York: Free Press.

———, and Robert F. Bales. 1955. *Family, Socialization and Interaction Process*. Glencoe, IL: Free Press.

Paul, Daniel. 2006. *We Were Not the Savages*, 3rd edn. Halifax: Fernwood.

Pearce, Tralee. 2006. 'Want to move up? Marry down', *The Globe and Mail*, 13 May.

Pérusse, Dominique. 2003. 'New maternity and parental benefits', *Perspectives on Labour and Income* (Statistics Canada) 15, 2: 12–15.

Phillips, A. 1993. *The Trouble with Boys: Parenting the Men of the Future*. London: Pandora.

Phillips, C. 2003. 'Who's who in the pecking order? Aggression and "normal" violence in the lives of boys and girls', *British Journal of Criminology* 43, 4: 710–28.

Picard, André. 2007. 'Scientific breakthrough or unproven fix?', *The Globe and Mail*, 26 March.

Pierce, Jennifer. 2004. 'Rambo litigators: Emotional labor in a male-dominated occupation', in Michael S. Kimmel and Michael A. Messner, eds, *Men's Lives*, 6th edn, 241–57. Boston: Allyn and Bacon.

Pipher, Mary. 1995. *Reviving Ophelia: Saving the Selves of Adolescent Girls*. New York: Ballantine.

Polivka, Anne E., and Thomas Nardone. 1989. 'On the definition of "contingent work"', *Monthly Labor Review* 112, 12: 9–16.

Pollack, W. 1999. *Real Boys: Rescuing Our Sons from the Myths of Boyhood*. New York: Henry Holt.

Porter, Ann. 2003. *Gendered States: Women, Unemployment Insurance, and the Political Economy of the Welfare State in Canada, 1945–1997*. Toronto: University of Toronto Press.

Pratt, G., and S. Hanson. 1993. 'Women and work across the life course', in C. Katz and J. Monk, eds, *Full Circles: Geographies of Women over the Life Course*, 27–54. London and New York: Routledge.

Prentice, Alison. 1999. 'Three women in physics', in Elizabeth Smyth et al., eds, *Challenging Professions: Historical and Contemporary Perspectives on Women's Professional Work*, 119–40. Toronto: University of Toronto Press.

Prentice, S. 1994. *Sex in Schools: Canadian Education and Sexual Regulation*. Toronto: Our Schools/Our Selves Education Foundation.

Pruett, Kyle. 2000. *Fatherneed: Why Father Care Is as Essential as Mother Care for Your Child.* New York: Broadview Press.

Purvis, Trevor, and Alan Hunt. 1993. 'Discourse, ideology, discourse, ideology, discourse, ideology. . .', *British Journal of Sociology* 44, 3: 473–99.

Quart, A. 2003. *Branded: The Buying and Selling of Teenagers.* Cambridge, MA: Perseus.

Rajiva, M. 2006. 'Brown girls, white worlds: Adolescence and the making of racialized selves', *Canadian Review of Sociology and Anthropology* 43, 2: 165–83.

Ramazanoglu, Caroline. 1989. *Feminism and the Contradictions of Oppression.* London: Routledge.

———, and Janet Holland. 2002. *Feminist Methodology: Challenges and Choices.* London: Sage.

Rankin, P., and J. Vickers. 2001. 'Women's movements and state feminism: Integrating diversity into public policy', in *The Integration of Diversity into Policy Research, Development, and Analysis*, at <www.swc-cfc.gc.ca/pubs/pubspr/index_e.html>.

Ranson, Gillian. 2005. 'No longer "one of the boys": Negotiations with motherhood, as prospect or reality, among women in engineering', *Canadian Review of Sociology and Anthropology* 42, 2: 145–66.

Razack, Sherene H. 1998. *Looking White People in the Eye: Gender, Race, and Culture in Courtrooms and Classrooms.* Toronto: University of Toronto Press.

Rezai-Rashti, G.M. 2005. 'Unessential women: A discussion of race, class, and gender and their implications in education', in N. Mandell, *Feminist Issues: Race, Class and Sexuality*, 83–99. Toronto: Pearson Education.

Rhode, Deborah L. 1989. *Justice and Gender: Sex Discrimination and the Law.* London: Harvard University Press.

———. 1990. *Theoretical Perspectives on Sexual Difference.* New Haven, CT: Yale University Press.

Rich, Adrienne. 1986. *Of Woman Born: Motherhood as Experience and Institution.* New York: W.W. Norton.

Ridley, M. 2003. *Nature via Nurture: Genes, Experience and What Makes Us Human.* Toronto: HarperCollins Canada.

Rigby, Ken. 2002. *New Perspectives on Bullying.* London and Philadelphia: Jessica Kingsley.

Risman, Barbara J. 2004. 'Gender as a social structure: Theory wrestling with activism', *Gender and Society* 18, 4: 429–50.

Rose, D. 2001. 'Revisiting feminist research methodologies: A working paper', at <www.swc-cfc.gc.ca/pubs/pubspr/revisiting/index_e.html>.

Rosenberg, J., and G. Garofalo. 1998. 'Riot grrrl: Revolutions from within', *Signs: Journal of Women in Culture and Society* 23, 3: 809–41.

Rothman, Barbara Katz. 1989. *Recreating Motherhood: Ideology and Technology in a Patriarchal Society.* New York: W.W. Norton.

Rubery, J. 1997. 'Wages and the labour market', *British Journal of Industrial Relations* 35, 3: 337–66.

Ruddick, Sara. 1983. 'Maternal thinking', in J. Treblicot, ed., *Mothering: Essays in Feminist Theory*, 213–30. Totowa, NJ: Rowman and Littlefield.

———. 1995. *Maternal Thinking: Towards a Politics of Peace.* Boston: Beacon.

Salih, Sara. 2002. *Routledge Critical Thinkers: Judith Butler.* New York: Routledge.

Scheper-Hughes, Nancy. 1992. *Death without Weeping: The Violence of Everyday Life in Brazil.* Berkeley: University of California Press.

Scobie, Willow. 2007. 'Adulthood and other horizons: The complexities of temporalities and orientations to the future', PhD dissertation, Department of Sociology and Anthropology, Carleton University, Ottawa.

Scott, J.W. 1999. 'Some reflections on gender and politics', in M.M. Ferree, J. Lorber, and B.B. Hess, eds, *Revisioning Gender*, 70–96. Thousand Oaks, CA: Sage.

Scott, N. 2007. 'The social dynamics of Canadian protest participation', MA thesis, Carleton University, Ottawa.

Seccombe, W., and D. Livingstone. 1996. ' "Down to Earth people": Revising a materialist understanding of group consciousness', in D. Livingstone and J.M. Mangan, eds, *Recast Dreams: Class and Gender Consciousness in Steeltown*, 131–94. Toronto: Garamond.

Seidler, V.J. 1997. *Man Enough: Embodying Masculinities.* London: Sage.

Seiter, E. 1998. 'Children's desires/mother's dilemmas: The social contexts of consumption', in H. Jenkins, ed., *The Chidren's Culture Reader*, 297–317. New York: New York University Press.

Sevenhuijsen, Selma. 1998. *Citizenship and the Ethics of Care: Feminist Considerations on Justice, Morality, and Politics.* London: Routledge.

Shalla, Vivian, ed. 2006. *Working in a Global Era: Canadian Perspectives.* Toronto: Canadian Scholars' Press.

Shandler, Sara. 1999. *Ophelia Speaks: Adolescent Girls Write about Their Search for Self.* New York: HarperCollins.

Sharma, Ursala. 1986. *Women's Work, Class and the Urban Household: A Study of Shimla, North India.* London: Tavistock.

Sheras, P. 2002. *Your Child: Bully or Victim? Understanding and Ending School Yard Tyranny.* New York: Skylight.

Silman, Janet. 1991. *Enough Is Enough: Aboriginal Women Speak Out.* Toronto: Women's Press.

Siltanen, Janet. 1986. 'Domestic responsibilities and the structuring of employment', in Rosemary Crompton and Michael Mann, eds, *Gender and Stratification*, 97–118. Cambridge: Polity.

———. 1994. *Locating Gender: Occupational Segregation, Wages and Domestic Responsibilities.* London: UCL Press.

———. 2002a. 'Full wages and component wages', in S. Jackson and S. Scott, eds, *Gender: A Sociological Reader*, 133–6. London: Routledge.

———. 2002b. 'Paradise paved? Reflections on the fate of social citizenship in Canada', *Citizenship Studies* 6, 4: 395–414.

———. 2004. 'Inequalities of gender and class: Charting the sea change', in J. Curtis et al., eds, *Social Inequality in Canada*, 4th edn, 215–30. Toronto: Pearson Education.

———. 2006. 'Gender, diversity and the shaping of public policy: Recent aspects of the Canadian experience', *Scottish Affairs* 56 (Summer): 88–101.

———. 2007. 'Social citizenship and the transformation of work: Reflections on past and future possibilities', in V. Shalla and W. Clement, eds, *Work in Tumultuous Times*, 349–79. Montreal and Kingston: McGill-Queen's University Press.

———. 2008. 'Inequalities of gender and class: Charting the sea change', in Edward G. Grabb and N. Guppy, eds, *Social Inequality in Canada*, 5th edn. Toronto, Pearson Education.

————, et al. 1995. *Gender Inequality in the Labour Market: Occupational Concentration and Segregation—A Manual on Concepts and Methods.* Geneva: International Labour Organization Publications.

————. 2008. 'Separately together: Working reflexively as a team', *International Journal of Social Research Methodology* 11, 1: 45–61.

Simmons, Rachel. 2003. *Odd Girl Out: The Hidden Culture of Aggression in Girls.* New York: Harvest Books.

Sippola, L. 1999. 'Getting to know the other: The characteristics and significance of other-sex relationships in adolescence', *Journal of Youth and Adolescence* 28, 4: 407–18.

Smith, D. 1974. 'Women's perspective as a radical critique of sociology', *Sociological Inquiry* 44, 1: 7–13.

————. 1987. *The Everyday World as Problematic: A Feminist Sociology.* Milton Keynes, UK: Open University Press.

————. 1989. 'Sociological theory: Methods of writing patriarchy', in Ruth A. Wallace, ed., *Feminism and Sociological Theory*, 34–63. London: Sage.

————. 1992. 'Remaking a life, remaking a sociology: Reflections of a feminist', in W. Carroll, et al., eds, *Fragile Truths: 25 Years of Sociology and Anthropology in Canada*, 125–34. Ottawa: Carleton University Press.

————. 2005. *Institutional Ethnography: A Sociology for People.* Lanham, MD: AltaMira Press.

————. 2006. *Institutional Ethnography as Practice.* Lanham, MD: Rowman & Littlefield.

Snarey, John. 1993. *How Fathers Care for the Next Generation: A Four-Decade Study.* Cambridge, MA: Harvard University Press.

Spellman, E. 1988. *Inessential Woman: Problems of Exclusions in Feminist Thought.* Boston: Beacon.

Spitzer, Denise, et al. 2003. 'Caregiving in transnational context: "My wings have been cut; where can I fly?"', *Gender and Society* 17, 2: 267–86.

Spock, Benjamin. 1960. 'A child's world', *Ladies Home Journal* (June): 50.

Stacey, Judith. 1990. *Brave New Families: Stories of Domestic Upheaval in Late Twentieth-Century America.* Boston: Basic Books.

Stack, Carol. 1974. *All Our Kin: Strategies for Survival in a Black Community.* New York: Harper and Row.

Stanley, L. 2002. 'Should "sex" really be "gender"—or "gender" really be "sex"?', in S. Jackson and S. Scott, eds, *Gender: A Sociological Reader*, 31–41. London: Routledge.

Stasiulis, Daiva K. 1999. 'Feminist intersectional thinking', in P. Li, ed., *Race and Ethnic Relations in Canada*, 347–97. Toronto: Oxford University Press.

————, and Abigail B. Bakan. 2003. *Negotiating Citizenship: Migrant Women in Canada and the Global System.* Houndsmills, UK: Palgrave Macmillan.

Statistics Canada. 2002. *Labour Force Survey, Annual Average 2002/Family Characteristics of Single Husband–Wife Families.* Ottawa: Statistics Canada.

————. 2003a. *The Canadian Labour Market at a Glance.* Ottawa: Ministry of Industry.

————. 2003b. *Women in Canada: Work Chapter Updates.* Ottawa: Statistics Canada.

————. 2006. *Women in Canada: A Gender-Based Statistical Report*, 5th edn. Ottawa: Statistics Canada (cat. no. 89-503-XIE).

————. 2007. 'Labour force characteristics by age and sex' (modified 1 January 2007), at <www40.statcan.ca/l01/cst01/labor20b.htm>.

Status of Women Canada. 1995. *Setting the Stage for the Next Century: The Federal Plan for Gender Equality, 1995–2000*. Ottawa: Public Works and Government Services.

———. 2001. *Canadian Experience in Gender Mainstreaming*. Ottawa: Status of Women Canada.

Stephens, S. 1995. 'Children and the politics of culture in "late capitalism" ', in S. Stephens, ed., *Children and the Politics of Culture*, 3–48. Princeton, NJ: Princeton University Press.

Stephenson, M., ed. 1973. *Women in Canada*. Toronto: New Press.

Stevens, V., et al. 2002. 'Relationship of the family environment to children's involvement in bully/victim problems in school', *Journal of Youth and Adolescence* 31, 6: 419–28.

Stobert, Susan, and Anna Kemeny. 2003. 'Childfree by choice', *Canadian Social Trends* 69 (Summer): 7–10.

Sullivan, K. 2004. *Bullying in Secondary Schools: What It Looks Like and How to Manage It*. London: P. Chapman; Thousand Oaks, CA: Corwin Press.

Sussman, Deborah, and Stephanie Bonnell. 2006. 'Wives as primary breadwinners', *Perspectives on Labour and Income* (Statistics Canada) 7, 8: 10–17.

Sydie, R.A. 1987. *Natural Women, Cultured Men: A Feminist Perspective on Sociological Theory*. Toronto: Methuen.

Tanner, J., et al. 1995. *Fractured Transitions from School to Work: Revisiting the Dropout Problem*. Don Mills, ON: Oxford University Press.

Taylor, J.M. 1995. *Between Voice and Silence: Women and Girls, Race and Relationship*. Cambridge, MA: Harvard University Press.

Thiessen, V., and J. Blasius. 2002. 'The social distribution of youth's images of work', *Canadian Review of Sociology and Anthropology* 39, 1: 49–78.

Thompson, Linda, and Alexis Walker. 1989. 'Gender in families: Women and men in marriage, work, and parenthood', *Journal of Marriage and the Family* 51, 40: 845–71.

Thorne, B. 1993. *Gender Play: Girls and Boys in School*. New Brunswick, NJ: Rutgers University Press.

Tiger, L. 1969. *Men in Groups*. London: Nelson.

Tolman, D. 1994. 'Doing desire: Young girls struggle for/with sexuality', *Gender and Society* 8, 3: 324–42.

Tossutti, L.S., et al. Forthcoming. 'Family, religion, and civic engagement in Canada', *Canadian Ethnic Studies/Études ethniques au Canada*.

Tripp-Knowles, Peggy. 1999. 'The feminine face of forestry in Canada', in Elizabeth Smyth et al., eds, *Challenging Professions: Historical and Contemporary Perspectives on Women's Professional Work*, 194–214. Toronto: University of Toronto Press.

Tyyskä, V. 2001. *Long and Winding Road: Adolescents and Youth in Canada Today*. Toronto: Canadian Scholars' Press.

Ungerson, Clare. 1983. 'Why do women care?', in J. Finch and D. Groves, eds, *A Labour of Love: Women, Work and Caring*, 31–51. London: Routledge and Kegan Paul.

Veblen, Thorstein. 1953. *The Theory of the Leisure Class*. New York: Mentor.

Veevers, Jean. 1980. *Childless by Choice*. Toronto: Butterworths.

Vickers, Jill McCalla. 1982. 'Memories of an ontological exile: The methodological rebellions of feminist research', in Geraldine Finn and Angela Miles, eds, *Feminism in Canada from Pressure to Politics*, 27–46. Montreal: Black Rose Books.

———. 1992. 'Intellectual origins of the women's movements in Canada', in Constance Backhouse and David Flaherty, eds, *Challenging Times: The Women's Movement in Canada and the United States*, 40–60. Montreal and Kingston: McGill-Queen's University Press.

Vosko, Leah. 2000. *Temporary Work: The Gendered Rise of a Precarious Employment Relationship*. Toronto: University of Toronto Press.

———, Nancy Zukewich, and Cynthia Cranford. 2003. 'Precarious jobs: A new typology of employment', *Perspectives on Labour and Income* (Statistics Canada) 15, 4: 16–26.

Waite, Linda J., and Mark Nielsen. 2001. 'The rise of the dual-earner family, 1963–1997', in R. Hertz and N. Marshall, eds, *Working Families: The Transformation of the American Home*, 23–41. Berkeley: University of California Press.

Walby, Sylvia. 1986. *Patriarchy at Work*. Cambridge: Polity.

Wald, G. 1998. 'Just a girl? Rock music, feminism and the cultural construction of female youth', *Signs: Journal of Women in Culture and Society* 23, 3: 585–610.

Wall, Glenda, and Stephanie Arnold. 2007. 'How involved is involved fathering?', *Gender and Society* 21, 4: 508–27.

Wallace, Claire D. 2002. 'Household strategies: Their conceptual relevance and analytical scope in social research', *Sociology* 36, 2: 275–92.

———, and Ray E. Pahl. 1985. 'Household work strategies in an economic recession', in N. Redclift and E. Mingione, eds, *Beyond Employment*, 189–227. Oxford: Basil Blackwell.

Waller, Maureen M. 2002. *My Baby's Father: Unmarried Parents and Paternal Responsibility*. Ithaca, NY, and London: Cornell University Press.

Wallis, Claudia. 2004. 'The case for staying home', *Time*, 22 March: 51–9.

Ward, Jane. 2004. ' "Not all differences are created equal": Multiple jeopardy in a gendered organization', *Gender and Society* 18, 1: 82–102.

Waring, Marilyn. 1988. *If Women Counted: A New Feminist Economics*. San Francisco: Harper and Row.

Weisner, T. 2005. *Discovering Successful Pathways in Children's Development: Mixed Methods in the Study of Childhood and Family Life*. Chicago: University of Chicago Press.

West, Candace, and Sarah Fenstermaker. 1995. 'Reply: (Re)doing difference', *Gender and Society* 9, 4: 506–13.

———, and Don Zimmerman. 1987. 'Doing gender', *Gender and Society* 1, 2: 125–51.

White, Jerry, Stephen Obeng Gyimah, and Paul Maxim. 2003. 'Labour force activity of women in Canada: A comparative analysis of Aboriginal and non-Aboriginal women', *Canadian Review of Sociology and Anthropology* 40, 4: 391–412.

White, Julie. 1993. *Sisters and Solidarity: Women and Unions in Canada*, Toronto: Thompson Educational.

Whitehead, S.M. 2002. *Men and Masculinities*. Cambridge: Polity.

Williams, Cara. 2004. 'The sandwich generation', *Perspectives on Labour and Income* (Statistics Canada) 16, 4: 7–14.

Williams, Christine. 1999. 'The glass escalator: Hidden advantages for men in the "female" professions', in Michael S. Kimmel and Michael A. Messner, eds, *Men's Lives*, 6th edn, 227–40. Boston: Allyn and Bacon.

Williams, L.S. 2002. 'Trying on gender, gender regimes, and the process of becoming women', *Gender and Society* 16, 1: 29–52.

Williams, Raymond. 1983. *Keywords: A Vocabulary of Culture and Society*, rev. edn. New York: Oxford University Press.

Willis, P.E. 1977. *Learning to Labour: How Working Class Kids Get Working Class Jobs*. Farnborough, UK: Saxon House.

Willms, J.D., ed. 2002. *Vulnerable Children: Findings from Canada's National Longitudinal Survey of Children and Youth.* Edmonton: University of Alberta Press.

Wolf, Diane L., ed. 1996. *Feminist Dilemmas in Fieldwork.* Boulder, CO: Westview Press.

Wollstonecraft, Mary. 1992 [1792]. *A Vindication of the Rights of Woman.* London: Penguin.

Wotherspoon, T. 2004. *The Sociology of Education in Canada: Critical Perspectives.* New York: Oxford University Press.

Wrede, P.C. 1999. *Star Wars Episode 1: The Phantom Menace.* New York: Scholastic.

Wyatt, G. 1956. *Dale Evans and the Coyote.* New York: Simon and Schuster; Toronto: Musson Book Company.

Young, K., and P. White, eds. 1999. *Sport and Gender in Canada.* Toronto: Oxford University Press.

Zavella, Patricia. 1987. *Women's Work and Chicano Families: Cannery Workers of the Santa Clara Valley.* Ithaca, NY, and London: Cornell University Press.

Zawilski, V., and C. Levine-Rasky, eds. 2005. *Inequality in Canada: A Reader on the Intersections of Gender, Race, and Class.* Don Mills, ON: Oxford University Press.

Zuzanek, Juri. 2001. 'Parenting time: Enough or too little?', *Canadian Journal of Policy Research* 2, 2: 125–33.

Index